# THE LIMITS OF AUTOBIOGRAPHY

# The Limits of Autobiography

## TRAUMA AND TESTIMONY

*Leigh Gilmore*

CORNELL UNIVERSITY PRESS

ITHACA AND LONDON

Permissions may be found on the last page of this book.

First published 2001 by Cornell University Press

First printing, Cornell Paperbacks, 2001

Printed in the United States of America

Library of Congress Cataloging-in-Publication Data

Gilmore, Leigh.
    The limits of autobiography : trauma and testimony / Leigh Gilmore.
      p. cm.
    Includes bibliographical references and index.
    Contents: Represent yourself — Bastard testimony : incest and illegitimacy in Dorothy Allison's Bastard out of Carolina — There will always be a father : transference and the auto/biographical demand in Mikal Gilmore's Shot in the heart — There will always be a mother : serial autobiography and Jamaica Kincaid — Without names : an anatomy of absence in Jeanette Winterson's Written on the body.
    ISBN 0-8014-3799-7 (acid-free paper) — ISBN 0-8014-8674-2 (pbk. : acid-free paper)
    1. American prose literature—20th century—History and criticism. 2. Autobiography. 3. English prose literature—20th century—History and criticism. 4. Winterson, Jeanette, 1959– . Written on the body. 5. Autobiographical fiction—History and criticism. 6. Kincaid, Jamaica—Criticism and interpretation. 7. Allison, Dorothy. Bastard out of Carolina. 8. Gilmore, Mikal. Shot in the heart. 9. First-person narrative. 10. Self in literature. I. Title.
PS366.A88 G55 2000
818'.50809492—dc21

                                   00-010238

Cloth printing   10 9 8 7 6 5 4 3 2 1
Paperback printing   10 9 8 7 6 5 4 3 2 1

*for Tom, Finn, and William*

# Contents

# Acknowledgments

This project developed through conversations with Chris Castiglia, whose intellect, compassion, and humor inform my thinking at every turn. I thank Evan Watkins for his generous reading of the manuscript. The final form of the manuscript owes much to Tom Pounds, and I am grateful to him for all the ways he helped me to realize this project. I have benefited from the comments of extraordinary readers: I thank Melanie Rae Thon, Sandra Macpherson, Marcia Aldrich, Jennifer Terry, and David Hoddeson for their generosity and helpfulness. Alison Booth, Paul John Eakin, Françoise Lionnet, Sidonie Smith, Julia Watson, and Kathleen Woodward have all given encouragement at different stages of this project. My current and former students have deepened my thinking on this topic, especially Gillian Harkins, Marlene Kenney, Joanna Piepgrass, and Jamie Lampidis. For keeping the conversation going, I thank my geographically too-distant friends Diane Stevens, Ed Cunningham, and Anne Skalley Van Cleve. For their invaluable contributions to making work and family possible, I gratefully acknowledge Jennifer Mangler and Erin Shipley. Many thanks to my able research assistant Beth Marshall. Thanks also to Jane Dieckmann, Suzanne Sherman Aboulfadl, and Bernhard Kendler for their careful work with the manuscript.

   I acknowledge the special contributions of my family, especially my parents, Don and Natalie Gilmore, whose example lies at the center of my thinking on this subject. Finally, I dedicate this book to my husband, Tom Pounds, and our children, Finn and William, who are my joy.

LEIGH GILMORE

# THE LIMITS OF AUTOBIOGRAPHY

# INTRODUCTION

# The Limits of Autobiography

*Every theory is the fragment of an autobiography.*
—Paul Valéry

*One writes in order to become other than what one is.*
—Michel Foucault

Suddenly, it would seem, memoir has become *the* genre in the skittish period around the turn of the millennium.[1] Book reviewers ritualistically cite its ubiquity as more publishers expand their lists to include memoir, more first books are marketed as memoir, and even academics, perhaps the group considered the least likely to cross over, are producing personal criticism, hybrid combinations of scholarship and life writing, and memoir proper.[2] Previously associated with elder statesmen reporting on the way their public lives parallel historical events, memoir is now dominated by the young, or at least youngish in memoir's terms, whose private lives are emblematic of a cultural moment. In 1996 a *New York Times Magazine* special issue announced nothing less than the "triumph"

---

[1]  A crude analysis using the Worldcat database shows the number of new English language volumes categorized as "autobiography or memoir" roughly tripled from the 1940s to the 1990s. The growth pattern over that period was approximately linear, rising from fewer than 1500 in the 1940s to more than 3000 in the 1970s, to over 4000 between 1990 and 1996. Thanks to Maureen Stanton for collecting this data.

[2]  See, for example, Alice Kaplan, *French Lessons* (Chicago: University of Chicago Press, 1993); Frank Lentricchia, *The Edge of Night* (New York: Random House, 1994); Nancy K. Miller, *Bequest and Betrayal* (New York: Oxford University Press, 1996); Susan Rubin Suleiman, *Budapest Diary* (Lincoln: University of Nebraska Press, 1997); Marianne Torgovnick, *Crossing Ocean Parkway* (Chicago: University of Chicago Press, 1994); Jane Tompkins, *A Life in School* (Reading, Mass.: Addison-Wesley, 1996); and the collection *Confessions of the Critics*, ed. H. Aram Veeser (New York: Routledge, 1996).

of literary memoir and linked its ascendancy to the therapy-driven "culture of confession" with which it was a perfect fit.[3]

This brief sketch of the memoir boom meshes with the historical description of autobiography as a Western mode of self-production, a discourse that is both a corollary to the Enlightenment and its legacy, and which features a rational and representative "I" at its center.[4] This version has been displaced from within and without autobiography itself as critics argue that the tradition was never as coherent as it could be made to appear, its canonical texts formally unstable and decidedly multivoiced, and its variety as much a critique, parody, or mimicry of the Western self as evidence of it. So, too, what I have described as the discourses of self-representation include an astounding range of autobiographical practices which, in their diverse traditions and histories, give evidence that the West possesses no monopoly on the kinds of cultural work autobiography can perform.[5] Thus a "culture of confession" and a culture of testimony, which Gayatri Spivak has defined as "the genre of the subaltern giving witness to oppression, to a less oppressed other,"[6] coexist with a certain tension: both insist on the centrality of speaking of pain, but emerge from different contexts which are themselves impure.

Indeed, anxieties about purity and danger, to use Mary Douglas's terms, characterize efforts to understand the place of trauma in contemporary memoirs. While the developing answers to the questions "why memoir? why now?" differ, the cultural awareness that something significant was happening around and through memoir crystallized in relation to the recognition of trauma's centrality to it.[7] I am interested in this coin-

---

[3]    In "The Age of Literary Memoir Is Now," James Atlas focuses mostly on the way writers are shaping this age, but he also indicates the formation of a readership in his subtitle, "confessing for voyeurs" (*New York Times Magazine*, May 12, 1996, 25–27).

[4]    For corrective readings of this version of autobiography's history see Françoise Lionnet, *Autobiographical Voices* (Ithaca: Cornell University Press, 1989), and *Postcolonial Representations* (Ithaca: Cornell University Press, 1995); Caren Kaplan, "Resisting Autobiography: Out-law Genres and Transnational Feminist Subjects," in *De/Colonizing the Subject*, ed. Sidonie Smith and Julia Watson. (Minneapolis: University of Minnesota Press, 1992), 115–38; Doris Sommer, "Sacred Secrets: A Strategy for Survival," in *Women, Autobiography, Theory*, ed. Sidonie Smith and Julia Watson (Madison: University of Wisconsin Press, 1998), 197–207; Gayatri Spivak, "Three Women's Texts and Circumfession," in *Postcolonialism and Autobiography*, ed. Alfred Hornung and Ernstpeter Ruhe (Amsterdam: Editions Rodopi, 1998), 7–22; Sidonie Smith, "Memory, Narrative, and the Discourses of Identity in *Abeng* and *No Telephone to Heaven*," in *Postcolonialism and Autobiography*, 37–59; Sidonie Smith and Julia Watson, Introduction to *De/Colonizing the Subject*, xiii–xxxi.

[5]    Leigh Gilmore, *Autobiographics: A Feminist Theory of Women's Autobiography* (Ithaca: Cornell University Press, 1994).

[6]    Spivak, "Three Women's Texts," 7.

[7]    Here is a sampling of recent trauma memoirs: Jean-Dominique Bauby, *The Diving Bell and the Butterfly* (New York: Vintage, 1997); Linda Katherine Cutting, *Memory Slips* (New York: Harper Perennial, 1998); Sylvia Fraser, *My Father's House* (New York: Ticknor &

cidence of trauma and self-representation and will examine what it reveals about autobiography, its history, and, especially, its limits. My account of trauma's centrality to contemporary self-representation, however, redirects attention from the most prominent contemporary memoirs to texts about trauma that test the limits of autobiography.

For the writers I study here, autobiography's project—to tell the story of one's life—appears to constrain self-representation through its almost legalistic definition of truth telling, its anxiety about invention, and its preference for the literal and verifiable, even in the presence of some ambivalence about those criteria. As a genre, autobiography is characterized less by a set of formal elements than by a rhetorical setting in which a person places herself or himself within testimonial contexts as seemingly diverse as the Christian confession, the scandalous memoirs of the rogue, and the coming-out story in order to achieve as proximate a relation as possible to what constitutes truth in that discourse.[8] These contexts are reproducible; repetition of the forms that characterize them establish expectations in audiences. Yet conventions about truth telling, salutary as they are, can be inimical to the ways in which some writers bring trauma stories into language. The portals are too narrow and the demands too restrictive. Moreover, the judgments they invite may be too similar to forms in which trauma was experienced. When the contest is over who can tell the truth, the risk of being accused of lying (or malingering, or inflating, or whining) threatens the writer into continued silence. In this scenario, the autobiographical project may swerve from the form of autobiography even as it embraces the project of self-representation. These departures offer an opportunity to calibrate our attention to the range of demands made by autobiography and the silencing or shaming effects they impose.

The recent example of 1992 Nobel Peace Prize winner, activist for the rights of the Quiché people in Guatemala, and author Rigoberta Menchú is instructive here. At the end of 1998, the *New York Times* broke the story that Menchú's celebrated autobiography was filled with inaccuracies and

---

Fields, 1987); Sandra M. Gilbert, *Wrongful Death* (New York: Norton, 1997); Lucy Grealy, *Autobiography of a Face* (Boston: Houghton Mifflin, 1994); Kay Redfield Jamison, *An Unquiet Mind* (New York: Knopf, 1995); Mary Karr, *The Liar's Club* (New York: Viking, 1995); Susanna Kaysen, *Girl, Interrupted* (New York: Turtle Bay Books, 1993); Caroline Knapp, *Drinking: A Love Story* (New York: Dial, 1996); Frank McCourt, *Angela's Ashes* (New York: Scribner's, 1996); Nancy Venable Raine, *After Silence* (New York: Crown, 1998); Lauren Slater, *Prozac Diary* (New York: Random House, 1998); William Styron, *Darkness Visible* (New York: Random House, 1990); and Tobias Wolff, *In Pharaoh's Army* (New York: Knopf, 1994).

[8] In *Autobiographics*, I argue that autobiography draws its authority less from its resemblance to real life than from its proximity to discourses of truth and identity, less from reference or mimesis than from the cultural power of truth telling.

downright misrepresentations. In his book *Rigoberta Menchú and the Story of All Poor Guatemalans,* American anthropologist David Stoll concluded after a decade of research that *I, Rigoberta Menchú: An Indian Woman in Guatemala* "cannot be the eyewitness account it purports to be" because Menchú describes as her own "experiences she never had herself."[9] Stoll does not dispute whether the events Menchú reported occurred, but whether they happened to her in the way she represented. He concluded that Menchú had often achieved a larger symbolic truth through her condensation of several events into one, her substitution of herself as eyewitness to events at which she was not present, and her depiction of the murder of someone else as her brother's murder. But the exposé was, of course, scandalous. Menchú and her defenders have said that accusations about her truthfulness are political in that they mean to discredit her and thereby her efforts to raise international concern for the indigenous Guatemalan Indians of whom she is one and whom she represents.

Criticism of autobiography is often political in just this way. It offers writers the opportunity to promote themselves as representative subjects, that is, as subjects who stand for others. It also threatens writers with unsympathetic scrutiny, as Menchú knows well. Public and private life are interwoven in such a way that either legitimation or shaming is always possible. Within the volatility generated by representativeness, the private becomes ambivalent as it transforms into public discourse. Menchú's autobiography is caught up in this dynamic: even as she expands her sense of what happened in her life to include things that did not happen to her *as if* they did, with no acknowledgment of this imagined transformation, she leaves her autobiography vulnerable to charges of lying and, at the same time, elevates it into an expansive sympathetic endeavor in which knowing about violence done to others allows her to imagine herself as the one to whom violence is done, and in which hearing about violence makes her into a witness who then represents herself as having seen the violence.

Stoll's adversarial account is hardly the first to notice the complexities structuring Menchú's testimony. As Doris Sommer points out, it is difficult to miss them. For Sommer, Menchú's overt silences and repeated insistence that she is keeping secrets constitute a strategy for calling attention to the context in which the testimony is given, to the shaping presence of an interrogator, and to the informant's ambivalence.[10] Gayatri Spivak

---

[9]  *I, Rigoberta Menchú,* ed. and intro. Elisabeth Burgos-Debray, trans. Ann Wright (London: Verso, 1984), first published in Spanish in 1983 at the height of the civil war in Guatemala; David Stoll, *Rigoberta Menchú and the Story of All Poor Guatemalans* (Boulder, Colo.: Westview Press, 1998).

[10]  Sommer, "Sacred Secrets," 197–207.

keenly describes this strategy and the pressures it entails: "Persons in that space of difference usually had to be interpellated or hailed as testifiers for some truth of the dominant, although not necessarily to mobilize for resistance, which would be to bring subalternity to its own crisis. It is well to keep that possible distinction in mind—testimony and resistance. The resistant subaltern may sometimes agree to be hailed to testimonial in the belief that resistance will thereby find effective consolidation" (9).

Clearly, then, when the issue is narrowed to the legalistic question, "Did she lie?," almost none of the complexity of representing the self in the context of representing trauma can be retained without seeming to sink into massive ethical relativism and equivocation. A different question would focus on the way her testimony tests a crucial limit in autobiography, and not just the one understood as the boundary between truth and lies, but, rather, the limit of representativeness, with its compulsory inflation of the self to stand for others, the peculiar way it operates both to expand and to constrict testimonial speech, and the way it makes it hard to clarify without falsifying what is strictly and unambiguously "my" experience when "our" experience is also at stake. Spivak points to the overlapping if distinct valences in testimony: if it is not exactly resistance, it certainly can be resistant and lead to further consolidation of other resistant practices. So, too, testimony refers not only to bearing witness, but to the protocols in which it must be offered; it evokes legal testimony and its juridical framing as a ready context for any testimonial speech.

The recent skirmish around Menchú's autobiography indicates one reason why not all writers choose autobiography as the mode in which to tell stories of personal pain. Consider the following: in collections of essays published between 1988 and 1995, Dorothy Allison referred to her experience of childhood sexual abuse by her stepfather. In 1992 she published *Bastard Out of Carolina*, a novel in which the child narrator is sexually assaulted by her stepfather. The experience as Allison describes it in her nonfiction closely resembles the one she narrates in her novel. In *Shot in the Heart*, Mikal Gilmore weaves his own autobiography within the vivid biography of his brother, executed murderer Gary Gilmore, and includes his parents' stories, Mormon history, and reflections on the American West. In a series of fictional texts published between 1986 and 1996, Jamaica Kincaid returns to the enigmatic and disturbing relationship between what seem to be different versions of the same mother and daughter. In interviews, Kincaid describes the relationship as autobiographical. Finally, in a text profoundly concerned with the body's meaning in a love affair that includes illness, separation, and grief, Jeanette Winterson creates a first-person, unnamed narrator whose gender and sexuality are never given. These cases describe a significant contour within the contemporary boom in first-person writing about trauma, and by focusing on them, we are able to discern the limit testing about form and subjectivity that the self-representation of trauma entails.[11]

The limit-cases I study here offer a means of thinking about the way autobiography is partially structured through the proscriptions it places on self-representation. Trauma, from the Greek meaning "wound," refers to the self-altering, even self-shattering experience of violence, injury, and harm. Crucial to the experience of trauma are the multiple difficulties that arise in trying to articulate it.[12] Indeed, the relation between trauma and representation, and especially language, is at the center of claims about trauma as a category. Something of a consensus has already developed that takes trauma as the unrepresentable to assert that trauma is beyond language in some crucial way, that language fails in the face of trauma, and that trauma mocks language and confronts it with its insufficiency. Yet, at the same time language about trauma is theorized as an impossibility, language is pressed forward as that which can heal the survivor of trauma. Thus language bears a heavy burden in the theorization of trauma. It marks a site where expectations amass: Can language be found for this experience? Will a listener emerge who can hear it? Attempts to meet these expectations generate incompatible assertions that both metaphorize and literalize trauma. For example, to take one view, trauma cannot be spoken of or written about in any mode other than the literal. To do so risks negating it. In this construction, language may merely record trauma even as its figural properties and the speaker's imagination threaten to contaminate trauma's historical purity. In another view, trauma, it is claimed, does not exist until it can be articulated and heard by a sympathetic listener. This view swings to the other extreme to claim that without language, experience is nothing. Yet such a view regards

[11] Dorothy Allison, *Bastard Out of Carolina* (New York: Plume, 1993); Mikal Gilmore, *Shot in the Heart* (New York: Doubleday, 1994); Jamaica Kincaid, *At the Bottom of the River* (New York: Farrar, Straus and Giroux, 1983), *Annie John* (New York: Farrar, Straus and Giroux, 1986), *Lucy* (New York: Farrar, Straus and Giroux, 1990), *The Autobiography of My Mother* (New York: Farrar, Straus and Giroux, 1996), *My Brother* (New York: Farrar, Straus and Giroux, 1997); and Jeanette Winterson, *Written on the Body* (New York: Knopf, 1993).
[12] See especially Cathy Caruth, ed., *Trauma* (Baltimore: Johns Hopkins University Press, 1995) and *Unclaimed Experience* (Baltimore: Johns Hopkins University Press, 1996); Shoshana Felman and Dori Laub, *Testimony* (New York: Routledge, 1992); Ian Hacking, *Rewriting the Soul* (Princeton: Princeton University Press, 1995); Judith Herman, *Trauma and Recovery* (New York: Basic Books, 1992); Lenore Terr, *Too Scared to Cry* (New York: Harper & Row, 1990) and *Unchained Memories* (New York: Basic Books, 1994); and Bessell van der Kolk, Alexander C. McFarlane, and Lars Weisaeth, eds., *Traumatic Stress* (New York: Guilford Press, 1996). A critical assessment of this consensus position has been published as my book is in press. See Ruth Leys, *Trauma: A Genealogy* (Chicago: University of Chicago Press, 2000).

public utterances and particular kinds of human relations as "language" in a way that suggests it isn't so much language that is sought as a public forum. The language in which one thinks to oneself, and the utterances within more fragile relationships, even temporary and/or anonymous ones, for example, do not amount to "language" under the previous definition. Survivors of trauma are urged to testify repeatedly to their trauma in an effort to create the language that will manifest and contain trauma as well as the witnesses who will recognize it. Thus the unconscious language of repetition through which trauma initially speaks (flashbacks, nightmares, emotional flooding) is replaced by a conscious language that can be repeated in structured settings. Language is asserted as that which can realize trauma even as it is theorized as that which fails in the face of trauma. This apparent contradiction in trauma studies represents a constitutive ambivalence. For the survivor of trauma such an ambivalence can amount to an impossible injunction to tell what cannot, in this view, be spoken.

Instead of claiming that language or representation is in an inimical or proscribed relation to trauma, I would argue for the importance of attention to specific formulations of trauma and to the range of settings in which they emerge. Because testimonial projects require subjects to confess, to bear witness, to make public and shareable a private and intolerable pain, they enter into a legalistic frame in which their efforts can move quickly beyond their interpretation and control, become exposed as ambiguous, and therefore subject to judgments about their veracity and worth, as Menchú discovered. Thus the joint project of representing the self and representing trauma reveals their structural entanglement with law as a metaphor for authority and veracity, and as a framework within which testimonial speech is heard. Although those who can tell their stories benefit from the therapeutic balm of words, the path to this achievement is strewn with obstacles.[13] To navigate it, some writers move away from recognizably autobiographical forms even as they engage autobiography's central questions.

Analyzed in the sequence I offer here, the limit-cases in this book offer a method for discerning when and how self-representation operates at a distance from the conventions of autobiography. In the first chapter I describe the current memoir boom as a pretext for thinking about limit-cases and develop a context for understanding the radical engagement with self-representation that characterizes limit-cases. This discussion has three parts; I preview it here at some length. In the first part I focus

---

[13]   The power of narrative to heal is cited broadly in psychiatric research, and also in feminist research through the efficacy of a range of practices that move women beyond silence.

on a convention in self-representation that predates the current boom and, arguably, is one of its most important precursors—namely, the paradox that the autobiographer be both unique and representative. While trauma has become a pervasive subject in contemporary self-representation, it is nonetheless experienced as that which breaks the frame. Because trauma is typically defined as the unprecedented, its centrality in self-representation intensifies the paradox of representativeness. Indeed, autobiography's paradox is foregrounded so explicitly that the self-representation of trauma confronts itself as a theoretical impossibility. I focus on representativeness advisedly and sketch the debates that arise around its invocation. I think it worth emphasizing insofar as it names a site of contention in self-representation where the limit-cases studied here contend with their own impossibility. In the second part of my discussion I connect the implications of representativeness to current debates about memory and trauma. Here I focus on the way the debate about false memory crystallizes the stakes around becoming representative. In the third part I examine two hard cases for representativeness in order to establish poststructuralism as a theoretical corollary to contemporary discussions of trauma and self-representation. I offer Foucault's uses of the memoirs *I, Pierre Rivière, having slaughtered my mother, my sister, and my brother* and *Herculine Barbin*, and Althusser's quasi-confessional *The Future Lasts Forever*, written in lieu of the testimony he was never permitted (or compelled) to provide in his murder of his wife, as companion limit-cases to the ones I explore in subsequent chapters.[14] These texts pose limit-testing questions about memoir and trauma and work to establish a lyrical position for the subject of trauma as one that entangles violence, memory, kinship, and law.

Subsequent chapters, which focus on single authors, work through progressively more opaque expressions of autobiography. In the second chapter I explore *Bastard Out of Carolina* in which Dorothy Allison questions the boundary between fiction and autobiography and in doing so challenges one of the central limits in autobiography: its separateness from fiction. The third chapter examines *Shot in the Heart*, Mikal Gilmore's 1994 auto/biographical narrative of kinship and culture, and the ways it tests the limits of telling one's own story when that story is indissoluble from a story about family, secrets, lies, and violence. In the fourth chapter I discuss how Jamaica Kincaid's autobiographical novels *Annie John* (1986) and *Lucy* (1990) analogize England's colonization of

[14]    Michel Foucault, ed., *I, Pierre Rivière* (New York: Random House, 1975) and *Herculine Barbin* (Paris: Gallimard, 1978); Louis Althusser, *The Future Lasts Forever* (Paris: Stock/ IMEC, 1992).

Antigua to a mother-daughter relationship. Here the limit between autobiography and fiction that Allison broaches coincides with the limits between autobiography and history and between the self and family that are Mikal Gilmore's focus. Additionally, Kincaid, like Allison and Gilmore, explores the limits of the child's perspective. Unlike autobiographers who handle this issue by narrating childhood from the remove of later adulthood, however, Kincaid immerses us in the child's inchoate and mysterious perspective on love, death, sex, history, and individuation. In the fifth chapter, Jeanette Winterson's *Written on the Body* reaches the furthest distance beyond the conventions of autobiography; this set of limit-cases provides a basis for understanding her work in its complex engagement with the demands of autobiography. These texts offer a way to theorize how self-representation and trauma reach into each other. By reading them as a sequence, they also provide a path to trace the relation between self-representational projects and the genre they rework.

For many writers, autobiography's domain of first-person particularities and peculiarities offers an opportunity to describe their lives and their thoughts about it; to offer, in some cases, corrective readings; and to emerge through writing as an agent of self-representation, a figure, textual to be sure but seemingly substantial, who can claim "I was there" or "I am here." Some writers, however, are more interested in the constitutive vagaries of autobiography, in how its weirder expansiveness lets them question whether and how "I" can be "here" or "there," what the self is that it could be the subject of its own representation, what the truth is that one person could tell it, and what the past is that anyone could discharge its debt in reporting it. While their responses to these issues bring their texts closer to what is typically called fiction, I will argue that the writers in this study find their way there via an engagement with autobiography. Dorothy Allison, Mikal Gilmore, Jamaica Kincaid, and Jeanette Winterson take autobiography's defining questions as what we might provisionally call autobiographical means to other ends.

While the current growth of memoir provides the pretext for this inquiry, we must also look to the history of self-representation for context. In the anthology he edited, *American Autobiography*, Paul John Eakin comments on the difficulty of writing a scholarly history of American autobiography due to the competing narratives of what it means to be American. As he posits in his introduction, the "true history of American autobiography and the culture in which it is produced and consumed may turn out to be the history of identifiable groups within the culture and the network of relations among them."[15] Thus African American and Native American representations of the self and culture contribute as significantly to the history of American autobiography as the Puritan legacy; yet, it is especially in the connections among varieties of self-representation that autobiography's history lies. Within the context of historicizing American autobiography Lawrence Buell traces American autobiography's two strains in his contribution in Eakin's volume. In one, texts more closely resemble Rousseau's *Confessions* in which the autobiographer offers "the detailed, complex secular narrative of the mind and fortune during a substantial portion if not the entirety of his or her life span." The earliest examples of this include Benjamin Franklin and Thomas Shepard. The other strain is found in texts that have "a strong autobiographical dimension—Emerson's major essays, Thoreau's *Walden*, Whitman's *Leaves of Grass*, many of Emily Dickinson's lyrics, Hawthorne's *The Scarlet Letter* (certainly "The Custom House" and, some would argue, even the romance proper), Frederick Douglass's *Narrative*, and all of Melville's novels through *Pierre*."[16] As Buell notes for the second strain, which includes a dazzling variety of texts, "the autobiographical mode strongly marks this writing from the start" (97). Though not all the texts I study here are American, Buell's schema possesses significant value for any study of autobiography: literary histories that are organized differently from his (in terms of period, nationality, and the like) nonetheless frequently note how a "strong autobiographical dimension" characterizes texts that do not finally qualify as autobiography but reside at its limit. In Buell's examples the autobiographical mode is often preferred over the autobiographical genre by poets, novelists, and essayists—writers by trade and avocation. Yet even though they are more likely to push more for formal innovation than, say, the statesman who writes his memoirs after retirement, they are not, therefore, retreating from questions of history. The essays in Eakin's volume labor to make this clear: it is to the margins of self-representation that we should look anew for autobiography's history, in the past, as they suggest, and in the present, as I will argue here. The limits tell us what the genre alone cannot.

Contemporary writers find themselves working among a variety of autobiographical models. Autobiographical writing has a richly experimental past. Not only do autobiography's canonical heavyweights such as Augustine and Rousseau appear now less as dictators of form than as instigators of diverse practices, historically more proximate precursors

---

[15]    Paul John Eakin, ed., *American Autobiography* (Madison: University of Wisconsin Press, 1991), 12.
[16]    Lawrence Buell, "Autobiography in the American Renaissance," in *American Autobiography: Retrospect and Prospect* (Madison: University of Wisconsin Press, 1991), 47–69.

speak to the range of forms within which self-representation emerges. Modernists such as Gertrude Stein with her audacious *Autobiography of Alice B. Toklas* and *Everybody's Autobiography* shadow such recent efforts as Vladimir Nabokov's *Speak, Memory*, Mary McCarthy's *Memories of a Catholic Girlhood*, Frank Conroy's *Stop-Time*, Lillian Hellman's *Pentimento: A Book of Portraits* and *An Unfinished Woman*, and Maxine Hong Kingston's *Woman Warrior*. In their interest in and ability to combine fiction and non-fiction, one also recalls Charlotte Brontë, who subtitled *Jane Eyre* an "auto-biography," and Henry Adams, whose *Education of Henry Adams* demon-strates considerable ambivalence toward the autobiographical "I."[17] Even the close historical companions reveal the dispersed locations from which this movement builds: from the self-conscious and artful shaping of *testimonios* by Rigoberta Menchú and Domitila Barrios de Chungara to the literary experiments of Michelle Cliff, Assia Djebar, and Clarice Lispector.[18] In acknowledging this multiplicity, my study contributes to the ongoing historicization of the autobiographical motif in which a self-representa-tional "I" emerges in a range of genres.

The texts I study here offer implicit theories of self-representation which suggest the value of an expansive, even protean, view of self-repre-sentational discourse. My epigraphs offer an entry into the theoretical ter-rain. Foucault's dictum, "One writes in order to become other than what one is," suggests that autobiography offers an opportunity for self-trans-formation. Less a report with a fixed content summarized at the end of a long life, autobiography becomes a speculative project in how "to become other."[19] Valéry's provocative insight, "Every theory is the fragment of an autobiography," asks us to imagine the central if enigmatic relation be-tween the objective and the subjective. How might a revised understand-ing of the relation between theory and autobiography, where theory is un-

---

17  Gertrude Stein, *The Autobiography of Alice B. Toklas* (New York: Harcourt Brace, 1933) and *Everybody's Autobiography* (New York: Random House, 1937); Vladimir Nabokov, *Speak, Memory* (New York: Grosset & Dunlap, 1951); Mary McCarthy, *Memories of a Catholic Girlhood* (New York: Harcourt Brace, 1957); Frank Conroy, *Stop-Time* (New York: Viking Press, 1967); Lillian Hellman, *An Unfinished Woman* (Boston: Little, Brown, 1969) and *Pentimento* (Boston: Little, Brown, 1973); Maxine Hong Kingston, *The Woman Warrior* (New York: Knopf, 1976); and Henry Adams, *The Education of Henry Adams* (Boston: Houghton Mifflin, 1918).

18  See, for example, Michelle Cliff, *Abeng* (New York: Penguin Books, 1991) and *No Telephone to Heaven* (New York: Vintage, 1989); Assia Djebar, *Women of Algiers in Their Apartment*, trans. Marjolijn de Jager (Charlottesville: University of Virginia Press, 1992); and Clarice Lispector, *An Apprenticeship* (Austin: University of Texas Press, 1986).

19  Charles Ruas, "Archéologie d'une passion," *Magazine Littéraire*, no. 221 (July–Aug. 1985): 100–105; translated as "An Interview with Michel Foucault," in Michel Foucault, *Death and the Labyrinth: The Works of Raymond Roussel*, trans. Charles Ruas (London: Athlone Press, 1986), 169–86 (quotation on 182), quoted in David Halperin, *Saint Foucault* (New York: Oxford University Press, 1995), 228.

derstood to hew closer to the "objective" and autobiography closer to the "subjective," help to establish a new set of questions for the study of autobiography? Let's juggle Valéry's terms to produce another aphorism, which his formulation invites: Every autobiography is the fragment of a theory. It is also an assembly of theories of the self and self-representation; of personal identity and one's relation to a family, a region, a nation; and of citizenship and a politics of representativeness (and exclusion). How to situate the self within these theories is the task of autobiography which entails the larger organizational question of how selves and milieus ought to be understood *in relation to each other*. Such heuristics as "man and society" or "text and context" reveal a pattern of pushing an individual forward out of a dense set of relations, and a subsequent struggle to figure out where that individual came from. Given the ubiquity of the individual as a trope of Western consciousness, this habit of decontextualization is not surprising. It does, however, surface some persistent problems for the study of autobiography. Namely, if autobiography in the Western tradition focuses on the singular individual who is also representative, how to recapture the effaced relations out of which the notion of the individual and persons themselves emerge? The interface of singular and shareable goes to the issue of political representation, for the autobiographical self who is cut off from others, even as it stands for them, is a metaphor for the citizen. Once separated conceptually from a nation, a family, a place, and a branching set of contingencies, how does an individual recognize this disestablished self?

In this context, we could say that the cultural work performed in the name of autobiography profoundly concerns representations of citizenship and the nation. Autobiography's investment in the representative person allies it to the project of lending substance to the national fantasy of belonging. As Lauren Berlant has argued, citizenship entails a personal investment in the nation, which is for her a fantastic site of identifications and desires that subtends an erotics as much as a politics of affiliation.[20] The nation prompts fantasies of citizens, rendered real, embodied, and whole through their incorporation into the national. Berlant's description of how the nation produces the appearance of reality through the dynamics and the artifacts of citizenship resembles autobiography's simulation of real persons through the combined techniques of the documentary and the imagined: fiction, historiography, testimony, and so on. In autobiography, a person, solid and incontestable, testifies to having lived. An autobiography is a monument to the idea of person-

---

[20]    Lauren Berlant, *The Anatomy of National Fantasy* (Chicago: University of Chicago Press, 1991).

hood, to the notion that one could leave behind a memorial to oneself (just in case no one else ever gets around to it) and that the memorial would perform the work of permanence that the person never can. A self-memorial says: "I remember, and now, so will you." But the fantasy of autobiography, like the fantasy of nationalism, never quite fulfills its promise in local terms. It is considerably more partial and exclusive as a practice, though as a fantasy it seems "free" and available to all. Although autobiography's association with and participation in dominant constructions of the individual and the nation seem to taint it ideologically, some postcolonial scholars and writers, for example, value it as a mode in which to represent oneself as a speaking subject. While any control over these dynamics by the nondominant is, of course, tricky, many, nonetheless, apprehend its fungibility.

The contemporary self-representational texts I explore in this book articulate the relationship between representativeness and a range of more local notions and experiences of the personal, in terms both of what it means to aspire to and achieve personhood and of exploring the interpenetration of the private and the public. The writers I discuss explore representations of personhood that are skeptical of dominant constructions of the individual and the nation. All are concerned with the interpenetration of the private and the public, and how its impact is registered in personal, aesthetic, and legal terms. Through her representation of incest within a working-class milieu marked by power relations, for example, Dorothy Allison explores not only the personal impact of incest on Bone, her protagonist, but also the legal ramifications of this crime in the context of her family and her social world. Mikal Gilmore's representation of his family and his brother, Gary Gilmore, draws on the techniques of autobiography and biography to render what U.S. law and custom induces us to think of as private life, but he does so in the context of the state-sponsored execution of his brother, the public spectacle of the execution and the national fantasy it plays out, and the bloody history of the American West as the shaping presence out of which this violence emerged. While Jamaica Kincaid in book after book writes about the intensity of the mother-daughter bond with a focus on daily details, she places this private relationship within the context of colonialism, and her critique of it, such that the two must be thought of together. Ultimately, in the trajectory of this logic, Jeanette Winterson questions what sort of story can be told in the absence of the seemingly indispensable public *and* private identity markers of name and gender.

It is important to notice how against-the-grain engagements at the limit of autobiography reveal those limits in ways that more conventional autobiographies obscure. In projects in which autobiography is implied but not faithfully reproduced, the strain of a writer's experimentation will demonstrate that a departure from the form is less agnosticism than heresy. I invoke religious language here in part to recall Western autobiography's debt to the confession, a practice that institutionalizes penance and penalty as self-expression. The confession welds together an official and a spiritual discourse in a way that conflates a functional boundary between the public and the private. This boundary dissolves under scrutiny in the confession, for just as one is compelled to express one's private self, the official rules for doing so are always foregrounded. The major legacy of the confession for autobiography here is the extent to which autobiography has reproduced the confession's double nature: its official and secret languages merge in self-representation such that any self-representational act is fully burdened by its public charge to disclose a private truth. The limit-cases I study demonstrate there are other ways to bear this burden.

Thus, I can summarize the goal of this book as twofold: (1) I offer the limit-case paradigm as a means to analyze the ways several contemporary self-representational texts about trauma reveal and test the limits of autobiography, and (2) I situate these limit-cases within a history of autobiography and a theory of self-representation. Within the outlines of these goals, I demonstrate that an engagement with autobiography (its conventions, problems, questions, and demands) is both a recognizable and significant feature of texts that do not readily conform to the genre of autobiography. The texts I gather are less concerned with enumerating the boundaries to which one can point between autobiography and fiction, autobiography and history, autobiography and legal testimony, autobiography and psychoanalysis, or autobiography and theory. Rather they confront how the limits of autobiography, multiple and sprawling as they are, might conspire to prevent some self-representational stories from being told at all if they were subjected to a literal truth test or evaluated by certain objective measures. Questions that could be posed of these texts imply judgments at the ready: "Was your mother really that cruel?" "Did your father really beat and rape you?" "Why are you writing this now when you were silent for so long?" "How can you be sure of what you remember?" In the imagined encounter with such judgments, many writers seek grounds other than the explicitly testimonial for self-representation. In swerving from the center of autobiography toward its outer limits, they convert constraint into opportunity.

Perhaps more surprising than the discovery of a negative limit in autobiography, then, is the productivity of the limit. As writers refuse autobiography's constraints, they grind away at them, sometimes relentlessly, and force difficult questions to the fore: Where does autobiography end and fiction begin? How do the fictive and the autobiographical traverse each other, and what prompts—or bars—their crossing? Where does collective history abandon an individual to a space of historical amnesia? Where does speculation end and evidence begin when the question is what did *you* do to *me*? Confrontations with the limits of autobiography also produce engagements other than open conflict. Some writers seem simply to decline autobiography's constraints, to slip by them gracefully without being caught up in their demands, and in doing so reveal the potential for self-representational writing without the explicit presence of its most familiar requirements. In their complex self-representational engagements, limit-cases point to persistent and constitutive issues in autobiography itself: What is the self that it can be represented in writing? Who am I and how did I become who I am? What does skin have to do with autobiography? What is the relationship between the self and others?[21] What sort of muse, guide, or judge is memory? Further, and crucially for the texts I study here, can writing transform the limits on trauma, the person, and her or his engagement with the world? In their embrace of autobiography's impossibility and revision of the testimonial imperative, limit-cases reveal how not writing an autobiography can be an achievement.

While other sets of limit-cases would produce different insights into self-representation's limits, I have chosen these to demonstrate that an engagement between self-representation and the representation of trauma lies at the heart of this limit testing. Whether the violence in question is limited in duration, repeated, or persists via a prolonged threat, trauma produces a range of bodily, perceptual, and neurological effects. While continuing scientific and psychoanalytic research into trauma ought to provide an improving understanding of helping people to heal from it, I hope that studies in self-representation will also contribute to this effort. What we can learn from texts currently exploring trauma and self-representation should form part of the context for the continuing study of trauma, as should the history and theory of autobiography. Insights into trauma and healing may be found in limit-cases that differ from (whether they extend, complicate, supplement, or challenge) the insights developed through either clinical studies or the study of conventional autobiography. I offer this work toward those ends.

[21] Questions posed in my *Autobiographics*; Karl Weintraub, *The Value of the Individual* (Chicago: University of Chicago Press, 1978); Sidonie Smith, "Identity's Body," in *Autobiography and Postmodernism*, ed. Kathleen Ashley, Leigh Gilmore, and Gerald Peters (Amherst: University of Massachusetts Press, 1994), 266–92; and Mary Mason, "The Other Voice," in *Autobiography: Essays Theoretical and Critical*, ed. James Olney (Princeton: Princeton University Press, 1980), 207–35.

# 1

# Represent Yourself

Memoir is thriving, energized in no small part by a surge in the publication of personal accounts of trauma. Why should this be happening now? A range of contemporary and historical forces suggests how and
why the age of memoir and the age of trauma have coincided and stimu-
lated the aesthetic forms and cultural practices of self-representation that
mark the turn of the millennium. While I offer only a schematic account of
the central forces at play, I do so in an effort to illuminate the histories and
practices they partially obscure and to suggest an alternative jurisdiction
for the self-representation of trauma.

First, the current boom in memoir would be inconceivable were it not for
the social and political movements of the past thirty years that have made it
possible for a broader range of people to publish accounts of their life experiences. Women, people of color, gay men and lesbians, the disabled, and
survivors of violence have contributed to the expansion of self-representation by illuminating suppressed histories and creating new emphases.
While some of these autobiographical texts have been formally experimental, such as Audre Lorde's *Zami: A New Spelling of My Name*, Cherríe Moraga's *Loving in the War Years*, and Gloria Anzaldúa's *Borderlands / La Frontera*,
others have focused more on telling a different story than on telling the
story differently. While identity-based movements have shaped recent developments in autobiography, they have also defined critical and theoretical
studies in feminism, race, sexuality, class, and postcoloniality such that a
synergy has developed among theories, autobiographies, and testimonials.

Second, the media confessional, and also "real life" media that posit a naturalized speaker who is simply telling his or her story, have come to permeate contemporary culture. More conventional memoirs have neither lost their audience nor their practitioners. Self-penned and "as-told-to" accounts, as well as the diaries and journals of the famous, continue to appeal. Now, however, the general is likely to be edged out by the movie star as celebrity confessionals mark a significant overlapping of factors: the media confessional saturates contemporary life and celebrity is capital. Confessional practices pervade and, arguably, define mass culture (at least in the United States) and extend into scientific, legal, and political statements and studies about the person. The efflorescence of talk shows and their mutating confessional forms has pushed forward another representative: neither celebrity nor statesperson, but the dysfunctional and downtrodden, the cheated-on and cheating, the everyman and everywoman of the bad times that keep on coming.

Third, categories such as "personal criticism" and "creative nonfiction" indicate the appearance of the autobiographical "I" in places it has not appeared previously. These hybrid texts are more difficult to situate along the fiction-nonfiction continuum, but they include the interdisciplinary crossover texts of, for example, scientists who write nonfiction animated by a recognizably autobiographical "I." So, too, professors of literature have produced a discourse of "personal criticism" that levers the autobiographical "I" to the fore, sometimes in essays published in scholarly journals or anthologies, and sometimes in memoirs per se. Woven throughout these innovations is poststructuralism. With its reconception of language, agency, and the human subject, poststructuralism is significant for writers whose interests in the self are closely linked to an interest in what language about the self can be made to do.

Finally, the literary market has proved a shaping force. Although it is unclear whether the market has led or followed, market demand currently encourages marketing practices such as subtitling an author's first book "a memoir" when in previous years it might have been classified as fiction, or selecting for publication a memoir by someone whose story would not have previously been expected to appeal to a so-called general audience. The extent to which the current expansion is driven more by marketing and publishing choices ("memoir sells! let's have more memoir!") than by writing practices is not clear. Thus political and social movements, the forces of popular culture, developments in academe, and the market all contribute to and are shaped by the current hothouse of ideas about telling the story of the self. From the newly ubiquitous literary memoir to first-person accounts of trauma, and a range of autobiographical projects beyond these, the current emphasis is on a person telling his or her story.

This schematic account suggests snapshots of the contemporary landscape as the North Atlantic in winter: over there is the tip of the political and social iceberg; here are publishing practices and market forces; there goes Derrida; here comes Oprah. While my account names the major factors animating the current production of memoir, memoirs themselves provide ambiguous evidence of what has caused their popularity. Why, exactly, should Susanna Kaysen's *Girl, Interrupted* and Mary Karr's *Liar's Club* be so successful? The memoirs themselves are incompletely contextualized by current cultural forces; they emerge from literary and cultural precedents that are partially, and sometimes fully, occluded by the crush of the new. Indeed for many writers the current renaissance in first-person writing provides an occasion for reconceiving autobiography as it has been known, even to the point of moving altogether through and beyond it into uncharted territory where what "one" or "I" once was is a matter of radical reinterpretation.

Innovation in contemporary memoir derives in no small part from a history of literary and autobiographical experimentation. Autobiography as a genre has always been defined by formally experimental works, even when critics focused more on its formal and ideological coherence. The course of self-representation has been shaped by formally dissimilar texts: Maxine Hong Kingston's *Woman Warrior* is not at all out of place in the company of Augustine's alternatingly anxious and confident assertions of self, or seen next to Whitman's, Emerson's, and Thoreau's inquiries into the possibilities of a representative, national "I."[1] In this century alone, modernists such as Gertrude Stein, who contributed to this field both *The Autobiography of Alice B. Toklas* (1933) and *Everybody's Autobiography* (1937), questioned the preeminence of facticity in their experimentation with language and the self. More recent precursors such as Nabokov's *Speak, Memory* (1966), McCarthy's *Memories of a Catholic Girlhood* (1966), Conroy's *Stop-Time* (1967), and Hellman's *An Unfinished Woman* (1969) and *Pentimento: A Book of Portraits* (1973) have demonstrated the potential to combine fiction and nonfiction. Serial autobiographers such as Lillian Hellman, Mary McCarthy, Maya Angelou, Richard Rodriguez, and Kim Chernin reveal ways to prolong what was once considered a one-time-only performance.[2] In short, contemporary factors provide only a partial

---

[1]    I argued in *Autobiographics* that innovation and experimentation have always characterized self-representational writing; so, too, other scholars have demonstrated the varieties of self-representation that even traditional autobiographies exhibit.

[2]    Kim Chernin, *In My Mother's House* (New Haven: Ticknor & Fields, 1983), *In My Father's Garden* (Chapel Hill: Algonquin Books, 1996), and *My Life As a Boy* (Chapel Hill: Algonquin Books, 1997); and Richard Rodriguez, *Hunger of Memory* (Boston: D. R. Godine, 1982) and *Days of Obligation* (New York: Viking, 1992).

context for the current boom. To develop a deeper context for my following discussions of limit-cases, I offer here an account of how the notion of representativeness informs contemporary self-representation and illuminates current debates in the study of trauma and memory, and the way this rather traditional notion is woven through poststructuralism's apparently aggressive anticonfessionalism via the examples of Foucault's and Althusser's interest in memory, violence, law, and self-representation.

## Represent Yourself

American individualism is informed by a democratic ideology of *e pluribus unum*. Stand up, it says, and represent yourself. Or, sit back and designate someone else to represent you. This intertwining of individual and collective representation demonstrates the close relation between representing yourself and participating in a representative structure in which one may stand for many. There is a long tradition in autobiography of representing the self as utterly unique and, on precisely this basis, able to stand for others through acts of self-inspection and self-revelation. Self-scrutiny enables an autobiographer to be representative more than any particular set of experiences. In fact, having an unusual life better suits one to stand for others in this tradition. The general, the president, the philosopher, and the saint are all better equipped than you or I to represent a life. Read and learn about me, they suggest, and you will learn more about history and, perhaps, yourself and what you are capable of. The didactic strain sometimes offers an exemplum, as in Benjamin Franklin's *Autobiography*, and sometimes welds it to a cautionary tale, as do the earlier models of Augustine and Rousseau. Both reveal the autobiographical paradox of the unusual or unrepresentative life becoming representative.

When self-representation entails the representation of trauma, the autobiographical paradox of representativeness is intensified. By definition, trauma names an unprecedented experience, but contemporary writers have revealed trauma's prevalence and capacity to signify representativeness. When self-representation and the representation of trauma coincide, the conflicting demands potentially make autobiography theoretically impossible: How can the exploration of trauma and the burden it imposes on memory be representative? How can the experience of a survivor of trauma stand for many? How can one tell the truth, the whole truth, and nothing but the truth, when facts, truth, and memory combine in the representation of trauma to undermine rather than strengthen representativeness? In her discussion of testimony and autobiography, Gayatri Spivak comments on this paradox: "And Rigoberta [Menchú], an organic intellectual taken for the true subaltern, represents herself as representative even as she points out she is not representative. The deliberate and powerful play of the individual and representativity is the impossible signature of the ghostly witness in all autobiography."[3] The writers I treat here cast a wary eye on representativeness and the ethics attached to it, though less to repudiate than to contend with them. While they write against autobiography's grain rather than with it, they are no less in dialogue with autobiography because of this choice.

As Foucault suggested in his example of the Panopticon, the development of a self capable of scrutinizing its actions is an ambivalent legacy of the Enlightenment for it describes not only the rational self formed through self-regulation but also the prisoner who, through subjection to surveillance, learns to monitor himself.[4] Autobiography, as an artifact of an Enlightenment legacy, demonstrates this ambivalence. The self who reflects on his or her life is not wholly unlike the self bound to confess or the self in prison, if one imagines self-representation as a kind of self-monitoring. Thus, along with the dutiful and truthful accounting of a life one might find in autobiography, the self is not only responsible but always potentially culpable, given autobiography's rhetorical proximity to testimony and the quasi-legalistic framework for judging its authenticity and authority that is so easily mobilized. Where there is getting it right, there is also getting it wrong and a litany of skepticism and censure is ubiquitous in the critical tradition. In the cultivation of an autobiographical conscience, one learns to be, and even strives for a sense of being, overseen. Thus autobiography can be viewed as a discipline, a self-study in surveillance. The prevalence of surveillance not only characterizes a relation between the self and others but becomes, as it is internalized, a property of the self as self-reflexivity or conscience.

The question of who gets to be representative in this tradition only partially obscures who does not. The exclusions that authorize the representative man derive historically from other forms of exclusion. In U.S. history, for example, the contradictory logic of the person can be demonstrated in slave law where the enslaved both were and were not persons. Autobiography studies have been influenced by this contradictory logic and specific autobiographies have been pressed into its service as the form grew up in relation to an emerging democracy in the United States.

---

[3]  Spivak, "Three Women's Texts," 9.
[4]  Michel Foucault, *Discipline and Punish*, trans. Alan Sheridan (New York: Random House, 1977).

That the category of the person can be structured nonsensically creates the possibility for considerable exclusions, and attempts to define the representative man illustrate this well. In the 39th Congress, Senator Jacob Howard made a comment that would resonate for autobiography: "Everywhere mature manhood is the representative type of the human race."[5] This definition is not codified by statute, of course, but it is an attitude traceable in autobiography criticism. It is easy to cite the glaring omission of nonwhite authors from earlier autobiography scholarship, and the absence of women has been well documented, as have the silences around these exclusions. What does this mean for autobiography, which, as a kind of writing constituted through *self*-representation, is a genre of the person?

Several questions emerge in relation to this query: How might we rethink autobiography in the absence of the rights of man, the bourgeois individual, and the notion of self-possession required to formulate an answer to "who am I and how did I become who I am?" If autobiography helps to install a sovereign subject, what is risked and gained by deposing such sovereignty? How does autobiography's rhetoric of rights and privileges efface its narrowing constraints? Further, how does one lay claim to, or discover, a *non*representative self? The limit-cases I offer in subsequent chapters can be seen as responses to these questions and the logic of representativeness on which they depend. Sometimes they challenge representativeness directly, and sometimes they seem simply to decline its appeal, and thereby reveal its insufficiency.

A gender politics related to truth telling has developed in relation to the legacy of the rational man and the ambiguities within self-representation its related exclusions entail. While the entry of women into autobiography did not inaugurate a debate about women's truthfulness, it certainly revived the rhetoric of women's deceitfulness. Two questions hound women's autobiographical efforts: Can women tell the truth? Do women have lives worth representing? Efforts to undermine women's self-representation are consistent with the construction of other barriers. Could men and women who were criminals, mad, or poor be appropriate autobiographical subjects? How could people of color use and be used by autobiography? How could minority sexualities become autobiographical material beyond the scandal of belated revelation or sensationalism? In other words, could autobiography be turned in a nondeforming way toward the interests of those without a dominant story to tell or dominant

[5] Senator Jacob Howard, *Congressional Globe*, 39th Congress, 1st session, quoted in Saidiya Hartman, *Scenes of Subjection* (New York: Oxford University Press, 1997), 175.

identities to reproduce? These questions lead us to the margins of autobiography.

In his anthology *American Autobiography* Paul John Eakin argues that studying the margins helps to delineate "the values and assumptions of the dominant culture"(8). For Eakin, the difficulty of writing a scholarly history of American autobiography is that the story of the margins is, paradoxically, where the full story that scholars are trying to tell is located. In his essay in Eakin's volume Lawrence Buell has identified the centrality of fictional and autobiographical intermingling to the development of autobiography. He finds a tremendous amount of variability in self-representational writing. From Emerson's "representative man" to Thoreau's "I," Buell problematizes how such quirky writing has ossified into a genre. Thoreau revealed the limits (or at least some of them) in the personal. He claimed the personal as his autobiographical subject, but produced a prose that was not particularly introspective or self-revelatory. His failure, which is perhaps his refusal, prompts an important question: Why equate the personal with a particular content? Another shaper of this dynamic form, Frederick Douglass, invented a representative self to perform in autobiography what was socially and legally impermissible for him as an African American. These two autobiographers form a crossroads of nineteenth-century American autobiography, says Buell. Because both Thoreau and Douglass relied on invention in crucial ways to secure an autobiographical subject, Buell questions what regulates the crossings between autobiography and the fictive, how we came to think of them separately, and with what consequences for our constructions of the genre?

How, then, might the logic of representativeness work in trauma narratives given these insights into autobiography's margins? If you are an autobiographer, then you stand in the place of the representative person. Your position there enables the kind of identification that characterizes autobiography. If you act, then, as the mirror of the self (for me), then in my identification with you I substitute myself for you, the other. If I am barred from doing that by your nonrepresentativeness, I withdraw my identification and, quite likely, the sympathy that flows from it. Thus trauma narratives often draw skepticism more readily than sympathy because they expose the conflict between identification and representativeness. While this is a limited (and critical) view of sympathy, it goes to the dynamic instability caused by the coincidence of representativeness and identification in self-representation. Autobiography about trauma forces the reader to assume a position of masochism or voyeurism. The reader is invited to find himself or herself in the figure of the representative, or to enjoy a kind of pleasure in the narrative organization of pain, in the case of trauma accounts. Whether the reader is a moral witness, a curious onlooker, or an interested spectator, he or she runs the risk Mikal Gilmore raises in *Shot in the Heart* where Gilmore addresses the ways in which his brother's life has been consumed to stimulate and satisfy a range of passions (21). In her reading of Rigoberta Menchú, Doris Sommer writes of the salutary effects of being denied identification and cautions that empathy hardly represents an ethic. Through her artful refusal of questions and calculated assertion of secrecy, Menchú invites and rebuffs identification. Her refusal of the reader's searching scrutiny reveals what might previously have gone unremarked: the will to knowledge and power at the bottom of what Sommer calls "our craving to know."[6] Identification, then, marks a point of tension in autobiography for writers whose self-representational projects place them squarely within the dynamics of surveillance and who fall outside the most familiar operations of identification and sympathy. Such writers might seek to swerve from autobiography's constraints as they find the figure of the representative man an image they cannot, or do not wish, to project. How, then, to proceed?

For these writers, an answer lies to the side of the genre itself. Some writers find little to recognize in the representative man; some recognize him all too well and seek some estrangement. Think of Henry Adams's use of a third-person persona in *The Education of Henry Adams*, for example. By inhabiting self-representation's ambiguities, such writers as Adams indicate other currents in self-representation. They do not construct themselves as nonfictional representatives of the fictions of citizenship and personhood; instead, they offer a self organized in relation to an autobiographical "I" rather than to the criteria of representativeness. Yet, without nonfictional reportage, what would an autobiography be? Would it cease to exist? Why take the risk, or why take the risk in this direction?

In part, the risk is already there. Consider that first-person accounts of trauma by women, for example, are likely to be doubted, not only when they bring forward accounts of sexual trauma but also because their self-representation already is at odds with the account the representative man would produce. A first-person account of trauma represents an intervention in, even an interruption of, a whole meaning-making apparatus that threatens to shout it down at every turn. Thus a writer's turn from the primarily documentary toward the fictional marks an effort to shift the ground of judgment toward a perspective she has struggled to achieve. Even given the factual claims made in such memoirs as Kathryn Harrison's *The Kiss* about adult incest, Linda Katherine Cutting's *Memory Slips* about child sexual abuse, and Nancy Venable Raine's *After Silence* about

---

[6] Sommer, "Sacred Secrets," 201.

rape, these texts question whether the exclusive benefit of memoir to women lies in the access it gives to reality, to the lived rather than the imagined.[7] Instead, in Harrison's preference for the literary over the strictly documentary, in Cutting's emphasis on the centrality of music in her life, and in Raine's drive to connect trauma research and therapy with the centrality of writing in her recovery, we see examples of the ways invention and imagination (elements more frequently associated with fiction) make self-representation possible and desirable. Along with the important work each does in bringing forward a personal injury into the public sphere, these writers insist that their documentary and creative talents be honored in their shaping of the material.

One argues for the importance of fiction to autobiography, in part, to challenge the assumption that honesty lies in personal revelation where one assumes that testimonial transparency is not only necessary and desirable but possible. There may be ways some trauma narratives can never meet the strictest standards of evidence (involving corroboration, for example) and still come into being. Texts that are concerned with self-representation and trauma offer a strong case for seeing that in the very condition of autobiography (and not the obstacles it offers for us to overcome) there is no transparent language of identity despite the demand to produce one. As controversial as any evidence of shaping may be in a trauma text—and what text is not shaped?—part of what we must call healing lies in the assertion of creativity. The ability to write beyond the silencing meted out by trauma is an achievement I want to recognize here.

## Trauma and Memory

As Sidonie Smith notes, "the 'I' as an enunciatory site is a point of convergence of autobiographical politics and the politics of memory."[8] Here, the speaking subject emerges in relation to the possibilities and limitations on its construction. Of these, memory is crucial because it, like experience, is both what one possesses by virtue of living and what can be constituted as evidence only by submitting it to various tests and protocols of presentation. As evidence, memory is only as authoritative as the person who is remembering, and only to the degree permitted in particular contexts. There is, then, a politics of memory in the sense that a politics of persons and their actions is operating, as Foucault theorized, in a field of

---

[7]    Kathryn Harrison, *The Kiss* (New York: Avon, 1998); Cutting, *Memory Slips* (1998); Raine, *After Silence* (1998).
[8]    Smith, "Memory, Narrative," 41.

power. Here we also find self-representation informed by what Ian Hacking calls *memoro-politics*, which is "above all a politics of the secret, of the forgotten event that can be turned, if only by strange flashbacks, into something monumental."[9] Memoro-politics concerns pathological forgetting, the kind that has produced psychoanalysis's clinical vocabulary of dissociation, repression, and amnesia, as distinct from the typically more benign kind, like forgetting the poetry you memorized in grade school or where you left your keys. Hacking's discussion of the controversies that characterize the study of memory suggests that current debates about "false memory" and recovered memory are a contemporary instance of a lengthy battle over truth telling and identity.[10]

According to Hacking, trauma, which had always meant a physical or physiological wound, acquired a new meaning sometime between 1874 and 1886 in France when it came to designate a spiritual, psychic, or mental injury, what he calls a "wound to the soul" (4).[11] Trauma acquired this additional sense of wounding by being linked to memory, such that trauma's wound no longer injured only the body but the soul and, through it, memory itself. In this way, for Hacking, the notion of traumatic, and even traumatized, memory was born. I am interested in how the development of traumatic memory impacts on self-representation and how, specifically, the debate about "false memory" instantiates this. As my discussion will make clear, determining a true memory to set alongside an accusation of "false memory" is of less interest here than clarifying the debate's functioning in the production of knowledge about trauma and self-representation.

Two precedents to traumatic memory and their relation to each other are especially relevant here: hysteria, diagnosed primarily in women beginning with Jean-Martin Charcot's studies in the late 1870s in France, and shell shock, diagnosed almost exclusively in male soldiers starting in the first world war. In *Pillar of Salt* Janice Haaken has argued that research into trauma stalled around applying insights gained through the study of

---

[9]  Hacking, *Rewriting the Soul*, 214.
[10]  For discussions of traumatic memory, in addition to Ian Hacking's work, see Laura Brown, "Not Outside the Range," in Caruth, ed., *Trauma*, 100–112; Caruth, ed., *Trauma*; Jennifer J. Freyd, *Betrayal Trauma* (Cambridge, Mass.: Harvard University Press, 1996); James M. Glass, *Shattered Selves* (Ithaca: Cornell University Press, 1993); Janice Haaken, *Pillar of Salt* (New Brunswick: Rutgers University Press, 1998); Herman, *Trauma and Recovery*; Lawrence Langer, *Admitting the Holocaust* (New York: Oxford University Press, 1994); Douglas Paton and John M. Violanti, *Traumatic Stress in Critical Occupations* (Springfield, Ill.: Charles C. Thomas, 1996); Raine, *After Silence*; Terr, *Too Scared to Cry* and *Unchained Memories*; and van der Kolk, et al., *Traumatic Stress*.
[11]  While some historical sources cite Freud's work on hysteria in the 1890s as the earliest usage of the new meaning of trauma, Hacking suggests that Freud did nothing more than deploy "what had become current" (4).

hysteria in women to the treatment of shell shock in men. Hysteria and shell shock offered two models for understanding disruptions in memory. Despite the similarities of somatic effects in those diagnosed with hysteria and shell shock, the two diagnoses and their treatments remained isolated from each other. Haaken lays the blame squarely on gender politics: soldiers could not be described as hysterics because the analogy, however clinically apt, would strike a mortal blow at the war effort. Instead, with gender politics as an organizing grid, the field of trauma studies split its focus, internalized gender hierarchy, and now bears the mark of this division. But Haaken argues that hysteria is like the repressed and that it has returned in the claims of sexual abuse made by women and children. For her, the ascendancy in the 1980s of child sexual abuse as a paradigm for understanding women's trauma marked a specification of the sexual violence that had already functioned as the paradigm for women and trauma.

Haaken questions why incest has become such a resonant illustration for what causes women pain. For her, incest may be a metaphor for any number of imperfectly understood causes. Since there is some support for women to self-report as incest survivors and because incest may resonate with a less definable experience of boundary violation, incest diagnoses have become prevalent. Thus for Haaken, declaring oneself a survivor of incest tells a kind of truth, though not necessarily a literal one. Yet that may be clinically appropriate given the restrictions placed on the stories women can tell about sex. For her, then, incest and the harm it causes indicates both a clinical phenomenon and a social movement.

Haaken has pointed out that when sexual violence is the dominant lens through which women's trauma is viewed, women may be pressured to report their pain in these terms. For her, it is less that women are "lying" about sexual abuse than that they are seeking a way to express an as-yet-undefined injury. She cautions against the literalizing of every report in therapy of sexual violence because sexual storytelling is a complicated process for women; it necessarily and appropriately combines fantasy with memory, and it develops over the course of therapy. Thus Haaken is less concerned with whether any particular memory is true or false than with the way that memory functions in a therapeutic narrative about sexuality. In this aspect she is Freud's heir, but with feminist sympathies. She will not close the door on fantasy, but she is equally disinclined to distrust the high frequency with which women report sexual violence.

Laura Brown in "Not Outside the Range" suggests that much of women's everyday life should properly be viewed as traumatic. Brown contends that women's habituation to abuse does not diminish its damaging and chronic effects. For those who define trauma as necessarily outside the range of daily life and who hold to unprecedentedness as the criterion of trauma, such a redefinition is problematic. If daily life itself is traumatic, against what can we measure trauma? For Brown, this question is not far off the mark. When women's lives are seen as lacking access to a nontraumatic standard, or when women's lives can so easily be categorized as a chronic traumatogenic state, how useful are our psychoanalytic, therapeutic, legal, and social services for addressing this long-standing harm? The residue of incest or other sexual violence often underpins this sense of chronic trauma, but Brown does not limit her insight to this form of harm. For her the poverty to which women are vulnerable is as critical a factor in chronic trauma as experiences of sexual violence.

It is worth taking a moment here to point out the double meaning of trauma in Freud which surfaces in Brown and Haaken: it may signify either a new wound or the reopening of an old wound. The relation between the wounds, and the extent to which trauma can be understood as repetition, raises an important question: where does harm done in the past end? The power of trauma to outlast the duration of its infliction is crucial to the sense of wounding that makes the term so resonant. For example, as an historical event the Holocaust is over, but its power to harm is not. Slavery no longer exists in the United States, but the wound it represents has not healed. Certain historical harms as well as injuries done to children suit the doubled meaning of trauma especially well.

Some historical and personal episodes are not so much forgotten, then, as subjected to particular forms of memory. Psychologist Jennifer Freyd has questioned in *Betrayal Trauma* whether the same mechanisms that permit us to remember also allow us, or compel us, to forget. For Freyd there is a logic to forgetting childhood abuse. It is an adaptive response to an abusive situation; children need to trust the adults who care for them. When children are betrayed by these adults, their world is profoundly threatened but their options both for escape and for development are severely limited. According to Freyd, children isolate the knowledge of betrayal so they can function (23). Freyd prefers the newer and expansive concept and term "knowledge isolation" (26) to the existing and conflicting vocabulary of repression, dissociation, and amnesia, terms that carry with them a considerable amount of imprecision. Freyd schematizes that repression is a form of "motivated forgetting," dissociation entails the splitting-off from consciousness of traumatic knowledge and experience, and amnesia involves comprehensive gaps in memory, as if parts of the record had been erased. While all of these phenomena may be present in the memory of someone who suffered childhood sexual abuse, Freyd uses "knowledge isolation" to get at how information about abuse becomes unavailable to consciousness while other contemporary memories of the abuse are preserved. To this end, Freyd, like Freud, emphasizes the way conflict drives this dynamic: "I propose that the conflict is between knowing about a betrayal in the external world and maintaining a necessary system of belief in order to guide adaptive behavior" (25).

Freud's formulation that "in mental life, nothing which has once formed can perish" suggests that memory offers a permanent record of all that has happened which can be accessed through analysis.[12] It has also been caricatured by some memory specialists whose explicit target is memory and trauma. Psychologist Elizabeth Loftus has served as an expert defense witness in child sexual abuse cases brought by grown children against their parents / caregivers.[13] Her experiments in memory lead her to conclude that "false memories" can be "implanted" by malevolent or misguided therapists. This view is a basic tenet of the False Memory Syndrome Foundation, a group founded in 1992 by Jennifer Freyd's parents after she offered their abuse as the reason she severed ties with them.[14] Significantly, Freyd did not sue her parents or seek any other legal recourse. She did not initially publicize their abuse of her to friends, family, employers, or any other collective entity. She simply cut off contact with them. Her withdrawal was intolerable, and the Freyds organized other parents whose children had accused them of sexual abuse, recruited experts, and coined and promoted the term "false memory" in popular parlance.

The question of what "false memory" is must be posed in relation to the ways in which its credibility has been established. False memory syndrome is not recognized by the American Psychiatric Association and is not listed in the *Diagnostic and Statistical Manual of Mental Disorders* (1994), which does list amnesia, repression, and dissociation as disorders in memory unexplained by common forgetfulness. Absent from an official clinical vocabulary, "false memory syndrome" is a moving target. Yet the narrative circulated by the False Memory Syndrome Foundation of corrupt therapists, often under the sway of the best-selling text on child sexual abuse for survivors *The Courage to Heal*, who see behind every unhappy woman (especially) a sexual abuse scenario, has gained currency.[15] Boosted by the claims of Loftus, who asserts that memories may never be

[12]    Freud, quoted in Donald P. Spence, *The Rhetorical Voice of Psychoanalysis* (Cambridge, Mass.: Harvard University Press, 1994), 2.
[13]    Elizabeth F. Loftus and Katherine Ketcham, *Witness for the Defense* (New York: St. Martin's Press, 1991) and *The Myth of Repressed Memory* (New York: St. Martin's Press, 1994).
[14]    See Hacking, *Rewriting the Soul*, and Freyd, *Betrayal Trauma*, for critical accounts of the False Memory Syndrome Foundation.
[15]    Ellen Bass and Laura Davis, *The Courage to Heal: A Guide for Women Survivors of Child Sexual Abuse* (New York: Harper & Row, 1988).

retrieved in any intact or reliable form once they have been forgotten, "false memory syndrome" possesses a scientific status for its believers.

The science on which Loftus's work is based has been critiqued by others who work on traumatic memory. Among others, professors of psychiatry Bessell van der Kolk and Lenore Terr have stipulated that while Loftus's research may tell us something about memory, it tells us nothing about traumatic memory, the kind that expresses itself in flashbacks and fragments. Unlike Terr and van der Kolk, Loftus works with human subjects who are neither putative survivors of trauma nor sufferers of disturbances in memory. While Loftus's laboratory experiments show that people can be induced to say they remember details that are suggested to them, she has not demonstrated that people can be compelled to develop "false memories" of trauma. Despite its dubious application to traumatic memory, the rhetoric of false memory has gained a cultural foothold. It has been promoted by motivated parties to do a specific kind of cultural work—namely, to discredit testimony by survivors, to pathologize, specifically, memories of sexual abuse in childhood, and to stigmatize therapies related to this abuse. But it has also become associated with the debunking projects that swiftly followed the brief cultural accordance of attention to child sexual abuse. In this context, journalistic accounts that expose false or inflated claims of whole towns involved in ritual satanic abuse, for example, seem like healthy correctives to hysterical witch hunts, their ethics above reproach and disinterested. A backlash against reports of abuse now means that the position of "victim," and the sympathy it mobilizes, is more likely to flow toward the accused rather than the accuser.

According to the False Memory Syndrome Foundation and its advocates, what, then, is the remedy for "false memory"? One might imagine it would be truthful memory, yet the False Memory Syndrome Foundation seems to be looking instead for *less* memory. They seek for the disaffected son or daughter to assent to official family narratives. Insofar as he or she is a dissident from family narratives of harmony and normalcy, his or her narrative concurrence is sought. Thus, "false memory" presents less a conflict about memory than one about power and narrative, specifically, *which* and *whose* story will prevail, even as the crisis of who is to control the family narrative is played out as a conflict in the realm of memory. The apparent dichotomy between true and false memory correlates to a judgment about good and bad therapy. In "bad" therapy, the kind in which the patient discusses memories of childhood abuse, the "bad" therapist has implanted a germ, a false memory, from which grows a bad narrative of kinship. The consequences range from lawsuits against, typically, male relatives, to the severing of familial ties. This assertion of independence seems in many cases more grievous to the parents than litigation. On close inspection, therefore, it appears more likely that the preferred choice of the False Memory Syndrome Foundation is no therapy, the dominance of parental memories as the basis of family narratives and, crucially, the prevention of any self-representation developing outside or in conflict to that authority. Many children who have now reached majority age want the inconceivable, according to False Memory Syndrome Foundation parents: they want their parents to leave them alone.

In books on traumatic memories in children, Lenore Terr has described memory and trauma and her own experiences as both therapist and expert witness in legal trials. Her first major case study in children, trauma, and memory focused on the schoolchildren who were kidnapped in Chowchilla, California, in 1976. This event provided her with a group who had all suffered the same traumatic event. In *Unchained Memories* Terr, like Freyd, concurs with Freud that the key to repression is conflict. Repression is motivated forgetting. Remembering traumatic memory, as Terr theorizes, requires a ground and a cue. A ground alone—getting well out of hurting range, for example—is not sufficient. A cue is needed, like Proust's madeleine, to act as a trigger to retrieve the memory. The children who were kidnapped in Chowchilla manifested Type I disorders: they were traumatized by an experience and developed a range of symptoms including nightmares, heightened anxiety, and withdrawal. They also remembered details of the kidnapping with clarity. Type II disorders, as Terr describes them, are associated with the kind of ongoing, even fragmented, abuse that some children suffer. As an example of Type II disorders, Terr describes Eileen Franklin Lipsiker who, as an adult, initially recalled her father's murder of her childhood friend Susan Nason through fragmented flashbacks. When abuse is combined with nonabusive caresses, and when private horrors mix with relatively normal public displays of family life, then memory is preserved in the fragmentation associated with Type II. The specificity of trauma and memory research like Terr's exceeds the formulations propounded by the False Memory Syndrome Foundation and its allies.

Brain research forms a key part of the ongoing work on trauma and offers a way to think about the totality of the trauma experience. Discussions of memory and the brain focus on how the brain processes, stores, and retrieves information, as well as what needs to happen for these processes to work smoothly. The relations among brain chemistry (the effect of noradrenaline on the parts of the brain associated with memory and perception, for example), the psyche, and the body are difficult for the survivor of trauma to separate. For example, a flashback is both a somatic experience (the survivor of rape may experience disorientations in place and time through flashbacks that prompt a range of observable, physical symptoms such as shaking, sweating, and a trancelike gaze), and a mental phenomenon, a disorientation of mind. So, too, it produces and draws on psychic residue even as it derives from and produces changes in brain chemistry. Research focused on the brain locates the hippocampus as the seat of memory, and studies the changes that occur in it during and after trauma. Some research indicates that the hippocampus shrinks in response to trauma and that characteristic failures in memory result. A range of research is finding interesting links between the brain and trauma and advancing hypotheses about traumatic memory that give it an organic base. In the context of the larger cultural and historical project devoted to memory and trauma, this research may represent an effort to return trauma to the wounded body.

Testimonial projects that involve narrating that which breaks the frame require for some theories a listener no less than a speaking subject. In writing about trauma generally and the Holocaust specifically, psychoanalyst Dori Laub has claimed that one of the harms of trauma is the impossibility of saying "thou."[16] Trauma lacks an other who will return the story without violence to the speaker by listening to it carefully. What is the value of such repetition? For Laub, telling is crucial. He claims that trauma has not happened in the same ways to someone before and after she or he can organize the story in narrative terms and recount it successfully. Narrative not only contains trauma in this formulation, but is itself an experiential category. Laub recognizes here the pain of storytelling, but also privileges narrative over experience. Experience is an insufficient category for the description of trauma: narrative, with the requirement of what I would call here a good-enough listener, is necessary.

If we follow Laub, what, then, happens to trauma if it cannot be remembered? What is memory if it is purged of trauma? I use these questions to link personal and cultural memories and narratives of trauma and to suggest that cultural memory, like individual memory, develops characteristic and defensive amnesia with which those who have experienced trauma must contend. Trauma is never exclusively personal; it always exists within complicated histories that combine harm and pleasure, along with less inflected dimensions of everyday life. Remembering trauma entails contextualizing it within history. Insofar as trauma can be defined as that which breaks the frame, rebuilding a frame to contain it is as fraught with difficulty as it is necessary. Placing a personal history of trauma within a collective history compels one to consider that cultural memory, like personal memory, possesses "recovered" or "repressed" memories,

[16]   See Felman and Laub, *Testimony.*

and also body (or body politic) memories of minoritized trauma like racial and sexual violence. In this context the burden of trauma lies in the difficulty of saying "our" as much as "thou," for it entails situating a personal agony within a spreading network of connections. This problematic goes to the central role of first-person accounts, however dissident and dissonant, in remembering traumas that have been pushed to the cultural and symbolic margins. It also raises a difficult question: why, if memory and trauma are so intimately linked, does the presence of trauma in memory prompt so much anxiety about truth and lies? In response to this question, one finds a range of accounts seeking narrative form, appropriate contexts, and able listeners.

Our vocabularies about extreme experience are biased toward descriptions of trauma. In some cases, pleasure may produce some of the same memory effects as trauma. That is, memories of pleasure may be experienced as flashbacks, may induce emotional flooding, and may even remove a person from the present moment so fully as to come very close to dissociation. Can these disorientations be thought of in the same context as trauma without sacrificing the elements critical to the study of trauma and its focus on injury and suffering? No one, after all, goes to a therapist complaining about the disruptive presence of happy thoughts. Yet, the similarity between remembering happiness and unhappiness (or forgetting them) may indicate some incoherence in the way we remember any intense experience and find ways to incorporate intensity (the unprecedented, the unassimilable, if not the catastrophic) into lives and life narratives that allow them no room. For unhappy memories, we look to trauma studies; for memories of intense pleasure that break the frame of daily life, where do we look? To a soft-focus ideology of romantic love? To charismatic worship or human potential movements? If the phenomenology of recall and forgetting is similar across pleasure and pain, and if some version of the somatic effects of posttraumatic memory is present in memories of other intense experiences, then perhaps it is to narratives of the self that we should look as much as to narratives of the brain. When memory bars that which does not fit, as well as that which hurts too much, how are we to understand the project of telling a life story where it must be organized in terms of what is anomalous, difficult, and resistant to narration?

The study of traumatic memory is marked by a history of definitional instability that probably makes it permanently vulnerable to exploitation in the name of science, as the highly charged debate around "false memory syndrome" indicates. I have indicated two developments in the history of traumatic memory to suggest why this is so. First, when trauma acquired its additional meaning as a psychological wound, memory was made to signify a place where this wound lodged. Memory therefore became especially significant to the meaning and location of identity itself. Second, the separation of the developing theories and treatments of shell shock and hysteria perpetrated a politics of gender asymmetry that persists in the study of traumatic memory. "False memory" capitalizes on both trends: it acknowledges the power of memory through its efforts to discredit it and it promotes a stereotype of hysteria around women's memories of sexual abuse. Despite its own hypothetical status and many trauma researchers' considering it to be simply false, "false memory syndrome" exploits the instabilities in the study of traumatic memory to discredit claims of abuse within families that would dissent from official family narratives.

### Foucault, Pierre Rivière, and Althusser

A much-circulated rumor has it that after Foucault was diagnosed with AIDS, he vowed never to speak of it.[17] The rumor works because it seems to crystallize in a particularly theatrical way Foucault's self-actualization as an anticonfessional subject. In his refusal to "confess" to AIDS, or anything else, Foucault became emblematic of his own theories of confession, discipline, and discourse. His not talking would indicate his resistance, however incomplete, to a whole machinery of compulsory talk about sex, sexuality, and, in his case, the linkage they would afford to his own illness and death. It was a narrative not of his own choosing, so he declined it.

Or did he? The truth rarely gets in the way of a good rumor. Rumors shape up desired interpretations in the mode of historical anecdote; they substitute a telling example for telling the truth. Why does the rumor about Foucault's last silence resonate more than one about, say, his last words? For some, it indicates a seamlessness between Foucault's work and life: of course, he would refuse to be implicated in a confessional discourse that would equate his medical condition with his sexuality and his death as if it were underpinned by some logic of retribution. For others, Foucault's silence was equated with his shame, or, as in the iconography of AIDS protest, "Silence = Death," with his mortality. It is well enough to say that Foucault's choices about what he would say and to whom when he was ill are overburdened by others' needs and expectations. He was and remains, after all, a powerful advocate for thinking about sexuality and resistance. But the rumor floats above its context to instantiate something about Foucault's own refusal to confess. As someone whose earliest

---

[17]   David Halperin, *Saint Foucault.* In this context, see Halperin's incredibly helpful discussion of Foucault and biography, 126–185.

scholarly publications introduced the previously unpublished memoirs of a confessed murderer and a hermaphrodite who committed suicide, the complexity of self-representation was of lasting significance to Foucault. Why he didn't pen his own memoir may be impossible to answer, but his persistent interest in memoir never disappeared despite his critique of confessional practices and its possible application to memoir. For Foucault, memoir may have represented a practice of resistance, a counterdiscourse to the official compulsion to confess.

Foucault's early advocacy for memoir developed into an abiding interest in the uses of memory in self-invention. Perhaps most obviously in *Madness and Civilization*, *Discipline and Punish*, *The History of Sexuality*, and *Birth of the Clinic*, Foucault demonstrates how memory is required for the resistant political practices his work inspires and in which he participated.[18] At the heart of self-representation lies a process of self-construction for Foucault, the material of which is a mixture of memory and invention. Acts of remembering the past differently, through rogue confessions, scandalous memoirs, and an unofficial archive of protest, offer a different construction of the present. Such acts, in fact, remake the present into a site of a disallowed past's resonance. For Foucault, scenes of self-construction, whether via sexual self-definition and self-actualization or through disciplinary processes of power, involve looking back in order to look forward. Not only reminiscences but the problems of how to reminisce and how to understand the place of memory stand out in Foucault's work. The spectator before the scaffold, the penitent in the confessional, the knowing child: all are wide-eyed figures in his work who find themselves in scenes of subjection. Each brings to bear on these scenes what he or she already knows, even as disciplinary pedagogies of penality, confession, and sexuality seek to rework personal memory toward disciplinary ends. Memory, however, remains a remnant from which a counterdiscourse may emerge. It is at least partially unassimilable to power even as power attempts to conscript it to its own ends via official discourse. The radical meaning of memory may always be shouted down, but such documents as memoir provide evidence of resistance. Their contemporary influence is not their primary value; in fact, Foucault's chosen memoirs were decidedly marginal in their time. Rather, it is what memory (in this case, in the form of memoir) can offer the future that compels Foucault.

Although Foucault did not write his autobiography, he has been

[18]   Michel Foucault, *Birth of the Clinic*, trans. A. M. Sheridan (New York: Pantheon, 1973), *Discipline and Punish*, trans. A. M. Sheridan (New York: Random House, 1977); *The History of Sexuality*, vol. 1, *An Introduction*, trans. Robert Hurley (New York: Random House, 1978); *Madness and Civilization*, trans. Richard Howard (New York: Vintage 1988).

posthumously (mis)treated to biography.[19] Whether Foucault's own memoir would have intervened in his biographers' constructions of him is debatable, but the issue of why Foucault did not write a memoir goes beyond his desire not to be compelled to confess. One could, after all, imagine him finding pleasure in this constraint and reworking the demands of confession toward his own ends. I would suggest that Foucault understood his theoretical interventions into history, memory, power, and sexuality as consistent with an abiding interest in memoir. Instead of dropping his interest in publishing other people's scandalous memoirs and replacing it with more crisply focused analyses, Foucault continued to find the workings of memory everywhere. His own "memoir," in a sense, is traceable in his continuing interest in memory and in the developing linkages of past to present and future.

Although the centrality of memory may be obscured by the more frequently used terms in Foucault's critical lexicon, it deserves to be as central a term in the study of Foucault as power, discourse, confession, and sexuality, and may, as a technique of self-invention, offer a way to understand how they all work together. Much of this is adumbrated in his contribution to bringing *I, Pierre Rivière* to publication. *I, Pierre Rivière* is a dossier of materials related to Pierre Rivière's murder of his mother, who was pregnant, his young brother, and his sister in 1835. It includes the case's official documents, among them, medical and legal opinions, accounts by Rivière's neighbors, court documents, essays by historians including Foucault, and a memoir by Rivière. In his brief introduction Foucault points to the important variety of discourses assembled in the dossier and, as one would predict, focuses on how these discourses demonstrate a convergence of psychiatry and criminal justice. What most compels him in *I, Pierre Rivière*, however, is less the assemblage of external documents than the memoir itself. He embraces its "beauty" (199) and, in the essay he contributes to the volume, directs his attention mainly to it. I would suggest that everything Foucault found compelling in the dossier materials was present in the memoir. The supporting materials contextualize the crime in important ways, but Foucault's introductory comments on the whole project are brief and schematic. It is not until he writes about the memoir that his interest becomes electric. The question is, what does he see in the memoir?

For Foucault, Rivière is author both of his memoir and his crime. This oscillation in authorship means that the crime and the memoir, the mur-

---

[19]  David Macey, *The Lives of Michel Foucault* (New York: Pantheon Books, 1993); and Didier Eribon, *Michel Foucault*, trans. Betsy Wing (Cambridge, Mass.: Harvard University Press, 1991).

ders and the writing, keep changing places. That they can do this reveals one of the constitutive dimensions of self-representation: a person's writing and a person's living contribute, in a sense, different legacies. This is a strange and absolutely characteristic feature of autobiography: the self becomes oddly multiple just at the time one might think it was most organized and coherent—the moment of telling its own story. It is precisely this organizational task of autobiography—the effort to set it all out in writing—that reveals how the self can never be quite where it ought, or where it is expected, or where it wants to be. Saying "it" here entails some alienation, though saying something more "personal" risks imprecision. We are not talking about "you" and "I," or "he" and "she" as persons only. To these pronouns we must add a metalanguage of identity in order to focus on what always threatens to disappear in autobiography: the writing. Foucault seizes on the relation between life and memoir and the disturbances in the "I" who must represent them. Whether Rivière is mad is of less interest to Foucault than the madness, or at least instability, around separating crime from writing, event from memory, the hand that wields the knife from the hand that grips the pen. What strikes Foucault is how the memoir was appraised by Rivière's judges: for them, the memoir is less an account of the crime than a part of it.

Foucault reads Rivière's memoir as a limit-case that highlights the boundary between memoir and history. On the side of history are accounts of battles and wars with sanctified and official actors; on the side of memoir are scandalous accounts of murders, brawls, and street violence. For Foucault, the activities on both sides are pretty much the same. The difference is that historical narrative elevates butchery to battle. "The frontier between the two is perpetually crossed," he writes (205): both describe murder, the only difference is with what degree of sanctification. Murder makes the hero famous and the criminal infamous, but both have blood on their hands. In this context, then, the focus shifts from what Rivière did to how his act will enter into discourse. Here Foucault points to an anticonfessional genre of last words: the criminal's "sorrowful lamentations," or the song of the one about to be executed. This is not the compelled contrition of the confessional subject. Instead, the murderer openly and freely confesses, even boasts, embraces the act and refuses to share it with anyone. The song falls between the murder and the execution. It is not confessional, therefore, in that the punishment has already been decided and will occur imminently. This is no plea; "it is, as it were, the lyrical position of the murderous subject" (208), a person on the verge of execution. Rivière described himself as one already dead when his death sentence was commuted and he was delivered to jail instead of the gallows. This was not the end he had composed for himself. He imagined his execution as a necessary and logical step in his crime. Following the commutation of his death sentence, he killed himself in prison.

Foucault applauds *I, Pierre Rivière* as an anticonfessional memoir. Foucault's sense of this genre was that only the criminal and the insane could sing the nonconfessional song of the condemned, poised as they were between deaths. But what does it mean to think of trauma memoirs more broadly as nonconfessional speech? If trauma memoirs are currently viewed as petitioning for belief from readers, then they do not fall into Foucault's category. Yet, is the readiness of many readers to render judgment sufficient to make a memoir into a confession, into speech that is compelled to petition someone for something? What if trauma memoirists are viewed not so much as asking to be believed as asserting their speech, as, that is, becoming lyrical subjects of trauma? The trauma memoirist's position differs, of course, from the soon-to-be-executed. He or she has done no harm and there is no closing frame of official punishment in place. These are crucial differences. But at a psychic level, trauma memoirists find a way to write themselves out of no-less punitive constructions of their "guilt" (a judgment frequently pounded into them by those who harm them) and punishment (what it is like to live with trauma inside the narrative the brutalizer authors). I read Foucault's glimpse into memoir as revealing something of the way confession can come off the tracks and become self-declaration. He also indicates the costs of the venture if speech itself is seen as a mad or criminal act consistent with other mad or criminal behavior.

Foucault is associated with another memoir of trauma and scandal and, as its publication comes later in his career, demonstrates his abiding interest in memoir. In *I, Pierre Rivière*, Foucault reaches toward his interests; in *Herculine Barbin*, he has found them. *Herculine Barbin* follows the first volume of *The History of Sexuality* almost as an illustration of Foucault's interest in sexuality, but nothing much in it surprises him. It is *I, Pierre Rivière* that catches him off guard and propels him into memoir's compelling strangeness. Perhaps it is simply easier, morally, to criticize Herculine Barbin's cruel treatment. Compelled to "become" a man but given no way to do so, forbidden to "remain" a woman but unable to throw off a whole lifetime and history, Barbin commits suicide. Nothing is decent, fair, or enlightened about this ending. One recognizes in the outlines of Barbin's life the issues about sexuality and politics that compelled Foucault. With Rivière, however, many of the details of his crime and life, despite involving his mental health, a trial and his imprisonment, do not suggest an immediate association with Foucault's interests: Rivière's memoir records in obsessive detail every presumed wrong his mother committed against his father as if this accounting would require and justify her execution. As if succumbing to the gravitational pull of Rivière's vendetta, Rivière decides his sister must be murdered because she sided with his mother, and that his young brother must be murdered because otherwise his father would be too sad to see Rivière punished. He, therefore, must murder his brother to spare his father any sadness over Pierre. The murders are vicious, the murderer remorseless, the murdered human and familiar. Thus, it is the beauty of the memoir and not of Rivière's crime that draws Foucault in, and the strange logic of anticonfessional self-representation he sees there.

Limit-cases in memoir need not, then, following Foucault, partake of the confessional. He offers a model of a reader who is not judge, jury, doctor, or priest. Yet, without the authority to evaluate, how do we read memoirs? How do we read self-representational texts, in other words, that challenge our familiar habits or protocols? Althusser's memoir *The Future Lasts Forever* moves us to this hard question. Because he reveals himself as a sufferer of bouts of depression and mania that often render him delusional, Althusser, as latter-day Pierre Rivière, confounds crime and writing, murderousness and memoir, family and law and makes us wonder how we are to read this memoir.

After Louis Althusser strangled his wife Hélène to death, he was immediately whisked by sympathetic friends at the École Normale Supérieure to a mental hospital. There, he was declared unfit to stand trial and was hospitalized. By declaring him unfit to plead, the French penal system allowed Althusser to go uncharged, untried, and unpunished for a murder he does not dispute committing due to his mental illness. *The Future Lasts Forever* is a quasi-confessional memoir that links the legal with the therapeutic. It is the "testimony" Althusser was neither permitted nor compelled to give, as well as a talking-cure-informed, psychoanalytically based memoir of the impact of childhood trauma on his later life. He elaborates a kind of causality around the murder that has its roots in his childhood and later experience as a prisoner of war. These traumas are adduced as evidence of his personality and they also define his focus as a memoirist. If his is a record of mental illness precipitated and realized, then what kind of an autobiographer is he? If trustworthiness and representativeness are traditional hallmarks of an autobiographer, can Althusser be an autobiographer, given his self-documentation of the mental illness from which he suffered and for which he was treated? Can his memoir withstand the test of accuracy, or must it, like Althusser, be whisked away from hostile judges? This question of whether Althusser can qualify as an autobiographer based on his own declaration of delusional episodes and other disorders strikes at many of autobiography's defining issues.

Written nearly 150 years after Pierre Rivière's crimes, *The Future Lasts Forever* forms a striking companion piece to *I, Pierre Rivière*. Yet, Olivier Corpet and Yann Moulier Boutang, who introduce *The Future Lasts Forever*, make the comparison explicitly in order to distance Althusser from it. Yet, Althusser himself embraces the comparison. For Corpet and Boutang, *The Future Lasts Forever* exceeds the analyses of madness and reason offered either in Freud's *Psycho-Analytic Notes on a Case of Paranoia* or in *I, Pierre Rivière* because of Althusser's position as an intellectual and a philosopher. Why they think his memoir is self-evidently superior to the account Rivière, or presumably any nonprofessional, could offer is unclear, but they elevate Althusser above an association with Rivière as madman and murderer and claim that Althusser's text should more appropriately be placed alongside Foucault's *Madness and Civilization*. Althusser is less squeamish about the connection to Rivière and declares a single precedent to his memoir: "No one before me has made such a critical confession (apart, that is, from Pierre Rivière, whose admirable confession Foucault published)" (29). His declaration of singularity, in fact, places him squarely within the autobiographical tradition, at least its Western and masculine side, and makes him into Rousseau's heir.

For Corpet and Boutang, Althusser's text should be distinguished from any genre that lays claim to historical accuracy. Althusser, too, is eager to dismiss models: "I give notice that what follows is not a diary, not my memoirs, not an autobiography. In discarding everything else, I simply wanted to remember those emotional experiences which had an impact on me and helped shape my life; my life as I see it and as others may, I think, see it too" (29). This is, however, a thoroughly satisfying definition of memoir or autobiography. It presses forward memory both as the central term, "I simply wanted to remember," and as a caveat. Yet Althusser suggests that there are expectations we ought to abandon about his self-representational text. In asserting the primacy of memory and emotional experience, what, exactly, are we diverting from? From historical documentation to memory? From actual to emotional experience? And for what reasons? Are they theoretical, or do they partake of the constraints that define Althusser's mental health? And if the shifts result largely in the context of the latter, would that obviate the theoretical insights they contain? For Althusser, the confusion that characterizes his murder of Hélène marks his experience of life. His memory is often at odds with what he knows to be the official record—he remembers things out of sequence, claims as memories events that did not happen to him but which he has, in a sense, adopted as his memories because they tell a symbolic

truth. He is, in short, an unreliable narrator of his own life, and self-de-
claredly.so. What, then, to make of this text? Located at the limit of fantasy
and hallucination on one side, and history and memoir on the other, *The
Future Lasts Forever* makes murder, madness, and memoir into a template
for the emergence of the subject.

Althusser's is an odd confession, if it is one at all. For him confession is
about the self in isolation, and in his case, the self before itself as no other
authority rises to the level of judge: "Here," he writes, "is the scene of
murder just as I experienced it" (15). Although he insists that being found
unfit to plead based on article 64 of the 1838 version of the penal code re-
lieves him of the obligation and deprives him of the right to tell his story,
he also recognizes the leniency that memoir permits: "I realise, of course,
that what I am attempting to express here conforms neither to the nature
nor the rules of a court appearance" (13). Instead, he assumes what Foucault described as the "lyrical position of the murderous subject." Althusser locates his writing, done like Pierre Rivière's in a concentrated
amount of time between the murder he commits and the death sentence
he feels has been imposed on him by being declared unfit to plead. He
faces no literal execution, but assumes one rhetorically: "Any individual
who is declared unfit to plead is destined to be placed beneath a tomb-
stone of silence" (14–15). Yet his protest is excessive. Although his silencing is complex, he is planning to publish his memoir. Rivière's memoir is
written explicitly within the context of a complicated legal proceeding
that takes as part of its process a determination about his sanity; Althusser
seems to seek this positioning.

The complexity of silence surrounding his speech goes to the isolated
privacy of the asylum. True, he has been protected from prosecution, but
the asylum offers a living death: few come to visit, the ones who do are
uncomfortable while there, and because Althusser's accounts of his actions are being heard in the context of clinical confidentiality, his story re-
ceives no public hearing. Like Pierre Rivière who found himself in prison
rather than on the gallows, Althusser feels out of place. For Althusser, the
experience suggests being a missing person in a war, not a prisoner of
war, which is something he experienced, but a blank, a gap in the record.
In what way, though, is Althusser being denied representation? Presumably a legal proceeding would require him to become a confessional subject, one whose privacy enters the public domain through the protocols of
law. Over this, Althusser would have had little influence or control. His
fate rests, nonetheless, within a system of influence and patronage—his
well-placed friends were able to circumvent any trip through the legal
system—which allows him to write the anticonfession of his choosing.

Althusser shares with Rivière a passionate misogyny. Mothers especially get rough treatment from both. Rivière admits to a horror of incest and promotes this obsession into a general avoidance of women. His mother's "crime" for which he punishes her with murder is to have made his father's life miserable. The son and father get rather mixed up here with respect to harm and revenge and young Pierre "goes Oedipal" with displaced sexual rage. Althusser diagnoses the roots of his pathology in his family and lays the blame particularly on women. Sexuality disturbs him, and, as he remarks as an adult to a friend, "The trouble is, there are bodies and, worse still, sexual organs" (36). What compels Althusser about the murder is himself. In comparison to his self-interest, Hélène is a bit player. To him, she is neither the cause of the murder nor the source of its most interesting effects. Rivière and Althusser build from the presumed wrongs done by women to their own murders of women. Yet the summaries of injury fail to persuade. The cases against the women are so obsessional in nature and so tangled up in the debates about madness that swirl around the authors that one's attention is pulled insistently toward the memoirist's "I." The murderer's perspective dominates as both sing the songs of murder, poised as Foucault wrote, between two deaths, murder and execution. Or, one could argue, between two silences: the silence each imposed on those they murdered and the silence they experience from listeners who cannot hear.

What does this position tell us about trauma, memory, and self-representation? Althusser and Foucault's Rivière occupy the margins of memoir. While their texts belong to a tradition of scandalous memoirs, they also illuminate the contours of confession, and reveal especially how confession might be resisted, how the talking-cure may offer a self-authorizing and anticonfessional position. Neither text sues for sympathy; instead, the memoirists seek self-revelation. In this context, how do poststructuralism and memoir mutually illuminate? For Foucault, the specialization of the modern state requires an intimate and fetishistic attachment to the nation. Citizenship depends on the interpenetration of public and private. Althusser and Foucault's Rivière are interesting examples of conformity and resistance to this model of citizenship. Although operating outside the law, they are nonetheless actors in a legal milieu who adopt the confession—with special mention of the legal confession—as their preferred mode of self-representation. Some strands of poststructuralism, especially Foucault's, have revealed that sexuality is the modern form of self-intelligibility. One knows oneself in and as one's sexuality. But sexuality is tethered to other related phenomena. It cannot escape their pull. Here it is madness, misogyny, criminality, and the juridical in which sexuality is saturated. These memoirs are extraordinary in that they demonstrate the interimplications of these discourses *as* identity. They do not hamper, constrain, or distort identity; they are not antagonistic to it; they are identity and thus the focus of self-representation.

Corpet and Boutang claim that "[i]f we enter the realm of phantasy and hallucination with [*The Future Lasts Forever*], it is because the subject-matter is madness" (8). Yet we also enter the realm of fantasy at least, if not necessarily hallucination, because the subject matter is autobiography. Memory's fragility, the enduring hold of trauma, and the complexity of self-representation do not simply make memoir inherently vulnerable to fantasy. Rather, the subject-who-remembers engages mental and narrative dynamics that partake necessarily of fantasy. These cannot be banished from the scene of memory, nor are they easily incorporated into working definitions of self-representation; perhaps especially where trauma is concerned and an implicit part of the project is to discern "what really happened." Thus dissimulation of the subject in the scene of fantasy parallels the dissimulation of the subject in the scene of memory, trauma, and self-representation. As limit-cases about murder and madness, *I, Pierre Rivière* and *The Future Lasts Forever* push us to the extremes of memoir. There we find dubious accounts by dubious subjects. Our reliance on the facticity of autobiography may become less relevant and it certainly becomes less secure, as the subject who emerges is no less a self-invention than in Rousseau or Franklin, yet not the representative we might embrace.

These limit-cases demonstrate poststructuralism's interest in the language through which the self may emerge (and is compelled to emerge), the institutions and discourses that not only impinge upon but make possible its emergence, and the protocols of self-representation in criminal justice and psychoanalysis. Althusser's and Rivière's texts are exemplary of how the self comes into being as a distinctive entity in memoir. After all, it was not the answers Rivière gave during his interrogation that resulted in the doctors having conflicting views about whether he was mad—it was his memoir that persuaded some of his sanity. Althusser's philosophical work does not introduce the burden of hallucination on self-representation, and his life does not speak for itself in framing the murder. For that, he turns to memoir, even if he disavows its name. Still, one can connect his philosophical concerns to those that characterize memoir: what is interpellation, arguably Althusser's best-known concept, if not a trope of autobiography?[20] For the self who comes into being as a subject at the moment of being hailed by an authority figure and signaling "It is I" in response to the policeman's "Hey, you" is structured in Althusser as a self-representational issue, a question of how the self knows

20    Louis Althusser, "Ideology and Ideological State Apparatuses (Notes Towards an Investigation)" in *Critical Theory since 1965*, ed. Hazard Adams and Leroy Searle (Tallahassee: University Press of Florida, 1986), 239–50.

itself. It is in these limit-cases that the constitutive vagaries of memory and trauma are asserted. We do not find here the caricature of a post-structuralism that would airily dismiss facts, reality, and history. In their tense documentation of events, states of mind, and rationalizations, both Rivière and Althusser seek to make sufficiently public and shareable what would otherwise be relegated to the realm of mad and criminal subjectivity, uttered by the dissonant other to whom one need not listen.

It may seem strange to get at the questions I am raising about trauma, self-representation, law, and kinship by focusing initially on two murderers rather than two survivors of such violence. I do so in order to uncover the presence within poststructuralism of an interest in memoir and memoir's capacity to represent trauma. Memoir is written in both cases in relation to law, but does not offer evidence within law's protocols. The crime, or "what I did," in both cases is subordinated to an autobiographical account of whodunit, which accompanies the erasure of the victims' accounts of trauma.

At the beginning of this chapter, I indicated my intention to describe an alternative jurisdiction for the self-representation of trauma. As a legal concept, jurisdiction concerns authority and the power to judge; administration, rule and control; and, at its most local level, the contexts in which this happens. Through my discussion of representativeness, I have shown how autobiography functions as a judicature, how self-representation exists within a juridical frame through the mechanisms of judging and assessment which inform its production of knowledge. Testimony names both a discursive demand in self-representation and the knot of resistance with which it contends: one is both abjured to speak and exposed to scrutiny, but the demand may be met with some degree of agency. In this context, not writing an autobiography can mark a movement toward an alternative jurisdiction within an enlarged frame of justice.

In the following chapters, I discuss texts that draw on a range of discourses and representational practices to tell complex stories of injury. Within these altered and expanded self-representational practices, trauma may be explicit or opaque, limited in duration or persistent, its complexities entered into, endured, and reworked. The stories are not the familiar ones; the trauma is not necessarily documented or documentable from the text at hand, the writer is not pressing for a specific remedy, and the boundaries of the trauma are not limited to an act or event. Rather, they grow to indicate how those boundaries reveal and restructure other boundaries and limits. In this sense and others I shall develop, the texts I discuss in the following chapters are limit-cases in self-representation; they challenge the limits of autobiography in the representation of trauma, and they reveal how complicated and entangled those limits are with still other boundaries. Limit-cases produce an alternative jurisprudence, a form of judgment drawn from the complexities of a legal, literary, and political past. As such, limit-cases neither aspire nor claim to be universal. If they offer a figure to rival the representative man, it is the knowing subject who inhabits locations and forms of knowledge for representations of the self and trauma that refuse the deformations of legalistic demands.

# 2

# Bastard Testimony

## Illegitimacy and Incest in Dorothy Allison's
## *Bastard Out of Carolina*

*Imagine vengeance. Imagine justice. What is the difference anyway when both are only stories in your head? In the everyday reality you stand still. I stood still. Bent over. Laid down.*

—Dorothy Allison, *Trash*

Dorothy Allison has been confounding generic categories and stretching the limits of self-representational discourse in a series of published works that combine autobiographical narratives, performance pieces, essays, and fiction sometimes under the heading "stories," as in *Trash*, sometimes as "memoir and performance" in *Two or Three Things I Know for Sure*, and sometimes as "fiction" in *Bastard Out of Carolina*.[1] Even careful readers, however, will have trouble parsing these generic distinctions because the same characters show up in the same places doing the same things in all these texts. Allison's insistent focus on telling the story of family, poverty, violence, and the persistence of love means that she will press any generic category into service. As she has insisted, her life depends on telling this story right.

Published in 1992 and the first of Allison's works to be called a novel, *Bastard Out of Carolina* immediately confronts a limit: Where does autobiography end and fiction begin in an autobiographical novel? While this question is certainly motivated by the context of Allison's work, it raises a larger question about how fiction and autobiography reach into each other, and whether they may, for some subjects, even require each other. A limit, like the one between autobiography and fiction, is not a simple divide. Like all territorial markers, it carves up terrain in an arbitrary, if mo-

---

[1] Dorothy Allison, *Trash* (Ithaca: Firebrand Books, 1988); *Two or Three Things I Know for Sure* (New York: Dutton, 1995).

tivated, way. When you cross a border, you often know you are some-place else because an apparatus presses upon your consciousness: there is a checkpoint, you answer questions, and produce documents. Difference does not establish itself all at once, but by degrees. So it is with limit-cases. You begin with what seems to be fiction, only to find more and more signs of autobiography. Yet, as with the passenger on a train who nods off in one country and awakens in the other having missed the border, it is hard to orient. Continuities and interpenetrations exist near the borders that are no longer tolerated or even recognized the farther you go in either di-rection. Due to the ambiguities it raises about genre and its contextualiza-tion within Allison's publishing history, *Bastard Out of Carolina* is situated in this borderland.

The limit between autobiography and fiction that *Bastard* straddles is not the only limit that characterizes it as a limit-case. Here we immedi-ately confront another characteristic of limit-cases: the most apparent limit may mask further complications and more intractable questions. While the generic question about limits implies that one ought to be able to provide a relatively certain answer to "where does autobiography end and fiction begin?" when pressed in the case of *Bastard Out of Carolina*, the question proves brittle: one pushes and it gives way. Beneath the surface of that question lie others that call our attention to how hard it is to tell the story of trauma. Here the initial question "Where does autobiography end and fiction begin?" can be reformulated as a struggle between what is real and what is imagined in the representation of the self and trauma. At stake is how antagonistic the monitoring of the real will be to the presence of the imagined. *Bastard*, therefore, points to a limit on realness and con-cerns the evidentiary and narrative limits that stake out the border around the query, "what really happened?"

No trauma narrative is easy to tell. Whether the narrative must take the form recognized and required by a particular institution (the law, say, or psychoanalysis), or whether audience expectations compel certain themes to emerge or insights to be arrived at, the subject of trauma refers to both a person struggling to make sense of an overwhelming experience in a par-ticular context and the unspeakability of trauma itself, its resistance to rep-resentation.[2] Trauma emerges in narrative as much through what cannot be said of it as through what can. Dorothy Allison's trauma narrative is no easier than any other to tell, and it offers some distinctive challenges. Alli-son organizes her narrative around two related injuries, illegitimacy and incest, and presents them as they affect Bone, the child narrator and pro-tagonist of *Bastard*, her mother, her family, and her milieu. In *Bastard*, how

---

[2]   See Caruth, *Trauma*; Felmar and Laub, *Testimony*; van der Kolk et al., *Traumatic Stress*.

to tell the stories of illegitimacy and incest reveals a further organizational challenge—intractable, surprising, and possibly unassimilable—how to focus such a story less on harm than on the persistence of love? As with the revelation that more complex limit-questions lie beyond the more apparent one, "how does love persist?" lies within Allison's narrative of trauma.

Even as *Bastard* initially claims our attention as a limit-case about autobiography and fiction, the way it presses beyond that limit indicates a network of related boundaries and prohibitions. They cluster around self-representation, impinge upon it when trauma is at issue, and raise intractable questions about autobiography: How do memory and imagination combine to form a historical record? Could a survivor of trauma offer a personal history of a collectivized experience—the Holocaust, for example—which incorporated invention? What does the autobiographer owe to history, and who will decide? These questions reveal how the line between what is real and what is imagined in a self-representational text can shift in the context of representing trauma toward questions about the ethics and morality of representation. They also help to contextualize why a self-representational project, Allison's in particular, might veer from autobiography when trauma is central. The complicity between autobiography and fiction, between a personal history and the imagination required to survive and tell it, raises a pointed question: "With what consequences does a self-representational account of trauma risk an alliance with fiction?"

In autobiography and trauma studies veracity is always at issue. Both share a skeptical orientation toward the inescapable element of fiction in self-representation. People make things up for a variety of reasons. Some fall within the domain of memory, some seem specific to trauma, and many point to some relation between the two. Are the mechanisms by which we remember similar to the ones that permit (or compel) us to forget? Is memory simply faulty, like a machine that breaks down from time to time, or does it fail because it must? Sometimes people augment memory by allowing context to supply missing information, sometimes the invented version is how they remember an experience, sometimes another's memories become one's own because they make a kind of symbolic sense that what really happened fails to provide. More controversially, perhaps, people invent because telling a story a particular way makes it "better."[3] Most controversial is the perennial claim that fiction offers truths that fact cannot. Once fiction's truth is preferred to fact's, the authority of both trauma and autobiography that derives from the eyewitness's credibility is thrown into a crisis of legitimacy.

[3]  Mary McCarthy, *Memories of a Catholic Girlhood* (New York: Harcourt Brace, 1957), 9.

Foucault's notion of the juridical is especially apt here not only for how it describes a network of judgments about legitimacy but because it names the site of Dorothy Allison's contention. She argues about the truth of incest and illegitimacy with the law, autobiography itself, and psychoanalysis: law, because incest and illegitimacy are legal terms with enforceable consequences; autobiography, because Allison questions how the limits of representing trauma shape, and are reshaped by, self-representation; and psychoanalysis, because incest, illegitimacy, and their mythologizing bear directly on her representation of desire, sexuality, harm, and the persistence of love. So, too, psychoanalysis offers a way to explore the shame and melancholia that shadow legal meanings. Bringing together law and psychoanalysis with the third term of autobiography offers the possibility of keeping issues in relational tension that might otherwise disaggregate into binaries: sex and violence, law and the unconscious, psychoanalysis and criminal statutes, love and pain. Such disaggregation is mandated within the juridical, but Allison's focus on self-representation and her choice to produce fiction within this context makes her work simultaneously vulnerable to judgments about veracity, yet also not accountable to the limited presentation of evidence that could be heard in a courtroom.

Even in the context of the juridical, Foucault held out the possibility that new stories could be told.[4] In texts such as *Bastard*, trauma is currently being represented in the borderland between autobiography and fiction where such writers as Allison use first-person hybrid accounts to contend with institutions and disciplines such as the law and psychoanalysis for authority and knowledge. Through this work, some previous discursive strategies for containing trauma are eroding. Trauma is no longer primarily represented within the clinic where case studies written by medical professionals dominate. Instead, self-authored, first-person representations of trauma seem to be everywhere: in identity politics, revisions of colonial histories, Holocaust studies, and historiographies focused on violence. Following the account I offered in Chapter 1 about how the convergence of certain discourses suggests a contemporary synergy around representations of the self and trauma, we can refocus the question of causality—"why trauma now?"—toward an exploration of effects. Here we would look to the new ways of representing the individual in relation to personal and collective histories of abuse that are becoming possible, to the new sorts of subjectivities, collective and personal identities, and the politics and aesthetics that emerge around self-representation and trauma. In this context, Allison's *Bastard* is a formal experiment in the

---

[4]    Michel Foucault, "What Is an Author?" in *The Foucault Reader*, ed. Paul Rabinow, trans. Josué Harari (New York: Pantheon, 1984), 101–20.

self-representation of trauma. What does formal experimentation make visible that repetition alone—telling another trauma story—may not? To be sure, repetition is valuable and the compilation of additional testimonies of trauma is important in all sorts of areas: establishing that injuries have occurred, documenting abuse, deepening existing accounts, extending traditions of reporting and testimony. This is cultural work that must be nurtured and continued. At the same time, an alternative and allied discourse of trauma that draws on less familiar (and authorized) forms of reporting risks in documentary believability what it recoups in a reconception of the subject of trauma.

*Bastard* reshapes our critical understanding of what autobiography is and what it can do. Allison articulates the relations among law, kinship, trauma, and love as the grounds of subjectivity. In so doing, she returns trauma to the set of relations from which its meanings emerge. The history of autobiography strongly suggests (in at least the American tradition) that autobiographical subjects are judged in part by whether they are appropriately representative. By uncoupling appropriate and representative, Allison makes the subject of trauma into a new figure of the citizen, where citizenship is inhabited by those whose histories of rights are fully interimplicated in histories of injury. In a text that everywhere questions the power of harm in the form of both illegitimacy and incest to define and delimit the person, *Bastard* asks: How are the claims of the traumatized and the illegitimate adjudicated in the public sphere?

Autobiography exposes a limit between the private and the public: it is a representation of personal experience meant to make a claim on public attention. It cannily introjects the private into the public and ensures that what is published cannot be considered exclusively private. While autobiography holds out the possibility that one might speak credibly to others about a life that challenges the assumption, for example, that law equals justice and that justice prevails, autobiography is Janus-faced. It can incite voyeurism and censure as readily as sanctification and respectability. Autobiography's negative capability is important here because it reveals that a self-representational text about incest and illegitimacy would lay the autobiographer bare to judgments about veracity and human value. Autobiography is a genre in whose name it is possible to make a declaration of illegitimacy. Allison insists on an alternative construction of the grounds of judgment by relocating truth from the legalistic jurisdiction of autobiography to the expansive borderland between autobiography and fiction. An alternative jurisprudence emerges as the bastard daughter rewrites her mother's legacy.

On the second point of how experimental self-representations of trauma open up new thinking about trauma itself, Allison has quite controversially linked her own childhood sexual abuse to her adult consensual practices of lesbian sadomasochism: not as a kind of false consciousness about desire and abuse that she "got over," but as sexual practices she insistently claims as her own.[5] Her refusal to pathologize sadomasochism as the detritus of early abuse, or to set it exclusively in a therapeutic discourse of recovery that would compel her to develop out of it, indicates that causal understandings of sexual pleasure are limited. To say the least, the sexual practices of those who have been sexually abused are not necessarily regressive or wrong. To say more, the achievement of sexual desire in adult consensual relationships, whatever form it takes, stands as a rebuke to the annihilation of consent and the violation of the sexual and the person that sexual trauma constitutes. There is more here to trauma than the suffering it imposes on all constructions of pleasure, but there is also more to sex, and Allison is willing to articulate it.

Finally, there is the third point: How might Allison's *Bastard* and other limit-cases like it loosen the hold of an institution like the law on the meanings of incest and illegitimacy? I turn to this issue immediately by drawing on a study that links the law to psychoanalysis to disclose the law's unconscious. In his analysis of what the law cannot know of itself but which it nonetheless carries with it, Peter Goodrich offers a useful way to think about how the law's conscious investments in incest and illegitimacy are underpinned by its less explicitly enunciated biases about women, children, and paternity.[6]

In *Oedipus Lex* Peter Goodrich describes a crucial mechanism of the law's power, namely, the positive value attributed to law shields from view the terrible exercise of its power: "The veil of legality, the bare image of law, hides innumerable traumas of enforcement and of powerlessness" (68). For Goodrich, the trauma beneath the veil of legality is not only the trauma of having the law work against you rather than for you ("traumas of enforcement"), but, more important, that the law effectively hides the violence constituted in and through its power and enacts "innumerable traumas . . . of powerlessness" in the process of constituting a subject before the law who is also subject to it. Goodrich does not see the law as decent at its core yet tragically miscarried by mere humans. For him, it is the opposite. Law consists inescapably in and of trauma in its very exercise, even as we assent to it; this, for Goodrich, constitutes the veiling of law. Similarly, Robert Cover asserts: "[T]he relation between legal interpreta-

---

[5]    For a discussion of this controversy in the context of the 1982 Barnard Conference, see Lisa Duggan and Nan Hunter, *Sex Wars* (New York: Routledge, 1995).
[6]    Peter Goodrich, *Oedipus Lex* (Berkeley: University of California Press, 1995).

tion and the infliction of pain remains operative even in the most routine of legal acts."[7] Also commenting on the false relation between law and justice, Wai-chee Dimock writes: "We worry, perhaps, about the local implementations of justice; but the idea itself—its ethical primacy and its descriptive adequacy—is almost never questioned. Justice, as our admiring idiom attests, is something that will eventually (and sometimes instantly) 'prevail,' not as a construct but as a kind of indwelling truth."[8] This line of argument requires the unyoking of law and justice: not only is the relation between the two not causal—the exercise of law does not produce justice—but law cannot produce justice if it produces harm as a matter of course. In the face of the insurmountable contradiction that law inflicts pain even as it seeks to adjudicate claims about pain, Cover and Goodrich conclude that law harms. One colludes in obscuring this harm by fetishizing law, by vesting in it all sorts of romantic notions about its ability to reveal the truth instead of focusing on its limitations and contradictions: its restrictive protocols surrounding the presentation of evidence, its prevailing notion of justice, and the authority it procures for itself through hypocrisy.

For Goodrich, law and other institutions no less than individuals should be understood as having an unconscious: "To understand the plenitude of law, to understand also what has been lost, involves the admission . . . that the institution internalizes its losses, that it carries a past obliquely on its surface, that it repeats, and that like all subjects it may be analyzed symptomatically in terms of the cultural work that its repetitions, its rites, and its symbols perform" (28–29). He identifies two "formative or constitutional repressions, namely those of image and of woman" in early British legal treatises. "Common law jurisprudence adopted to varying degrees the Continental doctrines of iconomachy (hostility toward images) and of the inferior condition of women through the influence of the Renaissance and the Reformation" (11). Goodrich connects the way discourses against rhetoric, images, and women combine to form the foundation of law, and insists that legal subjectivity develops from this foundation. That law is hostile to women has often been noted by feminists; Goodrich's contribution here is to identify the rhetoricity of this hostility and its pervasiveness in law: "The denunciation of woman in the early doctrinal and constitutional writings of common law was the repression of a figure of femininity, of a metaphor or face which represented the plurality or creativity of thought, an other scene of reason, a genealogy of myths or histories of difference" (12).

[7]  Robert Cover, "Violence and the Word," *Yale Law Journal* 95.8 (July 1986): 1607.
[8]  Wai-chee Dimock, *Residues of Justice* (Berkeley: University of California Press, 1996), 4.

I want to preview how this framing of law will become trenchant for *Bastard*. Law's legitimacy becomes questionable as it builds paternal authority from its unconscious violence toward and repression of women. If this insight into how paternal privilege builds upon an unconscious, partially repressed violence toward women is granted, then certain well-remarked-upon features of the law stand out in relief. Chief among them is law's often-remarked anxiety over what cannot be seen: paternity, hence legitimacy. Consequently, law's anxiety over the invisibility of the male contribution to reproduction finds its target in women and children. Law's protection of paternal privilege and legitimacy is also related to its views on incest. Law works to make the invisible (paternity) visible via the father's name and patrimony (legitimacy). Simultaneously, it veils the existence of incest because incest happens to a child, a subject who lacks full legal rights. Children are frequently prevented from testifying against adults, there are different rules for the corroboration of evidence a child and adult give, and there have been historical shifts in the adjudication of incest and the broader category of child abuse that reveal that the incidence of reported child abuse rises based on the strength of feminist movements although the incidence of abuse is thought to remain flat.[9]

Thus, the criminality of incest is sheltered by the differing legal statuses of criminal and victim. The criminal possesses not only the legal rights of men but to these rights are added the mystique of paternity, an issue in which the law's unconscious is deeply invested. The victimized child lacks legal subjectivity, and when she is a girl, she cannot aspire to the same degree of subjectivity a legal male subject attains upon reaching majority status. Qualifications emerge immediately in discussions of the crime of incest—and by crime I mean not simply its harm but its remedy, its actionability—because it is permitted, in part, by the deep cover offered to the father in the name of paternal rights and privacy, where the rape of girl children is allied with the privileges and the preservation of the law of the father and add up to (if not exactly the permissibility of this violence) an opacity around the legal standing of the victim. The law, therefore, cannot properly consider the trauma of incest or register the trauma of illegitimacy except through displacement because neither falls upon one fully endowed with legal subjectivity and both go to the heart of legal constructions of the family.

The legal definition of family has been contested by, among others,

<hr>

9   Linda Gordon, *Heroes of Their Own Lives* (New York: Viking, 1988); Ian Hacking, "The Making and Molding of Child Abuse" (*Critical Inquiry* 17 [winter 1991]: 253–88) and *Rewriting the Soul*; and Judith Herman, *Trauma and Recovery*, offer accounts of the relation between the incidence of child abuse and awareness of child abuse.

feminist legal scholar Martha Fineman.[10] Fineman has argued that the nurturing bond between mother and child should provide the legal definition of the family, and not the sexual relation between husband and wife. Fineman locates a transitional period in early nineteenth-century American law in which such a model operated as the legal family. For Fineman, the precedential logic of the law of the father eventually displaced this model, but, taking Goodrich's genealogical view, one would question whether such a moment could be fully excised, or whether this brief accordance of legitimacy to the mother-child bond wouldn't constitute a repression that might return in places like self-representational accounts of incest.[11] In this case *Bastard* can be read as demonstrating a residual if unconscious trauma in the law of the father arising from the demotion of mothers to vehicles of illegitimacy and the incestuous abuse of the children they cannot legally protect.

*Bastard Out of Carolina*, set in Greenville, South Carolina, in the late 1950s, records the cost of incest and illegitimacy to both the daughter and her mother. The text focuses on Bone, born Ruth Anne Boatwright, her mother Anney, the extended Boatwright clan, and Bone's stepfather "Daddy Glen" Waddell, whose terrible presence exemplifies the consequential interleaving of the law and the law of the father. The text opens with Bone's birth. Her mother, Anney, pregnant at fourteen, a mother at fifteen, delivers her daughter after an accident in which she is thrown from a car and lies unconscious in the hospital for three days. When she

---

[10]   Martha Fineman, *The Neutered Mother, the Sexual Family, and Other Twentieth Century Tragedies* (New York: Routledge, 1995).

[11]   The compounding of authority around the slippery term "law," as it applies to common law and codified, written law, the law of the father, the law as an anthropological term pertaining to kinship and the social form of the family, and so on, is significant to notice because of the way that density gives meaning to illegitimacy and incest. A semantics of legality abounds in the human sciences. I highlight it here to indicate the pervasive tendency to use law to denote order, authority, civilization, normativity, and penality. Remarking on such usage helps to restore some of the connections law shares with other disciplines in which semantics about "the law" and "the truth" are foundational. Controversies surrounding the interpretation of kinship take the law as a fundamental term through which to describe, for example, the exchange and circulation of people and objects (as gifts, in marriage, and so on). Many religions, especially in their more conservative expressions, become strongly law-based in an effort to anchor stricter social control to moral purity. In Lacanian psychoanalysis, the controlling principle of the symbolic order is "the law of the father," a term in which Lacan pithily compresses a millennial obsession of Western civilization. For a discussion of incest in relation to the many different "laws," see Vikki Bell, *Interrogating Incest* (New York: Routledge, 1993). For other discussions of law, kinship, and incest, compare Claude Lévi-Strauss, *The Elementary Structures of Kinship* (Boston: Beacon Press, 1969), and Gayle Rubin, "The Traffic in Women," in *Toward an Anthropology of Women*, ed. Rayna R. Reiter (New York: Monthly Review Press, 1975).

wakes up, she has a daughter whom her mother and aunt have named Ruth Anne. Her mother and aunt are distracted enough to spell "Anne," the child's middle name, which is also her mother's name, three different ways on the birth certificate. But when the mother and aunt give conflicting signals about the father's name, Bone is certified a bastard by the state of South Carolina. According to the 1952 Legal Code of South Carolina, a child is legitimate if born of a legal marriage, a common-law marriage, or a void marriage entered into in good faith (e.g. with an "incapable" spouse). If the parents of an illegitimate child subsequently marry, the child of that union becomes legitimate. The code specifies the state's economic interest in illegitimacy and outlines responsibilities for mother and father. A mother must declare paternal identity "if known," in the law's insinuating idiom. She can be brought before a judge if she is charged with bastardy and forced by warrant to testify based on the presumption that such a child is likely to become a burden to the county. As to the father's responsibility, the state is his unwilling surrogate if he fails to support the child. If the mother identifies the father, he can be detained by warrant and forced to pay support. A couple of decades after the years during which *Bastard*'s action takes place, the bastardy statutes were regularly dismissed as a means to make fathers pay child support. This dismissal was due in part to the statute of limitations which required that a paternity proceeding be executed against a father within three years following the birth of an illegitimate child.[12]

Anney spends the first chapter growing up fast, marked by what she believes is the indelible shame of illegitimacy. She repeatedly makes a lonely errand to the county courthouse to try to get a new birth certificate for Bone which will declare her "legitimate." Each time the clerk, who enjoys Anney's ritual humiliation, strings her along, but the outcome is always the same: "Across the bottom in oversized red-inked block letters it read, ILLEGITIMATE" (4). Anney has a second daughter, Reese, with her next boyfriend, the gentle Lyle, and dreams of the possibility of replacing Bone's absent paternal name with a live stepfather and the seal of legitimacy. But Lyle dies unexpectedly and tragically, leaving Anney with another hard chapter in her story: "Mama was nineteen, with two babies and three copies of my birth certificate in her dresser drawer" (7). The

---

[12]   According to common-law tradition, states still define children as possessions of the father, though in South Carolina and generally, the state has separated out its economic interest. Prior to 1960, South Carolina courts are sympathetic to a father's common-law right to custody in the face of competing claims by the mother in a divorce or in other unusual circumstances. In *Clardy v. Ford* (1943) for example, as held in common law, the primary right to the custody of a child is in the father, since the law requires him to support the child.

chapter concludes with an apocalyptic image: the county courthouse and hall of records burn to the ground and with them, of course, all official documentation of Bone's birth. Anney has her own private bonfire at home and sets fire to Bone's birth certificate in the kitchen sink. The family revels in Anney's unexpected deliverance. Although the burning courthouse appears as the spectacle of a fantasy come true, it is not an antidote to a legal culture that has already imposed a set of terms for self-knowledge. By the end of the first chapter, Allison has instituted a set of terms around sex, violence, law, and class on which she will build a complicated text about trauma. With this complex around illegitimacy in place, Allison introduces the man who will capitalize on Anney's shame about illegitimacy to marry her and commit incest. Although Glen does not adopt Bone and Reese, I use the term incest instead of the more general child sexual abuse to underscore the family as the context for his violence. Glen Waddell is unpredictable, violent, and needy; Anney is drawn to him and they marry. The rest of the novel details what can happen to a bastard girl and her mother.

To understand the daughter in this narrative, you must know her mother. The lessons of illegitimacy concretize Annie's class-based shame and make Bone literally and figuratively her mother's daughter. Mothers carry illegitimacy with them as their children's birthright; only a father can make a child legitimate. The violence of this law in its denigration of the mother and vaunting of the father marks a crisis in legal subjectivity. It is not merely the law's partiality that is at issue here; rather, its claim to universality lies in the codification of an unconscious violence toward the mother. The marker of illegitimacy is symptomatic of a judgment imposed by a paternal law on the power of mothers to protect children. Here, that judgment results in the creation of a legal status and identity for Bone: she is illegitimate. For women like Anney and children like Bone, justice is an abstract name for the harm done to them in the name of the law. Anney is particularly vulnerable to the shame of illegitimacy, about which no one else in the family seems to care in precisely the same way. Bone's Uncle Earle, Anney's charming and infamous brother, advises Anney to live with her second daughter's father for seven years: "you get the same result without paying a courthouse lawyer" (5). Yet even if other family members and "Granny didn't care, Mama did. . . . The stamp on the birth certificate burned her like the stamp she knew they'd tried to put on her—no good, lazy, shiftless" (3). One might have expected more sexually explicit epithets as the shaming terms for the mother of a bastard. But the one Anney fears most, in effect, sexualizes the class-based epithets that all suggest "trash." "Bastard" conflates a sexual and an economic judgment which is then imposed on the child as a legal identity. As such, "bastard" belongs to the nexus of economics, reproduction, and sexual violence from which cultural meanings of incest develop. Anney and Bone's shaming around illegitimacy prepares for the trauma and shame of incest that will unfold in the narrative. Because Anney is vulnerable to shaming around class (whereas other members of her family claim not to be), she errs tragically in marrying a man, in part, for the legitimacy he can give her daughters that she alone cannot.

"Bone," whose name evokes the biblical threat of patriarchal property, "bone of my bones," is sexually molested by her stepfather when she is five years old; the abuse entangles beatings with sexual abuse and continues until she is twelve, with the stepfather moving the family around during these years in part because of a series of failed jobs from which he is fired for losing his temper, and, in part, to escape detection. Yet as cast out and marginalized as Daddy Glen is by the Boatwrights, he still benefits from his association with the name and the law of the father. How else to account for his power over his family? He molests, beats, and brutally rapes Bone (and, as the text suggests, molests her sister, Reese), yet retains his place in the family. The paradox is that by molesting and beating Bone he strengthens his paternal glow(er). In his criminality (incest, battery) is his legality. We are deflected from the child's violation to the step / father's exercise of his rights. The father functions as the incest agent of the symbolic order, which depends on the separation of mother and child. The paternalism of law requires that the mother not be able to save the child. The threnody running through the comments by women in the family about Bone's exposure to Daddy Glen's violence is always the same, "What are we going to do about you, Bone?" They never ask, "What are we going to do about him?" Responsibility is thus displaced onto the object of harm.

Yet *Bastard* is less the story of the stepfather who brutalized Bone than of the mother she loves who neither saves her nor chooses her over the stepfather, and less still a study of mother or stepfather as singular, isolated influences than a thick description of enduring cultural formations. At issue are the multiple meanings of trauma that entangle incest and illegitimacy, especially their pervasiveness, to the subculture of poor, white, Greenville, South Carolina, in the late 1950s and early 1960s. For an earlier generation of criminologists, the concept of subculture as an explanation of violence was hegemonic.[13] After the late 1960s the relation of subculture to violence broadened beyond a narrow view of cause and effect. While subcultures explain much, it was argued, they fail to contextualize

[13]    Mercer L. Sullivan, "Biography of Heinous Criminals," *Journal of Research in Crime and Delinquency* 33.3 (Aug. 1996): 354–77.

incest, for example, within the more general cultural formations that permit it. Criminological analysis that situated subcultures within larger contexts, which, in effect, refused to exoticize and stigmatize the subcultural, asked how the rule of law and the legitimation of the state came about, and not only why some resorted to violence but why others did not. This distinction is useful insofar as it helps to build down the overwhelmingly class-based judgments that impose their mark on Bone and her family registered in such epithets as "those people," "they're all like that," and "ignorant trash."[14] The imposition of a subcultural identity shames Bone and makes her refuse to tell county doctors and sheriffs about her stepfather's violence. They all look to her like Daddy Glen in uniform: the same paternal privilege and imposition of male power makes them capable of the same mistreatment of her mother, and ultimately, of Bone herself. It is true that Bone's lessons in "who I am" are subcultural in the sense that they can be specified with some precision in terms of poverty, region, and whiteness. But they are linked to more general cultural formations around law, violence, family, and gender as well, in which Bone's sense of self entails an acquiescence to not-having, to loss.

How does the law collude in this pedagogy? In nineteenth- and twentieth-century common law, children were defined as property of the father. In the common law of these centuries, rape was defined as the forcible carnal knowledge of a female against her will and without her consent. Incest lies at the nexus of legal definitions of rape and family, in which children are construed as property. As property of the father, a child is barred from giving consent by a structural legal relation. She or he cannot withhold it because she or he does not possess the ability to give it. Nonetheless, incest is a crime, in part because of the threat it poses to middle-class notions of family that subtend the legal constructions of rape and property. At issue is how incest can become visible as a crime given the contradictory legal construction of consent for women in rape and children in incest. Rape is forced sex; sex to which women do not consent. Presumably there is sex to which women can consent. Incest is sex to which one can never consent, so the child does not gain the status of an agent through in-

---

[14]    As Elizabeth Wilson has argued, studies and commentators claiming that incest occurs mostly in the working class rely more on an ideology of the middle-class family than on data. Much recent data, in fact, suggest that incest occurs disproportionately in the middle and upper classes. As Wilson suggests, middle-class ideology about the family construes incest as the worst thing that can happen to a child; a lot of bad things can happen to children, however, and incest should not be fetishized as the worst possible abuse. Rather it should be understood, as it so frequently occurs, in relation to other forms of abuse and neglect. See her article "Not in This House: Incest, Denial, and Doubt in the White Middle-Class Family," *Yale Journal of Criticism* 8 (1995): 35–58.

cest law. She or he is property of the father which he may not use in certain ways, and, as such, is a world away from majority status.[15]

Given this construction, the child faces a structural dilemma: how to report the crime of incest.[16] Who is she when she does this, and what, exactly, has happened to her? Bone's pain, terror, and disorientation at the time of the initial molestation is compounded by the absence of a language in which to say what has happened and is continuing to happen to her, as well as the absence of a context in which to form this language. Not only is there no ready-made language that Bone can use to tell what Daddy Glen is doing to her, rather, that language is suppressed by the very law that would define and criminalize incest. The disavowal of incest, in this text and beyond, partakes of a silencing collusion of subjects and legal discourse around the contravened sites of sexuality, law, shame, family, and self-representation. That Bone cannot say what Daddy Glen is doing to her goes to her education in her mother's shame and Bone's desire not to compound it, but also to her (accurate) sense that Daddy Glen is structurally well positioned to continue his abuse. Who could or would be able to stop him without setting off what Bone believes are catastrophically sprawling consequences: the exposure of Anney as a "bad mother," the unleashing of county police on her family (not limited to Daddy Glen), no less than the appropriation by the law of her own anger and desire for revenge.

The trauma of incest points to a network of alliances and the child's compromised status with respect to consent within it. The ambiguous and

[15]   Incest is a crime to which a minor cannot consent. Majority age, after all, is called the age of consent. Thus a minor can never be an accomplice to incest, only a victim of it. Anyone over the age of consent can be considered an accomplice. Corroboration is not required of a victim's testimony about incest (*State v. Goff*, 86 S. D. 354, 195 N. W. 2d. 521 (S. D. 1972). Neither the common law nor early penal law required corroboration in a prosecution for incest (*People v. Gibson*, 1950, 301 N.Y. 244, 93 N. E. 2d 827). Although the court allows considerable leeway in asking children leading questions, the evidentiary standard for incest and child abuse is "clear and convincing evidence" (*Matter of Christine H.*, 1982, 114 Misc. 2d 475, 451 N.Y.S. 2d 983). The complications here compound upon whether this combination of factors removes or installs barriers to the successful prosecution of incest cases. Thanks to Joanna Piepgrass for locating representative cases.

[16]   In South Carolina in 1952, the torture or torment of a child was a misdemeanor punishable only by a fine not greater than $100 or a jail term no longer than thirty days. South Carolina's legal code defines incest as carnal intercourse between persons within certain degrees of relationship, not limited to family members related by birth but extending also to stepparents. By 1976 the crime of incest was punishable by a fine of not less than $500, or imprisonment of not less than one year. Changes in the law after 1976 appear to fall under a more inclusive definition of child abuse and neglect, which the earlier law differentiated from incest. In these statutes, the state declared its interest in protecting children from injury or harm, and included in its definition of harm both the direct inflicting of physical punishment (with numerous qualifications), as well as allowing a sexual offense, as defined narrowly by the state, to be committed against a child.

ungainly issues of consent and agency around incest are somewhat hidden beneath legal language about the state's interest in protecting children from harm. The state's stewardship of children until they reach "the age of consent" makes fathers into surrogates of the law while the child is a juvenile, and also makes the law an extension of the father after the child reaches what is called "legal age." This paternal umbrella under which children grow up produces some complications around personhood. While boys grow up to be men and can therefore negotiate their way into the role of the father, girls grow up merely to be women and thus never possess the symbolic and actual privilege accorded to men by law.[17]

What limit must be exceeded for the father's violence against the child to be legible in the law? In the case of a child who can neither consent to her violation nor is positioned to make it end, the law's circumscribed recognition of the harm of incest derives from the debased status it accords children. That the child can be made to submit, can in fact be held captive in and through a legal construction of family, is especially ironic in a narrative that consistently links illegitimacy to incest. Bone can be harmed not only because she is outside the law as a bastard but also because her mother so desires the legal familial relation that would place Bone within the law, a location, ironically, in which more harm may befall her.

A child who is terrorized through routine beatings, frequent molestation, and rape represents a spectacularization of crisis in the mode of family. "If only we knew what was happening, we would have stopped it" is the hand-wringing plaint of both bystanders and eyewitnesses, as *Bastard* points out. In this text all the signs of abuse are there, and no one protects Bone. Despite the law's declared interest in the protection of children, Bone and her family perceive its intervention in Daddy Glen's abuse of Bone as a threat. But the passions stirred by incest point in other directions. An erotics of violence emerges through the oblique and contorted language about seduction that is related to compromised consent. Despite her professed love for Bone, Anney's sympathy for and attraction to Glen mean that she frequently ends up having sex with him after scenes in which he has beaten Bone and Anney has been unable to stop him. Sex and violence go together for Glen, and Dorothy Allison insistently makes this connection. His beatings of Bone are sexual for him, his molestation of her is violent. When he beats Bone and Anney is present (yelling at him through a locked door to stop), he has sex with Anney after he has fin-

---

[17] Remember that *Bastard* is set in the 1950s, a full two to three decades before feminists are able to effect some changes in the law and pull back the veil of privacy shrouding the family that protected male violence against women and children from prosecution. By the early 1980s, child abuse was illegal, as was the rape of a married woman by her husband.

ished beating Bone. When Anney is not around, he molests Bone. Bone is taught through her mother's example and through Daddy Glen's terrorism that sex and violence go together, but it would be an oversimplification to conclude that they are the exclusive pedagogues here. Their actions are symptomatic of law and the violence it enacts via its construction of incest and illegitimacy, and their relation to consent, women, and children. The violence with which Bone's imagination resonates when she masturbates is not the same as the violence Daddy Glen visits upon her. She does not fantasize about beating, raping, and molesting those more vulnerable than she. She fantasizes about fire, which connects her to her mother's revenge-fantasy-come-true of the burning courthouse, and about taking revenge on Daddy Glen. Although she acquires the imposed linkage of sex and violence through Daddy Glen's abuse, she does not simply repeat his version of the formula. Consenting to her own sexual desire in the form of masturbation, Bone wishes for the apocalypse to come down on Daddy Glen. There is some catharsis here, if only temporary. His sex harms her, her sex harms no one, but in it she can imagine his ruin. The delicate realm of fantasy here allows us to see how sex emerges in relation to violence: it is a family legacy. Yet, Allison does not present Bone's masturbation fantasies as simply the detritus of abuse; rather, Bone's hunger, desire for the power to destroy, and neediness all contribute to a developing imaginary around sex, violence, and class. In this way, Allison complicates rather than therapizes her protagonist and by so doing points to a remnant of the imagination that exceeds the power of harm and preserves her love for her mother, and through it the damaged but still present capacity to love.

The second chapter represents Greenville, South Carolina, in 1955 as nothing less than "the most beautiful place on earth" (17). Images of lush landscape and familial love dominate and Bone is presented as happy in this place and with these people. This brief idyll is disturbed in the third chapter by Daddy Glen's menacing presence and with it comes Bone's confusion about love. Her love for her family certainly has plenty of contextual complications (the birth father no one will talk about, for example), but love for Bone pours out in an uncomplicated way. Daddy Glen introduces an incoherence into Bone's understanding of love. Suddenly it is a confusing code she is ill prepared to decipher: "Love, at least for a man not already part of the family, was something I was a little unsure about" (32). In observing Anney's need to have Bone, Reese, and other people imagine Glen as a "good man" and potential father, Bone notices a circuit of looks from Anney to Glen as Glen is being observed by others: "Maybe that was love, that look. I couldn't tell" (34). Allison indicates the deflections that will structure Anney's acceptance of Glen, how she persuades herself that the regard of others for him exists and justifies her complicated hunger for him. But the scene is filled with warnings about Glen. Granny doesn't like him, he has a terrible temper and desperately needy outbursts, and his middle-class family considers him a loser. He is a powder keg waiting to blow, his menace barely beneath the surface. In the fourth chapter, he and Anney, newly married and returned from the honeymoon, are expecting their first child together. The night Anney goes to the hospital to deliver the baby, Glen molests Bone in the car as they await the news and as Reese sleeps in the back seat.

I want to concentrate on how this scene of violation resembles and departs from Allison's other accounts of her own molestation by her stepfather and also from legal testimony in order to bring to the surface what this self-representational account of trauma can do that others cannot. In her nonfiction, Allison has offered her autobiography in several different registers, all of which develop the context for understanding how she survived her stepfather's violence. Dorothy Allison can offer her characteristic yoking of sexuality, kinship, violence, and love in a declarative register: "I have known I was a lesbian since I was a teenager, and I have spent a good twenty years making peace with the effects of incest and physical abuse. But what may be the central fact of my life is that I was born in 1949 in Greenville, South Carolina, the bastard daughter of a white woman from a desperately poor family, a girl who had left the seventh grade the year before, worked as a waitress, and was just a month past fifteen when she had me." Here, the elements that characterize *Bastard* are present, if in different form: the linkage of incest and illegitimacy and of poverty, class, and shame; and the centrality of her mother's biography in her own autobiography. The sentence that announces "the central fact of my life" emphasizes her mother, and Allison's nonfiction and fiction detail how a mother's shame about her illegitimate daughter compounds shame around poverty. About her family and herself, Allison would learn to say, "We were trash."[18]

There is also the storytelling mode in which Allison is the Southern spinner of tales. In describing how she learns to tell the story she would publish in *Bastard*, Allison writes: "I knew there was one story that would haunt me until I understood how to tell it—the complicated, painful story of how my mama had, and had not, saved me as a girl" (*Skin*, 34). She unfolds a complicated thematics of kinship and survival: home is the site of violation but also return, home marks out the location of a stepfather's violence, neighbors' scorn, and officials' contempt, but also the love among generations of mothers, daughters, sisters, and aunts. In her earlier work

---

[18]   Dorothy Allison, *Skin* (Ithaca: Firebrand Books, 1994), 14–15, 29.

Allison is concerned with how stories can lie, how humor can be used to evade the harder story rather than to deliver it more fully. In the manifest presence of her tremendous storytelling talents, she seeks the harder story, the one she must labor to tell well. In it she must find language for the grittiest parts of survival—their wretched dailiness and the destruction they seek: "When my stepfather beat me I did not think, did not imagine stories of either escape or revenge. When my stepfather beat me I pulled so deeply into myself I lived only in my eyes, my eyes that watched the shower sweat on the bathroom walls, the pipes under the sink, my blood on the porcelain toilet seat, and the buckle of his belt as it moved through the air."[19] Bone learns a lesson for surviving certain kinds of brutality: don't fight back. When, as an eight year old, a boy cousin tries to teach her and a girl cousin to wrestle, he is frustrated by their technique: the girls won't put up their hands and fight; instead, they curl up in a ball on the hard ground and cover their heads. Allison is taught by her mother and other family members, some of whom do stints at the county jail, that calling in the law is worse than whatever else is happening: "Don't tell anyone what is really going on. We are not safe, I learned from my mama. There are people in the world who are, but they are not us. . . . Tell no one that your stepfather beats you. The things that would happen are too terrible to name" (ibid.). Whether or not that is exactly true, Allison and her mother believe it is and have had enough to do with the law and the world of officialdom and its scorn that theirs is a functional truth. As Allison intimates in her early work, she had to learn to fantasize about revenge despite its impossibility: "Go stand still for him, his hands, his big hands on his little body. I would imagine those hands cut off by marauders sweeping down on great black horses, swords like lightning bolts in the hands of armored women who wouldn't even know my name but would kill him anyway. . . . Imagine vengeance. Imagine justice. What is the difference anyway when both are only stories in your head? In the everyday reality you stand still. I stood still. Bent over. Laid down" (ibid., 37–38).

In her published performance piece, *Two or Three Things I Know for Sure* (1995), written in the months after she completed *Bastard*, Allison pushes forward a "let me tell you a story" version of her life. No longer focusing on the incest material as it impacts her relationships with lovers and co-workers as she did in *Trash*, Allison returns to the women in her family, to class, race, poverty, incest, and illegitimacy. The impossible story is still the one she must tell, but because she has just told it in *Bastard*, she can reflect on the narrative structures the story required. First, there are the nec-

[19]    Allison, *Trash*, 36.

essary if unconscious evasions that yielded through writing: "I convinced myself that I was unbreakable. . . . That's the lie I told myself for years, and not until I began to fashion stories on the page did I sort it all out, see where the lie ended and a broken life remained."[20] Then there is the confrontation with writing itself: "But that is not how I am supposed to tell it. I'm only supposed to tell one story at a time, one story. Every writing course I ever heard of said the same thing" (39). Out of this confrontation with form and the prohibitions it imposes in the seemingly innocent name of craft, Allison finds a way to weld together the unimaginable and the unspeakable: "Behind the story I tell is the one I don't. Behind the story you hear is the one I wish I could make you hear. Behind my carefully buttoned collar is my nakedness, the struggle to find clean clothes, food, meaning, and money. Behind sex is rage, behind anger is love, behind this moment is silence, years of silence" (39). Her work, as she describes it, is transgressive in comprehensive ways. People are not supposed to live to tell her story. If they do, there are rules, writerly and social rules, conventions about presentation. If your "story" is the one no one wants to hear and which cannot be told given certain rules and expectations about form, then silence is your sentence. Allison indicates that achieving a form for telling the story requires going beyond the limit of prohibition. But what exists there? If it is no longer quite fiction, but something like nonfiction dogging fiction's every move, and it is not declaratively autobiography, how will it be read? "The man raped me. It's the truth. It's a fact. I was five, and he was eight months married to my mother" (39). Allison's use of both "truth" and "fact" as descriptions of her experience testifies that she knows that judgments will be brought to bear on her claims.

Allison's representation of molestation in *Bastard* differs from other published versions of her own rape in that it is told from the perspective of the child. The narration preserves the child's terror and confusion and, as such, differs sharply from the account either a child or an adult would be compelled to give in a legal proceeding. A court would require a language of body parts and acts, a description of what went where when. Allison describes the scene clearly but within the child's language and perceptions. Anney and Glen are expecting the birth of their first child, and Glen is desperate that it be a boy. In their Pontiac parked in the hospital lot, Glen, Reese, and Bone wait through the night while Anney is in labor. When Daddy Glen pulls Bone into the front seat of the car and begins to molest her, he talks about how well things are going, about how happy they will all be as a family. How can Bone understand this? With what

20 Allison, *Two or Three Things*, 38–39.

language would she describe it to others? What, for her, has begun to become terribly confused? When Daddy Glen moves from penetrating Bone
with his fingers and takes out his penis, Allison writes in Bone's voice:
"His hand was hard, the ridge of the wristbone pushing in and hurting
me. . . . He was holding himself in his fingers. I knew what it was under
his hand. I'd seen my cousins naked . . . but this was a mystery, scary and
hard. . . . He was hurting me, hurting me!"[21] As the rape progresses, he repeats, " 'It's all gonna be all right' " (47), which forces further incoherence
into a painful and disorienting scene. Glen's language of rape as the language of comfort—we will be happy; "it's all gonna be all right"—names
the rape as an instantiation of familiality such that Bone is left wondering
not exactly what happened, but what exactly it means.

All the characterization of Glen has pointed to his menace—his temper,
his proprietary and needy assertion that Anney and the girls are "all
mine," and his blurring of the difference between Anney and her daughters in his dangerous assertion of possession. No one in Anney's family
likes or trusts Glen; they are only willing to concede that Anney deserves
some measure of happiness. They doubt Glen will provide it, but if Anney
believes he might, they will acquiesce. In other words, all the signs are
there: a mistrusted and violent man enters the picture, a woman who desires love and a measure of relief marries him, and children unable to protect themselves are thrown into his path. Still, when Glen rapes Bone in
the front seat of the car while Anney is in labor, Allison makes the incomprehensible violence of that act both predictable, in a way, and shattering.
The child Anney is laboring to deliver does not survive. The coincidence
is palpable: one child does not survive, will the other(s)? As one child is
literally dying, another's childhood is being killed. Although Allison presents a deadly coincidence, she does not imply a cause: Daddy Glen does
not rape Bone in some contorted reaction to the death of his child. He
rapes her in the full confidence that Anney is in the hospital at that very
moment giving birth to, in his fantasy, his son. He is not in danger, not
pushed beyond some limit of human endurance into an incomparable act
of violence. On the contrary, he is having a great day.

Why doesn't Dorothy Allison offer a rationale for Glen's violence? She
uses certain techniques of characterization to flesh Glen out as a character.
He is neither a caricature of evil nor simply its symbolic representative in
an otherwise Edenic scene. Allison gives him a damagingly disapproving
family, shows how his temper gets him into trouble, makes him plausibly
beaten down and explosive, but she withholds from him an alibi that
would make his rape of Bone sympathetic. I do not read this as a flaw in

---

[21]    Allison, *Bastard Out of Carolina*, 47.

the text; rather, it is an indication of the way Daddy Glen's violence can be simultaneously inexplicable and familiar. Sexual violence in *Bastard* is permitted by a range of factors, none of which makes it comprehensible even given the other forms of violence that surround it. Has Allison, then, fetishized incest? If all other forms of violence and need that grow up in this working-class milieu get attached to at least somewhat sympathetic family members, why the limit on incest? In part, the other forms of violence are comprehensible in terms of Bone's milieu: fighting, stealing, lying, taking up with the wrong people, and so on, are consistent with the love she feels for her family. It is Glen's removal of Bone, Reese, and Anney from the protection of this more understandable world that is the problem. Incest in this text is not depicted as some sort of backward, trashy breakdown in kinship structures, as stereotype would have it. Incest is introduced through the same mechanism as legal and social respectability and precisely as an antidote to the class shame of illegitimacy. Anney marries Glen as a way to remove the stigma of illegitimacy. Through her entry into the law, she opens the door to incest. Allison therefore draws incest and legitimacy into a proximate relation. While she carefully presents Daddy Glen as the outsider in the family, he is nonetheless the bearer of paternal privilege.

To what extent is Bone's abuse invisible, and to what extent is it tacitly overlooked? She has multiple physical injuries that are not the stuff of daily life, no matter how rough and tumble that life is. She has the kind of injuries that a strong adult inflicts on a child, like broken bones, and smashed toes from tripping over the door jamb while running away and looking over her shoulder. Anney keeps this family secret from her relatives and Bone learns no language for articulating it. Signs of sexual abuse are sufficiently present that Aunt Ruth asks Bone as explicitly as she can: "Bone, has Daddy Glen ever . . . well . . . touched you? . . . Has he ever hurt you, messed with you? . . . Down here, honey. Has he ever hurt you down there?" (124). Bone's impulse is to tell her everything, but she cannot and does not. Daddy Glen's beating of Bone is disclosed when her Aunt Raylene sees bruises all over the child. She calls the uncles, who take Glen out and administer some potent kin justice (244–47). Nonetheless, the punishment occurs over Anney's shamed protestation of Glen's love for her and the girls and Anney's love for Glen, and Bone's apologies. Bone's body has provided a kind of evidence which she has not articulated and which she, in a sense, did not consent to provide.

The problem of telling is complex in *Bastard*. While Bone is coerced not to tell in a range of ways, there is also no formal, familiar, structural mechanism for telling. Telling and not telling do not represent an equal and balanced choice. Indeed, because telling is barred in numerous ways, not telling is structured as the inevitability. What, in fact, is Bone supposed to "say" in the face of Glen's effective terrorism? Daddy Glen has Anney's confused complicity born out of her shame and her desire for him, the power to remove Bone completely from any family member who might protect her, their fear of and disregard for any protection that would come from the law, and a child victim who has effectively been immobilized through shame and terror. Of her silence, Bone says: "He never said, 'Don't tell your mama.' He never had to say it. I did not know how to tell anyone how I felt, what scared me and shamed me and still made me stand, unmoving and desperate, while he rubbed against me and ground his face into my neck. I could not tell Mama. I would not have known how to explain why I stood there and let him touch me. It wasn't sex, not like a man and woman pushing their naked bodies into each other, but then, it was something like sex, something powerful and frightening that he wanted badly and I did not understand at all" (108–9). As Bone describes Anney, and as Allison has described her mother, this is a woman who actually had the capacity to understand. That Anney mostly reinforces Bone's lessons in shame by her own example instead of giving her language through which she could articulate harm goes to the heart of Anney's conflicted legacy to Bone and Bone's persistent love for a mother she has not learned how to blame or hate.

When Glen gets out of the hospital after the uncles beat him up, Anney moves out with the girls. The exposure of Bone's injuries precipitates a break in the narrative. Anney's complicity is also exposed and she must struggle to put some things right. Anney stays away from Glen for a while, then moves back in with him, taking Reese with her and leaving Bone with Aunt Alma. Daddy Glen realizes that Anney is grieving for Bone and determines that he will reunite the four of them despite Bone's reluctance. When he shows up at Alma's to induce Bone to return, his menace quickly surfaces. He brutally attacks and rapes Bone with a ruthless violence that Allison details explicitly. What she also does is have Anney walk in on the rape as it is occurring. There is a logic at work here to build down the mythology around rescuing children: people often say that if they only "saw" the violence that was happening, rather than suspected or surmised it, they surely would have taken care of things, protected the child, and so on. Anney's righteous anger and swift rescue of her child follows from that context, but what happens next signals Allison's doubt that knowledge is the main barrier to protecting children.

Anney takes Bone to the hospital, and returns with her other daughter to her husband. She abandons Bone and herself, in a way. Yet, as the text is at pains to show, Anney makes a limited effort to provide for Bone by leaving her with Anney's gay sister, Raylene. What Anney accomplishes for herself or her other daughter is, at best, opaque. The vision of Anney and Reese's departure in the company of Daddy Glen presents a striking image of the law. They appear not just as fugitives from kin-based vengeance and legal retaliation—after all, the rape is a crisis not only because Anney witnessed it, but because Bone is injured so badly she has to be hospitalized and thus falls under the full scrutiny of the law—but also as the legal family. Their togetherness is draped by the privacy that extends to the married heterosexual couple and family, and it is an utterly unsatisfying image. Perhaps this is the bastard's revenge on legitimacy, to make it feel illegitimate, flat, wrong. If this looks like family and legality, it feels like death.

While illegitimacy and incest name the key legal terms through which Bone's experience might be described, what escapes notice in law and psychoanalysis and many sociological studies, Allison places at the enigmatic center of her text: the daughter's love for the mother who cannot save her. This extralegal anomaly, this inconceivable standard, represents an alternative and persistent form of justice. Love involves for Bone the absenting of hopes for and claims to status because it entails loving her shamed family, especially her mother. Here is where self-representation and fiction combine to allow for the simultaneous presence of irreconcilables. In talking about Bone as subject, for example, I am compelled to use passive voice to describe a key feature of her life. I write, "Bone is raped by her stepfather." What is the subjectivity of such a grammatical subject? One whose autobiographical speech must turn in a critical instance to passive voice? The grammar of victimization indicates the limits on subjectivity around trauma. One no longer employs active voice, but must shift into the status of one acted upon by others and by external events: I was shot, I was hit by a car. Or exchange the active voice with the victimizer: he hit me, he raped me. The grammatical situation of the survivor reveals a significant dimension of trauma and its relation to self-representation. While the first meaning of illegitimate is "against the law," the second is "an incorrect grammatical usage." For the raped daughter to speak as a legal subject is contravened by grammar and by law. Self-representational speech about trauma seems to require the subject to work herself into the symbolic. Allison accomplishes this by focusing on the part of the story that is hardest to tell: how love persists even in the midst of damage, even as it permits harm, even as it opens the door to hell and calls it "home."

In so doing, the text is saturated with the mother's losses as much as her daughter's. In Freud's terms, melancholia names the morbid internalization of the loss of either a loved person or of "some abstraction that has taken its place."[22] Bone is downstream from so much mourning, based in the pervasiveness of sexual violence, poverty, and hopelessness that she registers her mother's displaced melancholia. Anney has lost the abstraction of legitimacy and what it might have offered her daughter. Shame is a symptom of the construction of desire in terms of the unlawful, the dishonorable, and the violent. As a structure of feeling, shame expresses the place of gender in sex, violence, and the family, as well as the devaluation of the child that makes her vulnerable to emotional and physical entrapment. Bone is mourning her lost mother, but it is the absence of the mother's ability to protect her child, codified even as Bone was born, that speaks to a larger absenting of legal subjectivity from Anney and, hence, Bone. At the end of the novel after Anney says good-bye, Bone wonders, "Who had Mama been, what had she wanted to be or do before I was born? Once I was born, her hopes had turned, and I had climbed up her life like a flower reaching for the sun. Fourteen and terrified, fifteen and a mother, just past twenty-one when she married Glen. Her life had folded into mine. What would I be like when I was fifteen, twenty, thirty? Would I be as strong as she had been, as hungry for love, as desperate, determined, and ashamed?" In their final encounter, Anney hands Bone her birth certificate. It documents three pieces of information. Name: "RUTH ANNE BOATWRIGHT. Mother: ANNEY BOATWRIGHT. Father: UNKNOWN." Unlike the original birth certificate, and the three copies Anney torched in the kitchen sink while the courthouse burned to the ground, there is no stamp bearing the judgment "illegitimate" at the bottom of this document. Of this "gift" to her daughter, Bone can only ask, "What had she done?"[23]

If, as Goodrich suggests, English law (canon law and common law) is founded upon the casting out of women as legal subjects, if it entails the denial of subjectivity to women as it constructs the binding code of social life, does not law undergo melancholia? How would this register? As I am doing here, if we think of a psychoanalytic jurisprudence as one that tries to historicize the unconscious of common law and jurisprudence, then it may be possible to remember the constitutive pain and trauma of law as a feature it repeats in its current enactments. In the case of *Bastard Out of Carolina*, the law fails to protect Bone, despite the state's interest in the child and the mechanisms of law designed to preserve that interest. It bifurcates into a kin-based and masculine form of vengeance represented by

[22]  Sigmund Freud, "Mourning and Melancholia" (1917), in *General Psychological Theory* (New York: Collier Books, 1963), 164.
[23]  Allison, *Bastard Out of Carolina*, 309.

the uncles and supported by many of the women, and the bureaucratic and classist authority of clerks, cops, prison guards, and doctors.

Dorothy Allison connects the damage of incest to the shame of illegitimacy; their relation underpins the complicated bond between mother and daughter. *Bastard Out of Carolina* demonstrates, in insights that resonate beyond the borders of Allison's text, how incest represents a critical dissonance in both psychoanalysis and law. In psychoanalysis, incest is a metaphor for kinship and also for narcissism. In this involution of self, other, and milieu, psychoanalysis's use of incest gestures toward a powerful dimension of the unconscious around the persistent mysteries of kinship in both personal identity and familial relations. In law, incest has a complicated history and can be described through law's inadequate effort to sort out incest's harm, the state's interest in protecting children, and the law's interest in paternal authority to the benefit of the victims. In Allison's text, we encounter the idea of law and justice neither as formal universals nor as the immanence of adequation and equitable resolution. Instead, justice is incomplete, even impossible, and haunted always by what it fails to accomplish. The view of law refracted through this subculture of poor, white Southerners, where men go to jail early and often, and women are forced young into heterosex and its consequences, is hard to ignore. It comes back without its burnished halo of universality and fairness; instead, it is a mechanism of force, an accomplice to trauma, an unworthy ideal. But *Bastard*, as the name implies, also suggests the lineaments of another jurisprudence, an alternative to the law of the father which is unconvincing, perhaps, when judged according to the requirements of the law's logic, but which is made persuasive in contrast to what in law is unsatisfying. This knowledge about law and justice is represented by the love of the illegitimate daughter for the mother who cannot save her.

Reading *Bastard Out of Carolina* together with insights about law suggests that in this genealogy there are other forms of law and justice, plural jurisdictions, which may promise justice for bastards and women, though not from a law that for centuries has required violation of them. Following from her interest in legitimacy, we could say that Allison develops a hermeneutics of illegitimacy, which suggests a meaning for the bastard form of autobiographical fiction. It is neither legal testimony nor nonfiction, and as fiction it claims a truth-value of an extralegal kind. Her preference in this project for a bastard form clarifies the survivor position vis-à-vis law and trauma. Here the bastard speaks, loses her mother, gains legitimacy through disinheritance, and asserts that "legitimacy" alters her not at all. She is already who she is going to be. As an indicator of the very possibility of legal subjectivity, the birth certificate tells her nothing about who she will be that she doesn't already know. It cannot compensate for her abandonment by her mother or her rape by her stepfather. It is a different legal name for a subject who came into being through an order of illegitimacy. The pronouncement of legitimacy that does not take the history of trauma into account has no power to transform.

# 3

## There Will Always Be a Father

### Transference and the Auto/biographical Demand in Mikal Gilmore's *Shot in the Heart*

*There will always be a father.*
                    —Gary Gilmore's last words before a Utah firing squad

*A story can't be told*
*Until a story's done*
    —opening lines of a poem Gaylen Gilmore was writing in the hospital
    where he died

*Shot in the Heart*, Mikal Gilmore's account of his family history and the execution of his brother Gary Gilmore, demonstrates the interweaving of the painfully clear and the unknown in trauma. In this case, Mikal Gilmore knows his family's violence intimately, yet its cause is presented in their narratives and mythology as the secret his father, mother, and brother Gary took to their graves. Given the spectacular violence inflicted within and by his family, and all that depends on understanding it, wouldn't you want to know the secret too? *Shot in the Heart* concerns the implicated viewer, the bystander who is never far enough away from the violence to remain undamaged. Mikal Gilmore explores not only how his family's violence shaped him but how violence, and identification with it, shapes autobiographical reading broadly, how it compels and repulses identification, and how voyeurism is catalyzed by the spectacle of pain and violence. In this cultural moment, will Gary Gilmore's crime and punishment again compel a generation of onlookers, or will Mikal's pain be more resonant?

Gilmore structures his narrative task as a combination of autobiography, biography, and family history. The inextricability of Mikal Gilmore's autobiographical story of pain from his damaged relation to his family's violence indicates how trauma ruptures the boundaries of the autonomous autobiographical "I," a masculine construct as earlier autobiography scholars implicitly defined it. No longer positioned to tell simply "my" story, this "I" must struggle to organize, even contain, trauma within narrative. Mikal Gilmore is well positioned to articulate the experience of the implicated witness, for he is at once biographer and autobiographer. This limit-case, then, initially concerns the relation between autobiography and biography. Clustered at this limit are related issues about the proximity and interpenetration of the story of the self, the story of a family, and the story of the nation. That these are interwoven for Mikal Gilmore indicates the extent to which autobiography entails kinship narratives, personal histories entail collective histories, and self-representations of trauma are embedded in the long-standing patterns of others' violence. The narratives through which the Gilmore family structures its violence form a central part of the family's legacy and indebt Mikal's own storytelling enterprise to his family's self-mythologizing enterprise.

To explore *Shot in the Heart* as a limit-case, I focus on how his task is structured through what I call the auto/biographical demand, in which the demands of autobiography (to tell my story) and the demands of biography (to tell your story) coincide. In many ways, it is impossible to satisfy this double demand because it yokes together a series of related and unrequitable tasks. First, the auto/biographical demand entails an irresolvable narrative dilemma because it both divides and doubles the writing subject with respect to the task (whose story is this? mine? ours? how can I tell them all?). While these questions and the dilemma they indicate are always present, however concealed, in biography, they also animate autobiography. The instability within the auto/biographical act produces constraints that the auto/biographer manages through form to some extent; yet, the writing subject is still caught up in, indeed emerges through, his or her implication in a family, a culture, even in a self. The auto/biographical subject is exposed in acute and untranscendable ways to the auto/biographical demand.

Second, Mikal Gilmore must speak to and for the dead. To organize his identification with them, rather than simply to be a living emblem of their pain, he must lay down a line between the living and the dead, between his story and their story—even if the line is thoroughly broached—in order to understand the claims the dead make on him. His book clarifies further the extent to which biography and autobiography emerge through the demands the dead place on the living, as well as the ambivalence of speaking to and for them. The dead stalk the unconscious and wait, in Gilmore's text, for any opportunity to appear: dreams, current relationships, the writing of his book. They make demands on him, and he issues them pleas. Tell me your secrets, he begs; never, they repeat. But they refuse to be still. Recalling Toni Morrison's brilliant evocation of the traumatized past that refuses to stay buried until it is properly mourned, the dead Gilmores, like the ghostly Beloved, will haunt noisily and threateningly until there is a reckoning.[1] *Shot in the Heart* aims to be that reckoning. The question, of course, of which Mikal Gilmore is aware, is how can it discharge this debt?

Third, his is a family whose haunting persists in the form of secrets. He must elicit his family's secrets if he is to be their biographer; yet, if he is to uphold the family code of loyalty, he must not reveal them. He must tell their story if he is to tell his; even if the former act entails infidelity, the latter is an act of survival. While it is clear that Mikal Gilmore must tell, it is also clear that he cannot ever hope to tell all. Secrets structure his family's narratives: apart from them, his family does not exist. Even having decided to tell the story, he cannot resolve why violence marked his family, or why he was spared certain forms of it, not only because such answers are hard for anyone to come by but because his family history is so intertwined with fiction. Given the implacability of the auto/biographical demand as Mikal Gilmore structures and is structured by it, the only words that comfort him are ones he repeats in an agony of insight about what it means to survive his brother's execution and still be a member of his family: "It will never be all right. Never. It will never be all right."[2]

Most biographers never articulate this degree of transference to their subjects. *Shot in the Heart* differs in that transference drives the project explicitly. Mikal Gilmore wants to understand his dead brother's life, to trace his family's lineage to see if he can read in it the story of how violence begins, and to retell it so that his story can include a chapter on how violence ends. Gilmore's explicit focus on his dead brother branches out to reveal the place of their father and the rest of the family in this story, which broadens into an account of his parents' pasts, and ultimately rewrites a larger historical narrative in the service of biography and autobiography. To tell his own and his brother's stories, Mikal Gilmore must confront the shaping power of narratives about violence, reckon with the centrality of the father to them, and settle up with the secrets and structural elisions in all these narratives. His project is as much an encounter with what it cannot say as with what it must.

[1] Toni Morrison, *Beloved* (New York: Plume, 1988). For an interesting discussion of trauma as haunting and the language of testimony, see Pamela E. Barnett's "Figurations of Rape and the Supernatural in *Beloved*," *PMLA* 112.3 (spring 1997): 418–27.
[2] Mikal Gilmore, *Shot in the Heart* (New York: Doubleday, 1994), 398.

## Telling on the Father

The story of Gary Gilmore reached into the unconscious of what seemed like the whole nation during the summer of 1977 when he insisted his death sentence be carried out. Gary Gilmore was the first person to be executed in Utah after the Supreme Court lifted the ban on capital punishment in 1976, and it is the catastrophe of his execution around which *Shot in the Heart* pivots. Gary Gilmore murdered two young Mormon men on consecutive nights in 1976; yet, the murders alone do not account for his notoriety. In choosing execution by firing squad and campaigning for his own capital punishment, Gary Gilmore seemingly took away a crucial feature of the state's authority over him, namely its ability to render him powerless in the face of its decision to execute him. Gilmore's way of realizing his punishment as his choice made "the nation," in its formation as an imagined community of those who will punish transgression through the cathartic spectacle of public execution, hate him, because Gary Gilmore transformed a national narrative of crime and public punishment into the final chapter of his private narrative of ruin and redemption.[3] How Gary Gilmore rewrote a narrative of state-sponsored violence into his autobiography is reported by his brother Mikal Gilmore in these words: "Through it all, Gary remained fierce and unswerving in his determination to die—he even tried his own hand at it twice—and he had put the State of Utah and death penalty advocates in a difficult, unexpected spot. He made them not just his allies, but he also transformed them into his servants: men who would kill at his bidding. . . . By insisting on his own execution—and in effect directing the legal machinery that would bring execution about—Gary seemed to be saying: *There's really nothing you can do to punish me, because this is precisely what I want, this is my will. You will help me with my final murder"* (xi).

Gary Gilmore was front-page news for the weeks leading up to his execution and the subject of tabloid coverage for years following it. Norman Mailer's treatment of Gary Gilmore's life, *The Executioner's Song*, based in part on hours of taped interviews with Gary Gilmore, his family, and his familiars, was a bestseller, as was Mikal Gilmore's effort to rework that ground from a point closer in.[4] The intensity and durability of interest suggests a national transference around how this particular narrative plays out crime and punishment. Or, to put it in Mikal Gilmore's terms, it offers up for national consumption a spectacle of blood and vengeance on

---

[3]    See Benedict Anderson, *Imagined Communities* (London: Verso 1983, 1991) for a discussion of the nation as an imagined community; and Lauren Berlant's elucidation of the libidinal dimension of citizenship in *The Anatomy of National Fantasy.*

[4]    Norman Mailer, *The Executioner's Song* (Boston: Little, Brown, 1979).

"America's favorite subject: families and murder."[5] At the heart of this durable subject is an inescapable figure, a principle of family narratives, psychoanalysis, and violence, and, arguably, the subtext of any discussion of auto/biographical transference: the father.

Through her discussion of the dead father in modernist narrative, Nina Schwartz explains how the father lies at the heart of transference: "[T]he trope of dead fathers is about the persistence of violence in disguised forms, a violence that is at the root of both the subject and the law. From the very beginning, the dead father is a screen. In the oedipal complex, the father who is already dead, beyond both (his) desire and (my) revenge, arises as a fantasy: through this fantasy, the child explains to himself or herself the loss of the mother, the death of the originally unified self, though such unity, of course, never existed. The myth of the dead father, appearing to explain death, in fact really *screens* a prior death, loss, violation. This myth and the subsequent transference that arises from it are mechanisms that work by enabling the subject to identify with that rage itself as a *paternal* legacy."[6] Transference, in Schwartz's view, offers an explanation of how the "persistence of violence in disguised forms" is connected to the figure of the (dead) father and to rage. Yet these also connect to love, and the complexification of love and rage names both the density of infantile emotions out of which transference emerges and the matrix for generating future emotions.

Because there are many ways to tell the story of the father, including telling the story of the brother, it is important to notice how Mikal Gilmore tells his. His representation of the past, and his father's place in it, is an argument about how violence begins, persists, ruins, and returns. Mikal's story contains a defining quirk. Gary Gilmore's story has a violent father at its core; Mikal Gilmore's story has both this father and a loving father. The paradox that Mikal Gilmore can neither resolve nor evade is that they are the same man. Mikal Gilmore's father brutalized Bessie—his wife and the mother of Gary, Frank Jr., Gaylen, and Mikal—and terrorized all his sons except Mikal, toward whom he was relatively solicitous and devoted, but whom he also used as a pawn in his general viciousness

---

[5]  Gilmore, *Shot in the Heart*, 11. In her early essay on feminist film theory, Laura Mulvey seized upon a crucial dimension of narrative when she wrote, "sadism demands a story." See her "Visual Pleasure and Narrative Cinema," in *Visual and Other Pleasures* (Bloomington: Indiana University Press, 1989), 14–26, at 22. A story also requires a listener. The narratives of Norman Mailer and Mikal Gilmore are consistent with this thesis but suggest that the listener is also a viewer. Further, two versions of looking may coincide in the same person who is both witness and voyeur. There is an uneasiness in reading a text about violence. One is implicated even if/as one turns away. If one is drawn to (or repelled by) this text, then it has already looped the reader into the transferential space it so fully occupies.
[6]  Nina Schwartz, *Dead Fathers* (Ann Arbor: University of Michigan Press, 1994), 157.

toward the rest of the family. As if the place occupied by the (dead) father were not already sufficiently charged, Mikal Gilmore's transference to his subject, father and brother, concerns this ambivalent, even contradictory, figure. It is in the representation of his father that the auto/biographical demand especially lays claim to Mikal Gilmore.

The mutually embedded stories Mikal has to tell of himself and his brother are structurally different with respect to the father. Gary's life can be narrated through his antipathy to his abusive father and the way the early tutorials in extreme punishment Gary received from his father connect to the long parade of institutional surrogates at whose hands Gary learned cruelty. Yet, Mikal must negotiate between two irreconcilable affective poles. This situation is literalized in a scene repeated throughout Mikal's childhood which he identifies as his training in how to love. His parents fought regularly and horribly with Mikal stationed physically between them. At some point the battle reached a familiar pitch and both parents demanded that he choose between them. Typically he chose his father. "This is the way I learned how to love: choosing between two loves that I could not live without and that I could never hope to reconcile" (176). His ambivalence about love is related to his urgent search for knowledge, and recalls another dimension of transference. As Jacques-Alain Miller explains: "[W]e would rather love than know, and that is the value of transference as obstacle: love, instead of knowledge . . . There is no desire to know. It is love, not the desire to know, that is directed toward knowledge."[7] Mikal Gilmore must struggle to wrest authority from his dead father and brother in order to gain knowledge of himself and them, but he must also learn how to claim his love for them.[8] The transference obstacle entails a struggle with the governing principle of the family, the law of the father, which is the obstacle to all knowledge insofar as Mikal, in his desire to understand and redeem his family, confronts a choice between love and knowledge.

The autobiographical dimension of *Shot in the Heart* allows Mikal Gilmore to record how transference arises as he writes his family's biography. His family seems larger than life to him, magnified not only by death, but by their spectacular violence, losses, and pain. These, their years of wandering, and their fictionalized biographies add up to some

[7]    Jacques-Alain Miller, "The Analytic Experience," in *Lacan and the Subject of Language*, ed. Ellie Ragland-Sullivan and Mark Brache (New York: Routledge, 1991), 91.
[8]    The mother whom he could not choose must also be honored, and Mikal Gilmore offers feminist arguments about her entrapment in her birth family and her life with Frank Gilmore. By making her more abused than abusing, and she is clearly both in his account, Mikal minimizes her role in the family's violence. Although he patiently traces her Mormon history and enters his father's story through hers, it is the father's mystifying and secretive story, the one Mikal Gilmore cannot tell, that has more power in this text.

formidable questions for Mikal Gilmore about identity and identification. His question, "why did Gary Gilmore choose death for others and then for himself?" is always shadowed by two related ones. First, when Mikal asks why Gary killed, he is always asking "why didn't I?" Second, when he wonders what it means that Gary was executed, he is always wondering how he survived. Mikal Gilmore's psychic gridding around identification takes place in the historical context his father has authored. While Mikal's questions would be poignant enough if his father's violence had been consistently directed at all his sons, in the face of the anomaly of his love, they are unanswerable. In other words, Mikal and Gary's differences from each other, which so concern Mikal, do not derive only, or perhaps even primarily, from the obvious—namely, that they were confronted with different circumstances, found and made different choices as children and adults, and Gary Gilmore spent the majority of his life in penal institutions with so little love and compassion that his multiple suicide attempts seem like reasonable responses to an intolerable life. What renders the distance between Gary and Mikal opaque to Mikal is their father. The man who devoted a couple of decades to abusing his wife and their three oldest sons, doted on Mikal, and effectively sentenced him to internal exile in the family. The father in this family, then, is the transferential object behind the more explicit biographical (Gary) and autobiographical (Mikal) ones. Yet it is not only the loving father whom Mikal has lost or been denied but the violent father who beat the rest of his family brutally, and who never touched Mikal in this way. The absence of this violent touch on Mikal is magnified by its presence in his family's daily life. How could he be spared the structuring principle of Gilmore family life and still be a member of the family? How can he be his father's son if he is not directly brutalized by him? How can he claim to have escaped when he is so traumatized? He is permitted no unambivalent feelings in response to these questions about kinship, violence, and personal identity. When they arise, as in the dreams in which his father appears and Mikal is happy to see him, he feels guilty. The limit, then, between autobiography and biography is stalked by the impossible stories of trauma, love, and family.

The book begins with a dream that suggests the fatality propelling Mikal Gilmore across the threshold toward his brother. It is a recurrent dream, years old and wretched. The family is back from the dead and inside the father's house. The father is there, too, and only Mikal is happy to see him. The house is represented as a transitional place: it is at the edge of a forest Mikal cannot enter, a track runs alongside it, and, although the dreamer hears the siren's howl, the train never comes. Frank Sr., the father; Bessie, the mother; and the brothers Frank Jr., Gary, and Gaylen are all present in death, although Frank Jr., absent from Mikal's life before the writing of this book, is still living. The family comes and goes from the house, but only to return to death. Mikal cannot leave the house either to join the family in death or to quit them and live. In the dream Gary offers Mikal a way to join them. He places a gun before Mikal and says, "See you in the darkness beyond." When Gary's offer comes, years into the dreaming, Mikal immediately chooses death and family: "I pick the pistol up. I put its barrel in my mouth. I pull the trigger. I feel my teeth fracture and disintegrate and pass in a gush of blood out of my mouth. I also feel my life pass out of my mouth, and in that instant I feel a collapse into nothingness." Repeating the terms of Gary's pact, Mikal continues: "There is darkness, but there is no beyond. There is *never* any beyond." When Mikal Gilmore awakens from this dream, he is deep in the grip of its ambivalence: "I want back into the dream," he writes, whether he has just glimpsed in it the "gateway to the refuge of my ruined family" or the "gateway to hell."[9]

While this dream images the dramatic pain Mikal Gilmore feels for a family he describes as ruined, it also contains a threat to his current project. As an image of the prohibition on telling family secrets, "I also feel my life pass out of my mouth" is potent. It implies that just as his brother was shot in the heart, so Mikal Gilmore will wound himself in the mouth with his brother's gun, even as he begins to tell the family's story. Telling and dying look the same in this dream. Following the italicized dream narrative, the prologue moves briskly to a declaration of the story's charge and its stakes:

> I have a story to tell. It is a story of murders: murders of the flesh, and of the spirit; murders born of heartbreak, of hatred, of retribution. It is the story of where those murders begin, of how they take form and enter our actions, how they transform our lives, how their legacies spill into the world and the history around us. And it is a story about how the claims of violence and murder end—if, indeed, they ever end. I know this story well, because I have been stuck inside it. . . . I know the dead in this story—I know why they made death for others, and why they sought it for themselves. And if I ever hope to leave this place, I must tell what I know. (x–xi)

In this passage, Gilmore formulates his text as a testimony that may earn him some absolution: "if I ever hope to leave this place, I must tell what I know." Yet in the bargain he attempts to strike, he inflates his knowledge, and claims to know the unknowable, "I know why they made death for others, and why they sought it for themselves." The book that

[9]  Gilmore, *Shot in the Heart*, x.

follows ultimately fails to resolve the mysteries of violence. The qualifier, "if, indeed, they ever end," signals Gilmore's doubt about the ability of narrative to order violence and murder into a story that began somewhere and can, therefore, end. Once he expresses doubt, he swerves in the other direction to make a claim that is more the book's wish than its fulfillment: "I know the dead in this story." In swerving from unknowability to knowability, Gilmore incises his autobiographical signature at the place in the text where the dead are not buried. Mikal Gilmore as auto/biographer stands at a yawning grave and embraces his task and the self to whom it falls, "I know this story well, because I have been stuck inside it. I have lived with its causes and effects, its details and indelible lessons, my entire life. . . . And if I ever hope to leave this place, I must tell what I know."

While Gary Gilmore was on death row, Lawrence Schiller interviewed members of the Gilmore family and became convinced that above and beyond the secrets they had disclosed, Gary and his mother Bessie were holding something back. He suspected it was a secret about Frank Sr. "Schiller sensed that something horrible had happened in the past, but Gary insisted that this was not the case, and he often met these questions with mockery or anger, even until the last hours of his life" (xi). Schiller followed up on his hunch with Bessie Gilmore: "Had something happened in Gary's childhood that later turned him to the course of murder?" "[M]y mother answered their inquiries with maddening riddles and outright avoidance."[10] While it is possible that both Gary and Bessie Gilmore were keeping a secret, it is also possible that there was no way for them to answer the question without seeming evasive.[11] Perhaps we read their resistance through the filter of Schiller's transference: because *he* believes they have the answer to the mystery of violence, he reads their failure to solve the mystery as their resistance and refusal to help him know them. Of the family's mythology Mikal Gilmore notes presciently, "whether any of these tales were true or not hardly mattered. We believed these claims

[10]  The phrase "maddening riddles and outright avoidance" is repeated on pages xi and 54.

[11]  There are, in fact, a lot of secrets, but who knows what they would explain. The one Schiller is certain Bessie is keeping is one Gary overheard on the phone, and Mikal is convinced it is the worst thing yet about his father. Neither Bessie nor Gary ever tell. Stories about the mother and father have different narrative economies of meaning. Bessie's stories are mostly ghost stories. But there is one that purports to be tethered to the realm of verifiable events. Bessie was traumatized as a child by being forced by her father to witness a public execution in Utah. At the moment the condemned man was to die, her father yanked her by the hair so she would have to watch. It was one of her most chilling memories, and like some of her other tales, it predicted a horror that would come. When Mikal Gilmore checks, he finds there were no public executions either at the time or in the place Bessie claimed.

about our lives, and we acted upon them" (70). Secrets are as powerful as any facts in the construction of meaning because of their function in the family's narratives of identity. Indeed, they remain implacable in the face of puny fact.

The family's secrets, which were also its lies, were overwhelmingly about patrimony, and had the power to shape the children's intimate self-knowledge. Bessie and Frank Sr., for example, whose dependence on the state-supported privacy surrounding what can be done in a family cannot be overstated, were not legally married when any of their children were born. Frank Sr. was married multiple times, under a variety of names, and had several children about whom Bessie knew little or nothing. More significantly in terms of the shaping power of narrative and the sense the family came to make of itself, the theme of fathers and sons cut off from each other is given allegorical centrality in the myth about Frank Sr.'s origins. Frank Sr.'s mother, Fay, told Frank that his real father was Houdini, that Frank's real last name was Weiss, Houdini's last name before he changed it, and that the tragedy of Frank's life was that his father kept his relation to his son a secret. As Fay tells Bessie, "The anger of the man is that he can never claim who he truly is" (68). Fay transforms this into an explanatory device for Frank Gilmore's violence and inscrutability which Bessie readily adopts and passes on to her sons. When Mikal does a little detective work, he discovers that the Houdini story could not be true. Mikal and Frank Jr. were left to absorb this information on their own.

Mikal claims to know with certainty that "[w]e all paid for something that had happened long before we were born, something that we were not allowed to know" (4). One of the "shockers," as Frank Jr. calls the big secrets, downstream from this prior debt concerns patrimony and paternity. Frank Jr., the first child of Bessie and Frank Sr. is not Frank Sr.'s son. Frank Jr. is the son of Bessie and Robert Ingram, Frank Sr.'s son whom Bessie met while she was staying with Frank's mother early in their marriage. Shortly after Frank Sr. took Bessie to meet his mother, he took off without explanation. Bessie found in Robert Ingram, who was nineteen years old at the time, a welcome companion, as well as a link to her husband's deliberately mystifying past. Bessie never told Frank Sr. about Frank Jr.'s paternity, and there is no indication in the book that Robert Ingram knew. Bessie told one of her sisters who ultimately told Mikal. In a displacement whose insight was its blindness, Frank Sr. became convinced that Gary was not his son, and treated him accordingly.

There are two photographs included in the book that offer a stunning visual image of this situation. One is a family portrait of the three boys, Frank Jr., Gary, and Gaylen in the foreground, with Frank Sr. and Bessie standing behind them. No one in the photo is touching. Mikal Gilmore zeroes in on Frank Jr.'s goofy look and reads it as a comment on the fakery of this group posing as a family: *"Isn't this ridiculous—all of us posing like a real family?"*(109). In the other photo, taken at the same time, Frank Sr. has stepped into Bessie's place (she had been standing behind Frank Jr.), and Robert Ingram now stands behind Gary. Little Gaylen, who had been grinning cherubically, now stares at the camera. Gary, who had been exercising a boyhood version of outlaw charm, just glares. Frank Jr. stands in front of Frank Sr., whose hands lie on Frank Jr.'s shoulders. All the energy has drained from Frank Jr.'s face and body. The camera catches a child who is dead in his father's grip. Mikal Gilmore offers this family photograph of fathers and sons, literally and figuratively unknown to each other, without comment.[12]

Mikal Gilmore sees the violence that animated Gary as his patrimony and figures it as the same blood flowing in their veins. Initially, Mikal Gilmore suggests that the origin of Gary's violence lies in an event, an external set of circumstances, or just the bad luck of being born into a particular family. But by the end of the prologue, murderousness becomes a heritable trait rather than the mark of a violent imposition (xii). Mikal's wish to identify with Gary, rather than to retreat from identification, causes him to swerve toward this claim about birthright. Mikal Gilmore's interest in probing the brother's wound, now found in his own psyche, as well as the multiple woundings authored by the father, complicates the task and requires Mikal Gilmore to enter the project as a subject himself, one who both does and does not know, who both possesses and lacks an epistemological privilege on violence and his family, and who is both a living member of the family that authored Gary Gilmore and its belated historian.[13] The doubleness of his positioning, the way he is never quite where he needs and wants to be with respect to knowledge, enacts a narrative specularity, or, put another way, evokes a kind of haunting that distinguishes this narrative as surely as the ghosts that keep showing up where Gary Gilmore is supposed to be. Again, the figure that seems to

---

[12]   The second photograph appears only in the paperback edition along with some additional photographs that were not in the original hardcover publication, which may explain why there is no mention of this or the other added photos in the text.

[13]   See Jacques Lacan, *Four Fundamental Concepts*, ed. J.-A. Miller, trans. Alan Sheridan (New York: Norton, 1978): "As soon as the subject who is supposed to know exists somewhere . . . there is transference" (232). As Lacan puts it, "the positive transference is when you have a soft spot for the individual concerned, . . . and the negative transference is when you have to keep your eye on him" (124). Transference involves the construction of a subject-supposed-to-know. While Freud focused on the way analysis elicits earlier passions to take shape in the present, it is clear now that transference is ubiquitous. To use Lacan's formulation, transference may be present wherever there is the construction of a "subject-supposed-to-know."

displace all other figures for knowledge about violence is the father. In a family in which kindness can be a form of brutality, how can Mikal Gilmore find his way across the threshold and into the haunted house where he waits for what he knows to catch up with what he can bear?

## Writing the Book of the Dead

For several chapters, Mikal Gilmore writes a history of the American West that connects Mormon settlement and Indian resettlement to the bloodthirstiness that defines U.S. history. The violence, massacres, losses, and upheavals that constitute this history also render it ghostly. In Mikal Gilmore's analysis, the history of the American West is dripping in blood, and these traumas transform history into haunting. Whereas historical personages are tamed by an official discourse of monuments and memorials that shrink the dead to a size the living can tolerate, trauma causes history to erupt from its manageable confines. In this context the dead are no longer persons who lived in the past, but angry, bitter, and mournful ghosts. The dead in this construction refuse to do the work of history, which is to stay buried, in effect, to "be" the past, and to maintain the rationality of time as past-present-future. Instead, the dead return because they were never properly buried. They impose on the living because the living still owe them something. As a Mormon elder tells young Mikal, "Never disrespect the dead, young man. . . . Remember that you live in their debt" (32).

What results is a negotiation about how the dead will be represented, that is, how they will permit, and be permitted by, the living to live on. Mikal Gilmore's effort to organize their presence entails nothing less than the reordering of time, via narrative, into a story with a beginning, a middle, and an end. Because haunting is a metaphor for the disordering of time, Mikal Gilmore feels belated in his task to restore history to its proper order. He is like Hamlet who, when given an impossible task by a ghostly father, declares that the ghost's demand has not only torn the veil between the natural and supernatural worlds, it has disordered time: "The time is out of joint. O cursed spite, / That ever I was born to set it right!" (1.5.188–89). For Mikal Gilmore, the cultural work of biographical narrative represents an opportunity to set time right, to alter the dominant construction of his brother's life, to place his family's biography into evidence, and to rewrite the traumatized past in order to thwart its endless reproduction.

Mikal Gilmore embarks on this task by framing his mother's story within the history of Mormonism. In this construction, Joseph Smith, the founder of Mormonism, becomes their fateful forebear. To see how Smith's legacy branches into his own, Gilmore focuses on Smith's persecution and death. By emphasizing that Smith was more punished than punishing, Gilmore makes the founder of Mormonism into a figure of retribution. Thus he feels for the *father* of Mormonism not as a *son*; rather, "I feel for him as for a brother" (15). Mikal Gilmore focuses more on the significance of the Mormon doctrine of Blood Atonement than polygamy when he turns to Gary, though both underwrite the family logic in crucial ways, and connects Blood Atonement to Gary's destiny. The doctrine of Blood Atonement offers an avenue of salvation for those who commit horrible crimes: you must offer yourself as a sacrifice for your sins by allowing your blood to be spilled out onto the ground. In the bleeding comes atonement. The insidiousness of this view in Gary Gilmore's developing imaginary around violence is signaled by his recurrent suicide attempts in prison. One prison doctor reported Gary's insight into his intrication in Blood Atonement in this report to a judge who had ordered a psychiatric evaluation of Gary: " 'he wanted to bleed to death, wanted to die, but more than that he wants [*sic*] to bleed to death' " (253).

Mikal Gilmore finds in narrative an opportunity to reshape history from the perspective of the storyteller. He writes: "[V]iolence always demands an explanation or solution" (11), and he wants the job. The subject position of narrator offers him the epistemological privilege that comes with access. He comes to know and to identify with his family through telling their stories and through reconfiguring history such that they are comprehensible actors within it. His effort to explain moves from Joseph Smith to a representation of Bessie Gilmore as a product of Mormon Utah. The narratives in the Book of Mormon help to construct the limits within which she and her family can know themselves and each other. At the heart of the Book of Mormon's account of the bloody and ruinous history of pre-America is the God who sets it all up, the angry and punitive father who authors a history of mass extinction. The sharpest instance of blasphemy in the Book of Mormon aims directly at this truth about the father, even as it punishes the blasphemer. The blasphemy occurs in a trial-like setting in which, as Gilmore writes:

> [A] charismatic atheist and Antichrist named Kohihor stands before one of God's judges and kings and proclaims: "Ye say that this people is a guilty and a fallen people, because of the transgression of a parent. Behold, I say that a child is not guilty because of its parent." For proclaiming such outrageous words, God strikes Kohihor mute, and despite Kohihor's full-hearted

repentance, God will not allow him forgiveness. Kohihor is left to wander among the people of the nation, begging for mercy and support, and the people take him and stamp upon him, until he lies dead under their feet. (12)

Transgression against the law of the father, in this parable, is unforgivable, and each story of an outlaw's ultimate punishment is another element in Mikal Gilmore's effort to build a narrative context in which his brother will become knowable.

After Mikal Gilmore reveals the tangled histories and narratives of his mother's and father's lives and lore, he turns to Gary Gilmore's life. With his narration of Gary's birth, Mikal refines the question that has organized the book to this point: "Could I locate one moment where everything went wrong, one moment—or period of time—that might have made all the difference? And if I could find such a moment, would it be one inside Gary's life? Or would it be one outside him—one, say, in the secret darkness of his father's history?" (86). In trying to answer, Mikal Gilmore identifies his obsession with this question as his mother's: "I can't help searching out our history for those answers, like my mother at the end of her days, examining each terrible link in the fateful chain" (86). Despite the appeal of his question—after all, answering it would solve so much—he concludes that there are too many terrible links.

Gary Gilmore is born when his parents are in Texas and Frank Sr. is running/has run a scam. When Bessie goes into labor, Frank tells her to let him do all the talking when they get to the hospital. Bessie awakens to find that Frank has named the newborn Faye Robert Coffman. The symbolic meaning of the name gets to Bessie: "You've . . . named your son after your *mother* and another one of your sons—somebody you don't even love. What the hell has gotten into you?" (85). Frank treats the legalities lightly: the birth certificate is not an identity card, it is a formality. While they are in Texas, he is Walter Coffman and his son is Faye. To a man with several aliases, and the wives and children to go with them, what's in a name? Yet Frank Sr. has spent a lifetime as a walking illustration of how the name represents a father's true relation to his son. The name offers a tether, however slight, from father to son. Gary is offered no connection. He isn't Faye and his father isn't Walter. Given the significance of the Houdini paternity myth to the family, its central lesson could not have been lost on Gary. Bessie's effort to repair the situation promotes further injury: she names the child Gary, which reminds Frank of a person he hates, a man named Grady who stole Robert's mother from Frank. Imagine the anxiety that swirls around any invocation of Robert Ingram, Frank's estranged son and the father of Frank Jr. Gary must bear the torsion of this displacement. Mikal offers his parents' last words on the subject as if they were an epitaph: "My father's last word on the subject: 'I'm not going to keep a son with that name.' My mother's last word: 'The name stays' " (86).

Frank Sr. becomes convinced that Gary is Robert Ingram's son, beats Bessie up about it, then a few days later, takes Gary and abandons Bessie and Frank Jr. Bessie makes it home to Provo with Frank Jr. where she gets a call from an orphanage in Des Moines. They have Gary. Frank Sr. had left him on a park bench while he tried to pass a bad check. Frank Sr.'s excuse for leaving Bessie and Frank Jr. points to the family secret Schiller was convinced they were keeping: "Somebody got too close that day," Frank answers (89). When Bessie presses him for details, he demurs, "It's a frightful truth, Bessie. You're better off not knowing" (90). However, we learn nothing that further addresses why he took Gary, or why he left the infant on a park bench after, presumably, he had gained the breathing space he left Texas to find. About that frightful truth, I'm inclined to think Gary Gilmore knew all he needed to.

The incident about Gary's name becomes significant to him later in his life, and to Mikal. The symbolic absence of any birth certificate for Gary Gilmore speaks to his cosmic dispossession. As Mikal puts it, Gary Gilmore was never born, he would only die. Gary confronts his mother with his actual birth certificate from McCamey, Texas, the one with the name Faye Robert Coffman. Bessie is evasive, but Gary has already drawn an inference: "Hell, Mom, no wonder the old man never liked me. I was never really his son, was I?" (251). Bessie insists Gary is Frank's son, but meaning has already clicked into place around this document, and he hands her back the birth certificate. A terse exchange follows:

> "You can keep it," she said to him, trying to force a smile.
> "No-*thank-you*," he said, biting off each word. It was the iciest way he had ever spoken to her.
> "Gary, there are some things you don't know, but this isn't what you think it is."
> He said nothing. He walked out of the house, slamming the front door behind him. It was the last time my mother ever saw Gary as a free man. (251)

In his last hours, Gary tells his Uncle Vern, "My father was the first person I ever wanted to murder. . . . If I could have killed him and got away with it, I would have" (143). To the end, the father haunts as surely as if Gary had killed him. There would have been no getting away with his murder, just as there is no getting away from his memory. The father casts a long shadow on Gary's life. His violent explosions, his inexplicable cru-

elty, and his capricious punishments structure the irrational and incoher-
ent patrimony within which Gary Gilmore tries to know himself. Gary's
struggle to answer the question "who am I?" is linked to one he cannot
answer, "who is my father?" His effort to locate the meaning of his
identity in the birth certificate is only one instance of this search. Another
is figured in a letter he wrote his mother from jail when he was twenty
years old and had started trying to kill himself by breaking the light bulbs
in his cells and slashing his wrists with the shards. He wrote his mother a
letter in response to her concern about his self-destructiveness.

The letter turns on a story set at MacLaren's, the reformatory where
Gary was first institutionalized, about a fourteen-year-old boy who was
brought there during Gary's stay. The boy's foster parents had given up
on him and he had no other relatives. MacLaren's was the last stop for this
orphan. The boy had a "pretty and fragile manner—a bad combination inside a jail. . . . He was one of those kids, Gary wrote, that both the coun-
selors and the inmates felt they could treat any way they wanted, because
nobody would speak for him." As an example of this maxim, Gary recalled watching ten boys hold this child down and gang-rape him. Gary,
who seems to have become a neutral observer to this assault, is implicated
enough to have refused "his turn" when it came. Gary's refusal earns the
boy's trust. The boy's mistreatment continues and his frailty deepens. He
often falls ill, but because he never improves, the supervisors conclude he
must be faking. One night when the night watchman refuses to take the
boy to the infirmary, he makes his way to Gary's bed and asks, " 'Can I
stay here with you tonight? I'm scared and I need somebody to hold me"
(158–59). Mikal continues the story:

> Gary lay in bed with the boy most of the night, holding him, running his
> hand over the boy's fevered brow, talking gently to him. "I just want to dis-
> appear," the boy told Gary, and then he tried to curl up into a ball in my
> brother's arms. "I want to disappear into the nothingness inside myself,
> where nobody can hurt me ever again." Finally, the boy fell asleep and so
> did Gary, holding him. When Gary awoke, he was still holding the boy,
> who was now curled up into himself, cold and dead. Gary said he stayed
> there and kept holding the boy, caressing his face. "This is what will hap-
> pen to me if somebody doesn't get me out of jail," Gary wrote. "I'm too
> healthy to die the way that boy died, so I tried to escape the only way I
> knew how. I'm sorry, Mom." (159)

When Mikal checks the records at MacLaren's, he can find no report
corresponding to this story. He concludes that Gary offered it to his
mother as a way to talk about the cost of staying alive in prison, and as a

farewell: "I think Gary was writing about his last night on earth, before he became as cruel as he needed to be to survive the rest of his life."[14] Mikal Gilmore recognizes this story as Gary's use of biography (even fictional biography) in the service of autobiography. He writes about this boy's life as a way to write about an emotional truth with no other ready illustration. In this example of the auto/biographical demand, Gary can discharge the demand of autobiography (to tell *my* story) in the mode of biography's demand (to tell *your* story).

Fifteen years later in a conversation with Mikal when he is on death row, Gary claimed the boy's statement as his own: "I want to disappear into the nothingness inside myself, where nobody can hurt me ever again." In this conversation, Mikal feels awkward as Gary tells him not to try to get a stay of execution. Mikal says, "It's hard to hear this stuff from somebody you love." Gary replies, "I won't let anything hurt me anymore" (328). He will now save himself, in effect, by taking the ultimate abuse. But there is another meaning in his words: what threatens to hurt Gary is Mikal's declaration of love coming too late, when it cannot change anything. Familial love, even brotherly love, is the enemy. When Mikal says "love," Gary hears "hurt" and says "no more."

There are few conversations between Gary and Mikal, and it is interesting that Gary Gilmore slips in and out of view in the sections of the book devoted to him.[15] The pressures of the auto/biographical demand account in part for this specularity as Mikal's effort to tell his story overlaps with his effort to tell everybody else's. Yet it is also the case that Mikal does not share in Gary's life outside the home and shares very little with Gary when he is home. Gary also disappears from Mikal's view when he is in reform school or prison. From interviews with some of the men with

[14] This anecdote on page 159, as Mikal Gilmore retells it, touches on a question that runs through *Shot in the Heart* about Gary Gilmore's sexuality. According to Mikal, Gary denied any homosexual relationships to Schiller. As a young man in Portland, Gary hangs out in gay bars which demarcate a liminal space with respect to law and convention, and there are remembrances of his kissing boys. He did some hustling and his circle was befriended by a gay man who let Gary and his friends use his apartment to do things they couldn't do at home. Mikal hypothesizes that a fellow inmate whom Gary tried to help escape and who double-crossed him in the process was Gary's lover. The thread of Gary Gilmore's sexuality is difficult to follow in the text, but the tenderness of the dead boy anecdote could be read for even more poignancy than Mikal offers here.

[15] Mikal Gilmore outlines Gary Gilmore's developing criminality, and suggests that while the early burglaries are done partly for cash, Gary's motive is strongly voyeuristic. He breaks into other people's homes because he wants to see how they live (167). Interestingly, whenever the police catch Gary, his father defends him pathologically, claims it is all a setup despite clear-cut proof of Gary's crime, then hires the best lawyers he can to get Gary off. Frank Sr. never tires of being the sole law for his family, and he tolerates no infringement on his claim.

whom Gary was incarcerated, and from his prison records, Mikal can re-construct some of Gary Gilmore's life in disciplinary institutions. Gary's battles with authority figures, particularly older men, make sense given his relationship with his father, but the simple fact that Gary spent over half his life locked up by and with men indicates another dimension of Mikal's study. The scenes in which Gary Gilmore appears form a record of his education in masculinity, a significant dimension of the patrimony he and Mikal share. The institutional surrogates of the father who fur-thered his education in the brutal side of masculinity do little to recon-struct Gary's notion that masculinity is punishment. In one of their rare conversations, Gary reveals to Mikal what he has learned about masculin-ity: " 'Promise me you'll be a man. Promise me you'll let them beat you.' I thought he was telling me how to survive in jail. I realize now that he was telling me how to survive in my family" (171).

## Last Words

In 1979 Paul de Man published an essay on autobiography in which he presented autobiography as an impossibility.[16] In its characteristic repre-sentation of the past, autobiography makes a demand on the dead to do what they cannot do: speak in their own voices. In any performance of the autobiographical voice, one speaks across a gulf to address an inanimate face, one's own, and to urge it to speak. Such an attribution of face to voice leads inexorably to a "de-facement" for de Man, for the thing itself is nei-ther "there" in the past nor in the text just waiting to speak. The autobio-graphical "I" is not the self in any simple way, it is necessarily its rhetori-cal surrogate. In other words the autobiographical "I" is no more your possession than are the other persons you compel to speak in your autobi-ography or their biographies. "You" and "yours" are not simply waiting off in the wings somewhere to be ushered onstage to speak. Such perfor-mances are fated and even fatalistic encounters with the impossibility of their fulfillment. Persons in the past, including you as you were, can only be bidden like discarnate spirits, and de Man's scrupulously deconstruc-tive reading ends with the self writing the text staring across an abyss to-ward the self in the text. Language seems to offer the possibility of having the dead speak directly, in their own voices, to the living and to the future. But this illusion is a property of language, a delusion, a ruse, a trope, in de Man's terms, passing itself off as the truth. In its effort to represent life,

---

[16]   Paul de Man, "Autobiography as De-facement," *Modern Language Notes* 94.5 (1979): 919–30.

autobiography comes inevitably upon its own impossibility. Its burden is to repeat this impossibility, but never to penetrate it, because it is constituted in and as this fatality.[17]

De Man's exemplary text is Wordsworth's "Essay upon Epitaphs," which he describes as turning "compulsively from [being] an essay *upon* epitaphs to being itself an epitaph" (923). In it, Wordsworth shifts from the epitaphs of others to quote from his own work. In this movement, de Man finds the sine qua non of autobiography: the language of mutilation that leads Wordsworth from one epitaph to another and then to his own work is bound to the language of self-restoration that is autobiography's hallmark. De Man identifies the rhetorical figure of prosopopeia as the trope of autobiography, and defines prosopopeia as "the fiction of an apostrophe to an absent, deceased or voiceless entity, which posits the possibility of the latter's reply and confers upon it the power of speech" (926). With not too much extension, it is possible to see how biography partakes of prosopopeia, too. In its restoration of subjects in the past, biography necessarily requires the same displacements that permit one to think that the self in autobiography has spoken in its own voice. Such "gliding displacements" lead Wordsworth to prefer the subtlety of prosopopeia to the blunt contrast of antithesis. De Man notices, however, that even in the face of Wordsworth's claim about prosopopeia's superiority to antithesis, "[w]henever prosopopeia is discussed . . . the argument becomes singularly inconclusive" (927). It cannot be otherwise because the subject conjured through prosopopeia is insubstantial, ghostly. It recedes into the medium (language, and here the rhetoric of autobiography and biography) through which it is made to appear.

While de Man's comments on autobiography obviously shed light on Mikal Gilmore's struggle to represent both himself and his family's ghosts, I want to link them to the conclusion of Freud's "Dynamics of the Transference," where he wrote: "[the transference-manifestations], and they only, render the invaluable service of making the patient's buried and forgotten love-emotions actual and manifest; *for in the last resort no one can be slain in absentia or in effigie.*"[18] If we follow de Man, no one in the past

---

[17]   Given de Man's posthumously revealed involvement with a collaborationist newspaper in Belgium for which he wrote anti-Semitic assessments of literature and culture, his association of autobiography with death, his emphasis on the impossibility of the self in the present uttering the truth about the self in the past, and his delineation of the specular noncoincidence between these versions and times of the self is as close to self-revelation as his public record approaches.

[18]   Freud, "Dynamics of the Transference" (1912) in *Therapy and Technique* (New York: Collier Books, 1963), 114–15. For an especially illuminating essay on transference, see "Dora: Fragment of an Analysis," Jacqueline Rose's contribution to *In Dora's Case*, 2d ed., ed. Charles Bernheimer and Claire Kahane (New York: Columbia University Press, 1990),

can be brought sufficiently to the fore to be slain at all. All figures from the past, including oneself, appear, in effect, as effigies. Executions are present-tense occurrences that cannot be staged outside their relentless moment. All else, including autobiography, biography, and history, confront this condition. The subjects of autobiography, biography, and history are present in absentia: they cannot testify in their own voices any more than Mikal Gilmore's family can. Transference, then, helps to explain how the past remains present, even if de Man places even greater restrictions on its resolution than Freud does.

Gary Gilmore's abbreviated autobiography is offered in the last words he utters before a Utah firing squad shoots his heart out onto the ground: "There will always be a father."[19] This utterance marks where Gary Gilmore disappears into an entangled past and the encrypted memories of others. Mikal confronts the insight represented by Gary's last words as if it were a mirror. Because of the difference in the way their father treated Gary and Mikal, Gary's claim, "there will always be a father," is especially

---

128–48. The case of Dora, in which Freud formulated transference as his own failure, instructs us about the complex constellation of real and imagined actors arranged in the analytic scene. Transference is permitted by the structural relation of analyst and analysand, but it is animated by memory, the dead, anxiety, and love. The present tense moment of the transference contributes no content; it offers a way to process it. Freud attributes the failure of Dora's analysis to his inability "to master the transference in good time." Transference appears in Dora's case as both something that is missing and a failure. Jacqueline Rose points out how the two are related, and reveals the incoherence at the core of Freud's formulation of transference. According to Rose, Freud's descriptive language misleads him for it suggests transference is both a relational element, it is what happens in analysis, and "a content, an object to be identified, placed, and resolved (transference as the recovery of an actual event)" (141). What resonates about Rose's discussion for Mikal Gilmore's historical search for answers is her pinpointing of Freud's "insistence that cure of the symptom and completion of memory were synonymous—psychoanalysis defined here as the creation of a full history to which the subject would be restored" (142).

19    At Gary Gilmore's trial, his lawyers presented no defense after the state presented its evidence. This prevented Gary Gilmore from offering the explanation he said he wanted to give and which may have further fleshed out his epigrammatic last words. Like Althusser and Allison, then, Gilmore has a vexed relation to the protocols of legal testimony and to the subjectivity granted and coerced by the confessional imperative. Althusser claims that he has been deprived of the opportunity to tell his story, specifically because he cannot address his culpability in a legal setting and not because he has been barred from publishing an account of his crime. Gary Gilmore had apparently prepared a statement, the delivery of which was mooted when he pleaded guilty. When the judge offered him a chance to speak, he declined to become a confessional subject or to speak from what Foucault called the "lyrical position of the murderous subject," a position into which he had moved by virtue of his plea and the sentence that would follow. In this context we should note that Dorothy Allison's stepfather was never brought to trial for his brutalization of her and that Allison never offered legal testimony as a child or an adult about his crime. The extent to which these stories do not enter into discourse via the law but are nonetheless presented in relation to it is crucial here for understanding the alternative jurisdiction these writers choose and the alternative jurisprudence they produce.

conspicuous. It suggests that even when the violent patriarch lays down his vocation, his previous excess represents a lingering patrimony and pedagogy. In this patrimony, the father's violence never ends, and there are plenty of fathers and father-surrogates willing to carry on the regime. Mikal Gilmore's focus on the family as the training ground of pathological violence resonates with the work done by many feminists that details how the family is embedded in a culture that makes the father's violence both permissible and invisible, both public knowledge and private, hence protected, activity. Gary Gilmore's last words gesture toward the futility of altering the legacy of fathers through biographical narrative. You can try, he suggests, but you can't rewrite the story. It always comes out the same: "there will always be a father."

As an analysis of temporality, "there will always be a father" implies an endless futurity to the patriarchal violence of the family, of kinship, and of the social. In contrast to Mikal Gilmore's efforts to fix time, that is, both to stabilize and to repair it, Gary Gilmore declaims an endless present to violence. Whereas Mikal Gilmore wishes to make time tell a different story, Gary Gilmore reports that the relationship between time and narrative is one of recurrence. For Mikal Gilmore, the brother who survives a violent family, the question concerns the necessary repetition of the story that violence tells: If my brother, why not me? If not me, why my brother? These are, at bottom, questions about the role chance plays in identity. Time and circumstance gave Gary and Mikal different experiences of family and violence, but it falls to Mikal to sort these out in the aftermath of violence. Gary Gilmore was brutalized by his father, grew up in reformatories and prison, and, by the time he shot two young Mormon men in Utah on successive nights, had become a living translation of that violence. As the witness to violence who did not commit violent acts, Mikal Gilmore struggles to transform violence into a narrative category structured through temporality. Like narrative, then, violence might be interrupted, or at least analyzable in its beginning, middle, and ending. Gary Gilmore, however, sees in time only the abyss. "There will always be a father." These words imply the persistent and structuring threat of the violent patriarch, of his recurrence, and deadly continuity.

Mikal sees how his other brothers responded differently to violence than Gary did, but he doesn't turn their versions of self-destruction into a triumph-in-the-face-of-adversity narrative. Of Frank Jr. he writes, "[T]he fact that my brother Frank wasn't a killer does not mean he did not also suffer a damage worthy of killing. There are all kinds of ways to die in this world. Some die without taking others with them. It's a victory, no doubt, but that doesn't make it the same as redemption" (194). Frank Jr., Gaylen, Mikal, and Gary Gilmore are different sorts of survivors. Mikal, on one hand, was not abused by his father, was able to sympathize with his mother, and internalized the family's violence. Gary, on the other hand, was brutalized, cast out, brought up in penal institutions, and through a saturation in a violence without end, came to choose murder and execution. Those facts, as Mikal Gilmore learns, do not explain everything.

In her chapter "Unclaimed Experience: Trauma and the Possibility of History," Cathy Caruth offers a general definition of trauma: "trauma describes an overwhelming experience of sudden, catastrophic events, in which the response to the event occurs in the often delayed, and uncontrolled repetitive occurrence of hallucinations and other intrusive phenomena."[20] This definition of trauma fits the experience of war, accidents, acts of violence, and loss that are limited in their duration, and are responded to later through disruptive recurrence, such as flashbacks and the range of associated symptoms grouped as post-traumatic stress syndrome. This kind of trauma can be thought of as injury to the person and to the person's sense of time because it splits time into before and after. Mikal Gilmore writes about the kind of violence that begins at an earlier age, has a longer duration, and gets connected to growing up in such a way that the boundaries of violence, or the location and limit of trauma, are overwhelmingly difficult to chart. The trauma that survivors of childhood abuse describe differs from Caruth's more general definition of trauma as a "sudden and catastrophic event," an event like no other. The ongoingness of violence within families, its incorporation into a family culture, renders it all too familiar. The endlessness of this trauma is frequently represented as haunting, in which the present feels stalked by a past that will not stay properly buried; or as dissociation, where the boundary between past and present, dead and living, is overwhelmed by a sense of their interpenetration, mutual incorporation, and simultaneity.

In *Admitting the Holocaust*, Lawrence Langer distinguishes between "chronological memory," which is fixed in the mind's narrative with a beginning, middle, and end, even if there are gaps in the sequence, and recedes in time; and "durational memory," which, in contrast, is related to events so harrowing and unassimilable that they persist as memories that exceed all others. The survivor of persistent family violence may find that chronological and durational memory melt into each other. Violence saturates time, reorders it from progressive movement into recursive movement via flashbacks and other time disorders associated with post-traumatic stress syndrome. The violence, in this construction, will not end. It recurs as the introjection of the past into the present which survivors describe rather more often as the introjection of the present into the past. It

[20]    Caruth, *Unclaimed Experience*, 11.

wounded brother as the vector though whom interpretation must flow. In this sense, the reader enters the brothers' bodies, lodges in their wound, and knows the father. I am working here with an impure and unstable metaphor for a transference that remains ambivalent, for as surely as the father is evoked, the wound, which is an opening, may become again the barred threshold one may not cross. "There will always be a father" beckons and bars the way to (self) knowledge. The installation of this figure, and its symbolic principle, at the threshold of knowledge about violence and love testifies to its intimacy no less than its ubiquity.

# 4

# There Will Always Be a Mother
## Jamaica Kincaid's Serial Autobiography

*I wondered then, for the millionth time, how it came to be that of all the mothers in the world mine was not an ordinary human being but something from an ancient book.*

—Jamaica Kincaid, *Lucy*

Several writers have taken the project of self-representation to be open-ended, susceptible to repetition, extendible, even, perhaps, incapable of completion. In their sustained multibook projects, the notion of an "end" to autobiography becomes ironic with each new publication. The multivolume autobiographies of Maya Angelou, Lillian Hellman, and Mary McCarthy, among others, demonstrate this pattern of returning to the autobiographical scene. It is somewhat heretical to structure the autobiographical scene such that it is one to which one may, or even must, return when for most writers autobiography is a one-shot deal. In its extension of autobiography beyond a single text, the practice of serial autobiography challenges the limits of the genre by raising the specter of endless autobiography. That there will always be (another) autobiography means there will be no last words and autobiography is a genre of last words.

I have been arguing that the most apparent limit a self-representational text crosses is a place where a range of related concerns are clustered together. In serial autobiography, the proliferation of texts questions the limit of any single text's self-sufficiency. Typically, one autobiography satisfies: it fulfills the contractual obligation to tell the truth. Its summary dimension, its claim to fullness and even accountability, militates against reenactment. With regard to the expectations Philippe Lejeune and others have identified as the pact or contract autobiography makes with the reader, writing *another* autobiography is more than slightly suspicious behavior.[1] But for some self-representational projects, once is not enough. Rather, autobiography seems to issue an open invitation to begin again. Autobiographical writing necessarily finds itself at the limit of representing life and death. For many, this is the spur to self-representation. Writing beyond the limit of one autobiography is a way to resist the little death that ending an autobiography represents. Writing multiple autobiographies offers a mode of writing against death even in its face, an ecstatic autobiography, to capitalize on my pun but to push it into an epistemology of space and self-representation, an ex-static autobiography that finds and moves itself progressively from its autobiographical enactments.

Such is the case, I would suggest, with Jamaica Kincaid's ongoing self-representational project represented by *At the Bottom of the River* (1983), *Annie John* (1986), *Lucy* (1991), *Autobiography of My Mother* (1996), and, to date, *My Brother* (1997). Perhaps the proximity of death to life in the autobiographical scene explains why Kincaid's texts are saturated with death imagery, especially as they open. In her absorption with the deathliness of self-representation, Kincaid reveals that a serial autobiographer returns to the scene because she has left a body there which requires further attention. Whether it is her own, her mother's, Antigua's, the body of childhood, or the psychic remnants of the pre-oedipal, the dead body calls to her as compellingly as the living one calls to other autobiographers. Thus the limit implied by seriality represents an engagement with the ultimate limit of life and death. Here, as with Gary Gilmore, that limit emerges in relation to kinship and speech. Gilmore, who never made a statement in court and whose chroniclers ultimately found him elusive, condensed autobiography to these epigrammatic and epitaphic last words, "There will always be a father." For Kincaid, whose position differs from Gilmore's in almost every way describable, there can be no last words because for her the organizing utterance would be, "There will always be a mother." Her focus joins fatality to its opposite and continually reconstructs the image of self-representation.

Kincaid's work illustrates that the limits of seriality and their association in (self-) representations of life and death combine to illuminate how a key figure emerges in the autobiographical scene. Constitutive of the autobiographical scene is a self-representational practice through which a subject-in-process is constructed. This construction occurs in two locations of becoming: in one is the subject-who-writes; in the other, the subject-in-the-text. They are joined to each other in this emergence-through-enactment, and form a representational figure capable of signifying

[1]   See Philippe Lejeune, *Le pacte autobiographique* (Paris: Seuil, 1975).

beyond any single text. This suturing and identification of two locations into a figure characterizes several experiments in serial autobiography, and allows for a particular kind of return to the scene. This new self-representational figure (not new to self-representational writing, but newly visible as a feature of serial autobiography), then, does not suggest a one-to-one correspondence between real and represented life. Instead, this figure, as a representation of identity, is capable of crossing all kinds of boundaries, including the boundaries of discrete texts, to extend the autobiographical into an intertextual system of meaning. The figure returns to the autobiographical scene, not exactly as a recurring fictional character or as the autobiographer at different stages of life; rather, this figure may be recognizable less for the features it shares with the autobiographer, or her textual simulacra, than for the preoccupations represented in and through it. Identifying its significance for autobiography opens up possibilities for understanding self-representational projects that exceed the confines of genre, and extend self-representation where the autobiographical subject has not been before and where it may be only dimly recognizable.[2]

Lest this sound too alien to the autobiographical project, let me assert that it is a central feature of autobiography that the author and protagonist (I use the literary term to clarify the textuality of this figure) tend to be collapsed through the feature of their shared name into the same entity despite their significant and demonstrable differences. To admit the difference between the writer of the text and the autobiographical protagonist threatens the truthfulness of the scene for some readers and critics. Such an admission reveals too clearly the constructedness of autobiography, both its inevitable affiliation with fiction and its recalcitrant realism. Nonetheless, the two locations of representation and identity I am describing emerge in relation to each other. Further, this relation becomes more significant in its intertextuality as additional autobiographies follow. In serial autobiography, the recurrence of this figure can be traced through preoccupations that persist across texts. These links may be simply thematic; or, situations, scenes, and images may recur. So, too, remnants of formal elements or familiar interests may remain as well, recognizable if altered. In this way, serial autobiography can be read within the ruins of textual memory. Among these marred, effaced, or revised elements, a larger self-representational project becomes visible.

---

[2]   Following Donna Haraway, we could ally this figure with the cyborg-as-autobiographer to clarify how the boundary between the fictional and real life is already thoroughly broached in self-representation. Or, following the postcolonial postmodern, we could identify a hybrid-as-autobiographer to amplify how the subject's location is simultaneously multiple and conflictual.

While Kincaid's oeuvre forms the context of my argument, I shall demonstrate here the way she constructs autobiographical scenes in two texts, *Annie John* (1985) and *Lucy* (1990), and discovers the autobiographical within biography in *My Brother* (1997). Both *Annie John* and *Lucy* present extended scenes from which the protagonist flees, but in which she leaves behind sufficient evidence to be read as the self-representational figure I have been anatomizing. Ultimately, to connect the previous discussion of serial autobiography to this reading of *Annie John*, *Lucy*, and *My Brother*, it is in the emerging intertextuality of Kincaid's body of work that the self-representational becomes most salient. In this reading, *Lucy* depends as much upon the texts that go before and follow it, as it, or any single text, depends on its similarity to Kincaid's life. My reading does not seek a one-to-one correspondence between the author, Jamaica Kincaid, and any single protagonist in her work as primary evidence of the autobiographical. Certainly such correspondences can be pointed out, but they offer a different kind of proof than I am interested in here. I am most concerned with how evidence of the biographical limits and contains the possibilities Kincaid finds in autobiography and how she reveals this protean view through her performance of autobiography as a discourse with an, as yet, limitless capacity for repetition or reengagement.

Let me preview Kincaid's biography before I take up specific texts in greater detail. As a West Indian woman living in the United States, Kincaid reveals just how complicated the task of literary and cultural history is. Her work is comprehensible within several traditions, including autobiography as I am proposing here, though none can claim her exclusively. Kincaid was born Elaine Potter Richardson in 1949 in St. Johns, Antigua. Her stepfather was a carpenter and cabinetmaker; her mother, Annie, a homemaker and a "well-known political activist."[3] In 1965 at age seventeen, she left Antigua for New York where she worked as an au pair and later became a staff writer for the *New Yorker*. *Annie John* and *Lucy* both appeared there in serial form. Then editor William Shawn nurtured her talent and published her work. In a significant overlapping of work and love, she met and married his son, Alan Shawn, a composer.

Most of her work has been reviewed as highly literary with the full rhetoric of universality, accessibility, and transcendence bolstering this

---

[3] This information is drawn from Donna Perry's "Interview with Jamaica Kincaid" in *Reading Black, Reading Feminist*, ed. Henry Louis Gates (New York: Penguin, 1990), 492–510). Further biographical background can be found in Diane Simmons, *Jamaica Kincaid* (New York: Twayne, 1994). Moira Ferguson identifies Kincaid's mother as an activist in *Colonialism and Gender from Mary Wollstonecraft to Jamaica Kincaid* (New York: Columbia University Press, 1993).

claim. Her first book, *At the Bottom of the River*, predicted some of this re-
ception, though its unconventional structure and poetic language strained
the criterion of accessibility. It was with the coming-of-age "novel" *Annie
John* that reviewers rushed in to award an elite culture seal of approval.
As a review from the *New York Times Book Review* used as a jacket blurb
put it: "Coming of age in Antigua—so touching and familiar . . . it could
be happening to any of us, anywhere, any time, any place." Not too long
after that endorsement, the long essay *A Small Place* appeared, a polemic
against the tourist's gaze and the practice of tourism as uninspected colonial privilege.[4] It was declined for serialization by the *New Yorker* as "too
angry," and reviewers castigated Kincaid for her unbecoming rage. As if
in too much contrast to *Annie John*, this, then, was *not* a story that could
happen anywhere and its particularity proved very troubling to some.

Some recent critical work on Kincaid has echoed her suggestion in interviews that her writing is autobiographical. While critics are following
Kincaid when they take up her self-description, as I too am doing here,
hers is hardly a transparent claim. What and how the autobiographical
signifies within and across her texts is fairly complicated. Invoking the
"autobiographical" as a dimension of writing raises, or ought to raise, as
many questions as it seems to answer. Unfortunately, its invocation seems
to settle things down rather than open them up, and I would agree with
the comment that "applying the label 'autobiographical' to all types of
writings—even when their titles announce them as memoirs, testimonials, confessions, or the like—tends to reduce and narrow our reading of
the text."[5] But this is not a necessary consequence or condition of autobiographicality. Quite the opposite is possible. The autobiographical may, instead, function critically as an expansive, extendible system of meaning,
one that enables readers to do much more than search out sources, proof,
or evidence of a corresponding reality. While it is accurate to say that Kincaid's texts have their differences from each other, their continuity is
rather more striking. It is not that Kincaid is writing the same book over
and over; rather, she is adding volumes to a series. The series compounds
the elements of experience and a political consciousness into a dense
mixture.

While we could provisionally identify Kincaid's work as first-person
fiction, it is also clear that she is calling into question the constructed division between autobiography and first-person fiction. Her method focuses
on a "problem" contained and obscured by that generic division; namely,

[4]    Jamaica Kincaid, *A Small Place* (New York: Farrar, Straus and Giroux, 1988).
[5]    Lee Quinby, "The Subject of Memoirs," in *De/colonizing the Subject*, ed. Sidonie Smith
and Julia Watson, 299.

the perpetual problem of truth telling as a criterion of judgment, and the equally persistent materiality of autobiographical writing practices, or the way autobiographical writing refers to the extratextual, if improperly. Kincaid maximizes the nonmimetic capacities of autobiography through her emphasis on autobiographical extension, a self-representational practice allied with and knowable through metonymy. Insofar as seriality depends upon returns and repetitions, it emerges through a pattern. Unlike metaphor, which depends upon a meaningful relation grasped, as it were, in an instant of identification, metonymy points toward the endlessness or extendibility of patterning. Metonymy stabilizes certain forms (whether they are habits of reference or rituals of the state) and renders them recognizable through time. Thus when autobiography studies focus on metaphor as the defining trope, they participate in the production of identity as the mirroring of an essential sameness (the self) in different forms (real life and autobiography). When autobiography studies focus on metonymy, they recognize the continual production of identity as a kind of patterning sustained through time by the modes of production that create it.

By looking at Kincaid's texts as interrogative of problems in self-representation, we have already taken a critical step across the line of genre and begun to regard the question of textual specificity in the light of the areas I define as central: autobiography's relation to truth telling (or cultural authority) and to representations of the real (via metonymy and metaphor). Autobiography's representation of the real is sufficiently central to autobiography studies to warrant coming at it from a new direction. The autobiographical subject represents the real person not only or even primarily as a metaphor of self, wherein the self in the text transcends it materiality and becomes an emblem for a person's striving. But by emphasizing metaphor, autobiography seems to represent or be represented by the metaphorical resonance of reality. Then, autobiography appears as a metaphor for truth beyond argument, of identity beyond proof, of what simply is. Yet, insofar as autobiography represents the real, it does so through metonymy, that is, through the claims of contiguity wherein the person who writes extends the self in the writing, and puts her in another place.

Such a conception of autobiographical extension gets at the limit represented by the text itself. Instead of respecting the sufficiency of each text unto itself (and why should she adopt that constraint without being able to rework it? and why should her readers?), Kincaid extends what appears to be the same character, with different names, into book after book. To pursue this seriality, I shall focus on two shared features of *Annie John* and *Lucy*: an interest in self-naming and renaming, and the centrality of the mother-daughter relationship as a site of enigmatic trauma. Attached to these are Kincaid's preoccupations with representing the legacy of colonialism in the Caribbean, as well as a persistent even signatory anger.

First, what's in a name? The function of a name is to identify, to stabilize meaning, to fix and hold in place. Except in Kincaid's work. Jamaica Kincaid may have initiated her experiments in naming when she renamed herself. Her parents named her Elaine Potter Richardson, but she changed her name when she began writing; or, to put it another way, she gave herself a new name for a newly explored identity. In an interview, Kincaid said she chose the name Jamaica to evoke the West Indies and her birthplace, Antigua, and the surname because it went well with the first. Kincaid has continued the recycling of names by naming her daughter Annie, which is her mother's name, as well as the name of the protagonist in *Annie John*. She reserves this opportunity in all her writing, and names shift and recur in her texts. In both her life and her writing, Kincaid takes the name as an occasion for experimentation, and thereby transforms its function. Recognizable relationships, especially that of mother and daughter, persist despite changes in the names of the characters. Autobiographical extension is enacted through the loss, or at least displacement, of names across texts to the point that the name functions as a self-representational sign at the limit of autobiography. That it keeps changing is what persists.

How does this interest in naming play out in the texts? The character Annie John is apparently modeled on Kincaid. The book chronicles Annie's growing up on Antigua, from age ten to seventeen, a period during which Antigua was a British colony. The book concludes with Annie sailing for London. The same character, then, seems to show up, in another text, in Kincaid's New York, where she is now "Lucy," with the same defining relationship with what appears to be the same mother. Both the island Lucy is from in the West Indies and the city to which she has fled go unnamed. Kincaid has remarked in an interview that "Lucy" is short for "Lucifer," yet it is Annie John who first identifies with a painting depicting Lucifer. Intertextual continuity is threaded throughout these texts and the signifier of change is the name. Hearkening back to Kincaid's given name, Lucy's full name is Lucy Josephine Potter, and, in *The Autobiography of My Mother*, it is not Annie, Lucy, or Jamaica who speaks, but Xuela Claudette Richardson. Kincaid's change of names raises the issue of literal truthfulness as the hallmark of autobiography. For those who insist upon autobiography's quasi-legal status, as a record to which one could and must swear, Kincaid's change of name rules it out as autobiography. But what of the antagonistic relationship between law (as official discourse) and truth (as unofficial and resistant discourse) that structures the self-representation of the colonized? To what law ought Kincaid submit in

her rendering of truth in and as autobiography? I suggest we read one dimension of her experimentation with a different discourse of truth telling as an effort to forge a more adequate representation of a "post"-colonial subject.

Kincaid avoids the ways autobiographical writing splits (or doubles) the "I" into "myself" and "herself" by coming up with different names for herself and her characters. In so doing, she exposes a crucial limit: that identity exceeds its representation, and the violence of splitting (or doubling, or extending) the "I" into autobiographer and character makes possible both alienation and nostalgia for the fictional unity of an "I," even as serial autobiography offers a textual environment for refusing this split. Serial autobiography permits the writer to take multiple runs at self-representation, more as a way to explore the possibilities present within autobiography than to produce a single, definitive solution to the problem of representing identity. I think of serial autobiography in the context of a project Foucault identified: "One writes in order to become other than what one is." Autobiography offers an opportunity to experiment with becoming a person. In order to think further about how the self-representational figure I am associating with serial autobiography enables this experimentation with becoming a person, this opportunity (or wish) to write "in order to become other than what one is," I want to turn to feminist legal theorist Drucilla Cornell's provocative thinking about the transformation of the experience of life into the (self-) representation and self-conception of oneself as a person.[6]

In sketching the legal frame of her argument, Cornell writes: "What we think of as 'individuality' and 'the person' are not assumed as a given but respected as part of a project, one that must be open to each of us on an equivalent basis. . . . Without minimum conditions of individuation, we cannot effectively get the project of becoming a person off the ground. . . . The equal worth of personhood of each one of us must be legally guaranteed, in the name of the equivalent chance to take on the project" (4–5). Cornell offers a way here to think about the complexities of Kincaid's project. In what conditions is Kincaid's project of individuation mired? What inhibits her from getting the project off the ground? There is the work of individuation from her mother, which Kincaid represents as trauma and to which she returns in multiple books. There is also the legacy of colonialism and its many shaping and lingering effects. What emerges in Kincaid's corpus is what Cornell articulates as the project of working through personae toward personhood: "A person is not some-

[6] See Drucilla Cornell, *The Imaginary Domain: Abortion, Pornography, and Sexual Harassment* (New York: Routledge, 1995), especially chapter 1.

thing 'there' . . . , but a possibility, an aspiration which, because it is that, can never be fulfilled once and for all. The person is, in other words, implicated in an endless process of working through personae. On this definition, the person is neither identical with the self or the traditional philosophical subject" (5).

The "person" for Cornell is analogous to the figure that Kincaid constructs in her intertextual project of self-representation. Kincaid explores how a colonial subject may refuse a certain imperial injunction to offer an account of herself that is intelligible within the structure of colonialism by refusing to engage the autobiographical to those ends.[7] Kincaid refuses to join the subject of that law and the subject of self-representation metaphorically; instead, her extended serial autobiography undercuts the command to "be" or "become" a delimited subject by merely repeating as her autobiography one version of her life, as if it were exhaustive of the project of self-representation (that is, of becoming a person, in Cornell's terms). When Kincaid chooses a series of names for a series of identities, she refuses this patterning and becomes an agent of self-representation running at cross-purposes to the figures of colonial identity.

In negotiating this effort to become a person, *Annie John* and *Lucy* take their emotional charge from a central theme of mother-daughter conflict, represented as a locus of enigmatic trauma and extending into a representation of identity. Here, repetition and trauma are welded to autobiographical extension and nostalgia. At stake seems to be nothing less than the daughter's aspiration for achieving personhood. In the context of modern fiction and culture, Laura Doyle has argued that the mother figure is entangled not only in "the gender identities, . . . but in the racial, ethnic, and national identities of the characters and narrators.[8] Doyle explains the formal experimentation that characterizes modernism as an outgrowth of a way of understanding the significance of the mother figure: these "mother-entangled complications of identity" prompt "the unorthodox narrative practices of experimental novels" (4). For Doyle, formal experimentation offers writers a way to elude some of the more negative, even pathologizing, theories of the mother by turning their energy to a revised intercorporeality. For this reason, she prefers Merleau-Ponty's more flexible notion of the "reversibility" of alterity to Julia Kristeva's theory of abjection whose work is mired in the "tragic drama and heart-breaking romance" of the split subject and the mother's imposed exile from knowledge, authority, and bodily proximity to the growing child.

---

[7]    See Françoise Lionnet's discussion of gender, race, and autobiography in "Of Mangoes and Maroons: Language, History, and the Multicultural Subject in Michelle Cliff's *Abeng*," in *De/Colonizing the Subject*, 321–45.

[8]    Laura Doyle, *Bordering on the Body* (New York: Oxford University Press, 1994), 4.

Kincaid's work, however, is sited in the child's consciousness and her experimentation is both syntactic (she is heir to Gertrude Stein's innovations in the long sentence) and conceptual (I describe her entire oeuvre as serial autobiography rather than first-person fiction, essay writing, and biography). In Kincaid's welding of these experiments to the representation of the child's view, Kristeva's work on abjection becomes especially useful for contextualizing Kincaid's insistence on the enigmatic trauma of the daughter's individuation from the mother.[9]

If Kristeva narrows the possible renderings of the mother, Kincaid embraces and revels in the constraints. She embraces abjection passionately, makes an erotics of it, and glories in its pains. In this way she is like the medieval mystic who so fully inhabits self-abnegation that she obliterates it and discovers narcissism in its place. Not ego-denying but ego-driven, if in oblique ways, Kincaid claims the child's perspective in relation to a desired and powerful mother whom she must, nonetheless, forswear. In *Powers of Horror*, Kristeva challenges Freudian psychoanalysis's emphasis on ego development over the pre-oedipal processes of drive organization. In its focus on the self who stands apart from objects, and who can manipulate symbols and representation, psychoanalysis has neglected the realm in which it would have had to confront the power of the mother, and failed to develop a theory that would speak to the gendering of the self. By neglecting the pre-oedipal structures which the mother primarily affects in favor of the law-giving father, psychoanalysis recasts the mother as a figure of horror rather than of sympathy.

In her earlier work, *Revolution in Poetic Language*, Kristeva introduced a distinction between the symbolic, and its affiliation with the father, and the semiotic, which she tied to the mother. Kristeva insisted that the semiotic's bodily, heterogeneous, even nonsensical "language" derived from the corporeal bond between mother and infant. To enter into language and become a self, the child must abandon the blissful continuity it experiences with the mother's body. In acquiring a boundary between self and (m)other, the child must expel the mother from its body/ego identity, must, in other words, force out what has been introjected. Abjection is the cost of this violent reconfiguration and recurs symptomatically in a range of boundary-testing situations. Thus the mother loses her position as the all-embracing matrix and becomes precisely that which threatens the establishment of an autonomous identity. The ambivalence of this disavowal structures abjection: "Because, while releasing a hold, it does not

---

9    Julia Kristeva, *Revolution in Poetic Language*, trans. Margaret Waller (New York: Columbia University Press, 1984; originally published in French, 1974); *Powers of Horror: An Essay in Abjection* (New York: Columbia University Press, 1982).

radically cut off the self from what threatens it—on the contrary, abjection acknowledges it to be in perpetual danger."[10] The abject recurs in "whatever disturbs identity, system, order. What does not respect borders, positions, rules" (4). Kincaid's representation of the mother inhabits this ambiguity and figures it through the body.

Annie John's and Lucy's changing conceptions of the body, both their own and the bodies of others, underlie Kincaid's self-representation. For both, the body becomes a central locus for working through personae related to the process of becoming a person. The first place Annie knows is her mother's body, and its power is never displaced, only written over in subsequent texts. The mother's body is an all-encompassing situation from which intercorporeality (of mother and daughter) emerges as a defining feature of self-representation.[11] Within the shelter of the mother's body and in the presence of her voice, the daughter learns the possibilities for and constraints upon who she may become. Each situation in which Annie John, and then Lucy, comes to know herself is suffused with the first: the intercorporeality of mother and daughter. Annie's and Lucy's understanding of colonialism is first glimpsed through this lens. Through it, Lucy also views Mariah, her white employer and miniaturized mother substitute. Superimposed upon this situation, and saturated with its meaning is Annie's representation of Antigua. It, like her mother, is paradise as a time bomb. Its beauty and power threaten to transform into something horrible, though both locations retain their identity as home. To use Freud's term, the appearance of these locations in each other evokes the uncanny. This repetition of the uncanny in Annie's relation to her mother's corporeality and her representation of the landscape bears upon Annie's own body.

In *Annie John*, the idyllic mother-daughter relationship falters permanently over individuation. Until the rupture in their seamless domesticity, Annie is happily patterned in the form of her mother who is represented as paradise. The details of the scenes Kincaid chooses to illustrate the dissolution of mother-daughter intimacy appear trivial; yet, the daughter reacts to each as severe, intolerable, and world-destroying abuse. During the summer when Annie turns twelve, for example, the break between mother and daughter is initiated when the mother calls a halt to their custom of mother-daughter dress: "Up to then, my mother and I had many dresses made out of the same cloth, though hers had a different, more grownup style." (25). Mother and daughter, too, are seemingly cut from

[10]   Kristeva, *Powers of Horror*, 9.
[11]   See Laura Doyle, *Bordering on the Body*, on intercorporeality, modern fiction, and the racial matrix in which mothers are represented.

the same cloth. Their shared fashion de-emphasizes the separateness of their bodies. When Annie chooses a piece of cloth for their new dresses, her mother unexpectedly intervenes: " 'Oh no. You are getting too old for that. It's time you had your own clothes. You just cannot go around the rest of your life looking like a little me' " (26). The mother's refusal is unprecedented; the daughter's reaction severe and dissociative: "To say that I felt the earth swept away from under me would not be going too far" (26). The difference in clothes signals a profound shift in identity, one that Annie understands in terms of her growing body which now seems strangely unmoored. Paradoxically, it is the body of girlhood that resembles the mother's and not the body of young womanhood. This metaphor of their difference describes their actual developing similarity as women. Annie, though, accedes to the logic of bodily metaphor and struggles for a way to stay different from, hence attached to and the same as, her mother: "I thought of begging my mother to ask my father if he could build for me a set of clamps into which I could screw myself at night before I went to sleep and which would surely cut back on my growing" (27).

In an effort to rework this trauma, Annie turns to the autobiographical scene and rewrites the outcome of another event in the mother-daughter breakdown. In an autobiographical essay she writes in school, Annie describes another symptom in the mother-daughter crisis of individuation that produces another moment of dissociation. She describes an afternoon of swimming which begins as her mother, a strong swimmer, lets Annie float upon her back. The sea buoys them up in a blissful embrace. Annie's infatuation with her mother's embodiment is limitless and Annie is fully satisfied. Later in the day, the mother swims and dives as Annie watches. Distracted by noise, Annie turns away to follow the sound of a ship's horns and cheering people, and when she looks back, she cannot see her mother: "My eyes searched the small area of water where she should have been, but I couldn't find her. I stood up and started to call out her name, but no sound would come out of my throat. A huge black space then opened up in front of me and I fell inside it. I couldn't see what was in front of me and I couldn't hear anything around me" (43). When Annie sees her mother sitting on a large rock, her reaction becomes clearer to her. She is not calmed by finding her mother; instead, she realizes that she is upset because her mother was not paying attention to her. She had been caught in a moment of separateness. That her mother does not know the pain Annie is suffering precipitates a second dissociative moment as profound as when "the earth was swept away" in the earlier episode of individuation. Yet Annie uses autobiography to alter the ending of this story. In the essay she writes for class, she recounts having a recurring nightmare in which this trauma is replayed, and concludes by having her mother comfort her and reassure her of her devotion. The nightmares end, the frightening memory fades, and all is well. The essay offers a way to reconstruct the idealized mother who is now available to Annie only in autobiography.

The trauma surrounding the mother-daughter relationship is enigmatic, the mother's desire opaque, the daughter's reaction dissociative. All compound to define a recognizable autobiographical scene when its recurs in *Lucy* (and is prefigured in *At the Bottom of the River* and revisited in *Autobiography of My Mother*). The repetition and linkage of sex and death imagery, and their pervasiveness, points to an oedipal crisis (for example, the mother turns into a crocodile—all mouth and teeth—at other times, she is possessed of a "black thing" that inhabits and is detachable from her). Looking again at the mother-daughter dress episode that precipitates the series of crises in individuation, each crisis seems to repeat a primary trauma, and each appears to cause a complete change in Annie's world. Certainly, an excess of emotion flows from these events. In what consists the trauma? Initially, there is a refusal of the mother to continue the patterning of the two as Big Me-Little Her (Annie is called Little Miss), or Big Her-Little Me, from the narrator's perspective, in which the mother serves as original and the daughter as copy. But is the mother the only one who generates an incomprehensible gravity-reversing dictum? The psychic structure in which the mother wishes to reproduce herself in-and-as her daughter seems at least to be emerging on Annie's part as well. The psychic structure, which is presented as suiting the mother's whim up to a certain moment and then being cut off utterly without the possibility of negotiation, parallels a change in the daughter. Annie represents the moment as forced individuation, but her own gestures toward separation, if ambivalent or even guiltily sought, are nonetheless present. I say this because the daughter's reversal is too sudden, thorough, and fully mapped onto her identity for it to have been exclusively externally imposed. She meets it with a vengeance, as if she has been awaiting it, even preparing for it. What Annie used to love (you are a little me), she is now told cannot be ("You just cannot go around the rest of your life looking like a little me"), which becomes not what she misses but what she hates: you are trying to turn me into a little you and I won't have it. Certainly there is conflict here; interestingly, its dimensions are opaque, submerged in the narrative voice and consciousness of a young girl whose crisis of boundaries with her mother is undecidable, even, in some ways, illegible.

Imitation of the "like mother like daughter" variety is recast in a third dissociative moment. Annie has grown into adolescence and is walking in the town. She glimpses herself in a shop window and struggles to recog-

nize this image as herself.[12] "I saw myself . . . , but I didn't know that I was I, for I had got so strange" (94). She describes this image, this new and abject self-representation, as follows: "My whole head was so big, and my eyes, which were big, too, sat in my big head wide open, as if I had just had a sudden fright. My skin was black in a way I had not noticed before, as if someone had thrown a lot of soot out of a window just when I was passing by and it had all fallen on me. On my forehead, on my cheeks, were little bumps, each with a perfect, round white point. My plaits stuck out in every direction from under my hat; my long, thin neck stuck out from the blouse of my uniform" (94). When she describes this image as looking "old and miserable," it reminds her immediately of a painting of Satan after he has been cast out of heaven, entitled *The Young Lucifer*. Annie identifies her image in the shop window with this image of Lucifer and, in that chain of associations, predicts the next name in Kincaid's serial autobiography: Lucy. Immediately following this meditation, Annie recognizes four boys she has not seen for some time. They greet each other in a scene strained with adolescent sexuality and flooded with Annie's memories of childhood games gone bad played with one of the boys. Annie has the sense that the boys are laughing at her and she leaves them. As she walks home, she begins to lose her bearings. Perhaps the memories have intruded too much and further disoriented her chain of identifications begun in the shop window and continued with the remembered painting of Satan. She enters into an Alice-in-Wonderland state of spatial confusion: "I thought that I had better get home quickly, for I began to feel alternately too big and too small. First I grew so big that I took up the whole street; then I grew so small that nobody could see me—not even if I cried out" (101). When she arrives home, her mother accuses her of "making a spectacle of herself in front of four boys" (102) and calls her a slut. This epithet, focusing as it does on Annie's sexuality and her mother's interpretation of it, forces another crisis in the mother-daughter pattern: "As if to save myself, I turned to her and said, 'Well, like father like son, like mother like daughter'" (102). The dissociative moment lifts and what emerges in its place is another identification. Annie sees her mother as "tired and old and broken." But when she realizes she is describing herself, Annie then sees her mother as "full of vigor, young and whole" (103), and she is moved by the desire to embrace her mother. It is all too late, though, and the finality of their separation leaves Annie with no place to

---

[12]   For a discussion of what happens in literature when a black woman sees herself, see Karla F. C. Holloway in "The Body Politic," in *Subjects and Citizens*, ed. Michael Moon and Cathy Davidson (Durham: Duke University Press, 1995), 481–95.

call home, no recourse to mother-daughter union, and no stable not-me to know herself in opposition to. The structure has been forced to crisis and has imploded. Annie falls seriously ill.

These events occur within a condensed frame and highlight the dangers implicit in imitation. Annie and her mother have become items in a series without a true and stable origin. The mother is already an implied copy of "the good mother." There is no true original mother upon whom Annie is to model herself; the imperative to copy (or model or imitate) is already in place, having been assumed by her own mother. The crisis of individuation follows from realizing this. At the point of the daughter's intimation of the sexual, the mother sees the copy she has been fashioning as illegitimate, or inauthentic, and denounces it. Yet it is equally possible that the copy is all too accurate in some of its dimensions, and Annie seizes upon this interpretation in order to hurt her mother. But what of the mother's desire?[13] Barbara Johnson has identified "the desire to create a being like oneself" as the "autobiographical desire par excellence."[14] Implicit in Kincaid's serial autobiography is the danger posed by this project for both mother and daughter. The mother denounces the copy, her daughter, not for its failure (as a "bad" copy) but for its success (as a good or lifelike copy). Her words are, "You just cannot go around the rest of your life looking like a little me." This indicates that in childhood a daughter may be a miniature of her mother, which is a way of containing and chastening the sexuality of both, though it is also clear that the technique of copying and imitation is supposed to produce development, which although alien to its functioning, is presumably its proper end. The irony here, even the impossibility, seems to structure the enigmatic situation, a situation animated to some degree by the desire of both mother and daughter for separation. When the mirroring no longer works, for the mother there is renunciation, for the daughter, abandonment. Annie internalizes both renunciation and abandonment as her psychic matrix and works them obsessively, taking those themes as the text for her technique of repetition, copying, and imitation. These lessons are saturated with an overwhelming bitterness toward her mother; as self-image, there is still too little of Annie. For the daughter, whose identity is primarily "not my mother," identity itself is threatened with annihilation when Annie falls ill. For the mother, "originality," even her identity, is thrown into crisis by the suc-

13   For an elaboration of mother-daughter rage that explores both sides of the dynamic, see Nancy Miller, "Mothers, Daughters, and Autobiography," in *Mothers in Law*, ed. Martha Fineman and Isabel Karpin (New York: Columbia University Press, 1995), 3–26.
14   Barbara Johnson, "My Monster, My Self," in *A World of Difference* (Baltimore: Johns Hopkins University Press, 1987), 146.

cess of her modeling. On this view, better for the daughter to be nothing than to become, through virtue of successful imitation and repetition, a substitute for the mother, a copy that is so good it stands in for the original (revealing that metonymy can read in two directions). The danger here for both mother and daughter is annihilation, figured throughout the narrative in the proximity of death. The risk of being swallowed up or engulfed haunts even the blissful scenes of union: this amniotic, erotic sea in which mother and daughter merge and are suspended also submerges difference and threatens drowning.

What was once for the mother a form of representation, even self-representation, has turned into a repetition of formal elements (activities, outfits), mere alterations on the surface. The mother's "autobiographical desire par excellence" has focused on her representation of her self in her daughter and her daughter as her self, and as such has become a kind of autobiographical production. Annie's outside is being modeled on her mother's, and, of course, the implication is that these activities are linked to "interior" qualities such as virtue, modesty, and chastity. As with Annie's colonial education, this technique structures rebellion as surely as it structures obedience. Once Annie rejects her mother as the desirable original upon which to continue her own self-fashioning, the very reality of the mother is thrown into question; she is negated, largely through the technique Annie has learned so well: repetition. Now Annie reworks herself as not-my-mother. Renunciation replaces adoration in her imitation. Trained as she is in the habit of repetition, she takes to it readily and renounces all that her mother represents.

How can we understand the place of the mother in this text? While she is central, her actions seem less like the cause of Annie's unhappiness than something more like the psychic force of individuation, the incomprehensibility of some forms of emotion, and deep emotion as itself a kind of trauma. In Annie's view that her mother has betrayed her by forcing individuation, the mother's desire is opaque. Kincaid veils the mother's desire through *Annie John*'s representation of childhood, which is steeped in the language, imagery, and even pathos of loss and nostalgia. The reader navigates the mother-daughter terrain as if in a dream of backward-looking desire. But as the text that intervenes between *Annie John* and *Lucy*, *A Small Place* clarifies the politics of Kincaid's rage and differentiates this intensity from its imbrication in the mother-daughter relationship. Our sense that the mother-daughter relationship is overdetermined with meanings it cannot disclose gives us the sense that there is a body of political meaning here. To discover it we must move between a representation of the psychic text and the social text. Moira Ferguson offers a psychoanalytic reading of the mother-daughter dissolution that clarifies how this relationship pulls the social text into its orbit.[15] Ferguson recognizes that Annie intuits and lives with but cannot yet identify "the multiple effects of colonization and oppression."While Annie's education within a colonial school system and her engendering at her mother's knee parallel each other in some ways, there are considerable differences. The daughter is the center of the universe in her home schooling. The world is structured by narratives about Annie's life which the mother tells and is illustrated by objects and fetishes that the mother curates. Artifacts of Annie's universe are carefully placed in a trunk, and from these her mother weaves narratives of Annie's primacy. Ritualistically, the mother removes objects from the trunk and lovingly retells their stories, all stories of Annie. This trunk of fetishes, itself a revealing image, anchors the narratives and gives them totemic substance. Annie never tires of hearing her mother tell the stories of Annie. The colonial system aims toward a different end. Annie is to become an object in a narrative in which she is made to know her place in the colonial order as strategically and necessarily marginalized. There is no love in this narrative. The mechanism of repetition works to different ends: it is to make the island of Antigua unrecognizable to Annie and her classmates as their home and to remap it as a colony, a little England. Annie intuits in both pedagogies, however, the psychic and structural presence of a too-powerful force.

Annie assumes her mother's representational strategies by the end of the text when she reconstitutes herself now as narrator of her own life, a position her mother has abdicated. She takes over her mother's function, which has been to constitute the daughter's identity by threading her life story through the totems that evoke it. On her last day on the island, Annie returns to the autobiographical scene for leave-taking: "If someone had asked me for a little summing up of my life at that moment as I lay in bed, I would have said, 'My name is Annie John' " (132). Annie takes in the house and its furnishings as extensions of her parents' labor, of which she, too, is a product: "I suppose I should say that the two of them made me with their own hands" (133). Continuing to respond in this imagined interlocution, Annie concludes: "If I had been asked to put into words

15    See Ferguson, *Colonialism and Gender*. In addition to her psychoanalytical reading, Ferguson shares Françoise Lionnet's critical model of situating postcolonial texts in dialogue with their colonial histories and the discourses of empire in order to understand the way writers "configure feminist, abolitionist, and post-emancipationist agendas" (2). Ultimately, in exploring the text's autobiographicality, Ferguson sees Annie as Kincaid's mouthpiece, as her puppet protagonist. Through Annie, Kincaid "ventriloquizes" her own struggle against marginality, and "how colonization, as well as gender, might have conditioned or constructed Annie John" (6).

why I felt this way, if I had been given years to reflect and come up with the words of why I felt this way, I would not have been able to come up with so much as the letter 'A' " (134). The crucial preservation of a single letter as all that she has at her disposal—no less than the alphabet in embryo—indicates that Kincaid will need to make it all up again in the next book. Her unmaking of "autobiography" back to its first letter works to necessitate a return to the autobiographical scene, to extend or repattern self-representational identity in additional books, to rename this set of narrative problems, and, like any serial actor, to prompt us to wait until she strikes again.

The self-representational figure that makes Kincaid's work intelligible as serial autobiography reappears in *Lucy*. In its return to the autobiographical scene, *Lucy* shares with *Annie John* a clarifying, if costly, moment of identification that follows a confrontation with the mother. It occurs when Lucy presses her mother to tell her why she was named Lucy. Her mother's answer welds *Annie John* to *Lucy*: " 'I named you after Satan himself. Lucy, short for Lucifer. What a botheration from the moment you were conceived' " (152). Lucy's feelings evoke Annie's response to her "like mother like daughter" confrontation, itself a scene about naming and identity. "I went from feeling burdened and old and tired to feeling light, new, clean." But the scene ends differently. Lucy does not fall ill; instead, she identifies: "I was transformed from failure to triumph," she now insists. "It was the moment I knew who I was . . . whenever I saw my name I always reached out to give it a strong embrace" (152–53).

In *Lucy*, the narrator mourns the loss of the mother-daughter relationship, but has physically removed herself from her mother's presence. In a sense, the mother's presence is no longer physically required in *Lucy*, and her absence allows Kincaid to press forward in her project. Of her mother's power over her, Lucy remarks: "I wondered then, for the millionth time, how it came to be that of all the mothers in the world mine was not an ordinary human being but something from an ancient book" (150). Obviously, the mother is no less powerful for being absent. She sends letters that the daughter refuses to open. These metonyms of the mother are too powerful for the daughter to risk opening. Finally, the mother sends another letter of sorts, her friend Maude Quick. Lucy, echoing Annie, surfaces the trauma still associated with mother-daughter intercorporeality. Though Lucy has attempted to claim some personhood outside her embeddedness in the mother-daughter relationship, her means for self-representation are still readiest and still primarily defensive within that relationship. As Lucy struggles to assimilate the shock of this visit from her mother's representative, and the news Maude Quick brings of her father's death, this exchange unfolds: " 'You remind me of

Miss Annie, you really remind me of your mother' " (123). Anything more ambiguous, and Lucy was on the verge of another Alice-in-Wonderland descent down the rabbit hole. However, she knows how to navigate expertly within the remark supplied by Maude: "She could not have known that in one careless sentence she said the only thing that could keep me alive. 'I am not like my mother. She and I are not alike. She should not have married my father. She should not have had children. She should not have thrown away her intelligence. She should not have paid so little attention to mine. She should have ignored someone like you. I am not like her at all' " (123).

Lucy's self-representation as not-my-mother is only one version of her identification with her mother; the flip side of which is "I am my mother." Lucy realizes that by crossing the ocean, she can remove herself physically from her mother, but she cannot leave behind the matrix of identification and intercorporeality in which her efforts to become a person have been shaped: "I had spent so much time saying I did not want to be like my mother that I missed the whole story: I was not like my mother—I was my mother" (90). "The whole story" of identity and self-representation both stalls and crystallizes in this articulation for it is both clarifying insight and perilous identification and recalls Mikal Gilmore's statement that overlaps his dream of dying with the autobiographer's imperative: "I . . . feel my life pass out of my mouth." As with Mikal Gilmore, the family threatens annihilation but also offers identity. The possibility and necessity of representing the family defines the autobiographical scene to which Kincaid has continuously returned. In a continuation of the project begun in *At the Bottom of the River* and extended through *Annie John*, *Lucy* offers more context on the traumatic break with the mother. In *Lucy* the mother has three sons and Lucy views the redirection of her mother's affection away from her and toward these boy children as a shameful secret (130). Lucy confesses that in the breakdown of her relationship with her mother and in her own fierce struggle for separation, she has been mourning the loss of the love of her life (132).

Such a powerful relationship cannot, in the terms of Kincaid's serial autobiography, be rendered in explicit terms; rather, Kincaid continues to come at the relationship from oblique angles, clarifying aspects of it while rendering other elements opaque. In Kincaid's serial autobiography, relationships with women are complex, disorienting, and risky, fraught as they are with over-identification and read by Annie and Lucy through the supervening presence of the mother. The men in these texts are distant, fully separate; they make almost no claim on the protagonists. Lucy's relationship with Mariah, the white woman for whom she works as an au pair, though still charged with intensity, is a diluted and manageable version of her relationship with her mother. Lucy reads her feelings for Mariah through her feelings for her mother: "The times that I loved Mariah it was because she reminded me of my mother. The times that I did not love Mariah it was because she reminded me of my mother" (58). Lucy fuses these feelings with a withering exposé of Mariah as witless oppressor, as a white woman who gives Lucy feminist books to help her to understand her situation, a solution Lucy finds pathetically off the mark. Lucy sees Mariah's privilege as uninspected and naive (41). In her harshest comment on Mariah's efforts to establish rapport with Lucy on the grounds of their shared "difference" (Mariah claims to have "Indian blood"), Lucy wonders: "How do you get to be the sort of victor who can claim to be the vanquished also?" (41) Yet two stories are told simultaneously: one of the strong attachment she is developing to Mariah, and the other of Mariah as complicit colonizer.

*Lucy* ends, like *Annie John*, in a self-reflexive return to the autobiographical scene. Lucy recalls the notebook Mariah gives her as a going-away present, an object that evokes the autobiographical scene: "Around the time I was leaving [Mariah] for the life I now led, I had said to her that my life stretched out ahead of me like a book of blank pages. As she gave me the book, she reminded me of that; and in the way so typical of her, the way that I had come to love, she spoke of women, journals, and, of course, history" (162–63). Both Annie and Lucy reach toward textual images and toward the task of summing up at the text's close. Both, that is, carefully prepare the final scene as autobiographical. Lucy claims her name, as Annie did: "At the top of the page I wrote my full name: Lucy Josephine Potter." Underneath that she writes the prophecy: "I wish I could love someone so much that I would die from it" (164). Again, in a gesture that echoes the ending of *Annie John*, Lucy offers a final moment in which she unmakes the autobiographical scene: "[A]s I looked at this sentence a great wave of shame came over me and I wept and wept so much that the tears fell on the page and caused all the words to become one great blur." The autobiographical scene with which the text concludes, then, can never be fully or finally written. The scene is unmade as a condition of its being reentered or returned to in subsequent texts. There will be no last words. There will always be a mother.

Kincaid's *Autobiography of My Mother* features a female narrator whose mother has died in childbirth, a mother who dies precisely at the moment her daughter is born. This offers a literalization and extension of the psychic structure first suggested in Kincaid's earliest work. Readings that would ultimately find meaning for this continuity, or repetition, in Kincaid's life to the undervaluing of its significance as a system of meaning throughout the texts perpetuate a fallacy. Namely, there is a true and authentic ground, real life, from which self-representational narratives necessarily emerge and to which they compulsorily refer. Given what Kincaid does with the mother-daughter relationship, with the representation of the legacy of colonialism, and given the textual transformations that her serial autobiography enables, any reduction of autobiography to the status of narrow proof is not only unnecessarily limiting, but inaccurate. Instead, autobiography as an intertextual system of meaning is an expansive and expanding network of associations that reaches across the boundaries of texts and lives. Kincaid's work, as well as her comments in interviews, can be read as this growing network of associations which expands in multiple directions and produces the uncanny sense that we have been "here" before. The "here" may well have been first glimpsed in another text, and we need not confirm its source in Kincaid's life to grasp its intrication within the autobiographical.

As one might expect, some dimensions of Kincaid's ongoing project are complicated by the declaratively nonfictional *My Brother*.[16] *My Brother* documents Kincaid's efforts both to get to know and to help her brother who was already desperately ill with AIDS in Antigua when she learned of his illness. She writes of her attempts to secure better treatment for him (drugs, doctors, information drawn from contacts in the United States) and also of the great distances between brother and sister that she never overcomes. She struggles, for example, with whether she loves him and decides she does not: "What I felt for him might have been love, but I still, even now, would not call it so" (58). She and her bother share an ambivalence toward the powerhouse mother at the center of this family. They see her in extremis: she is saint and villain, tireless caretaker and evil manipulator, good to be around if you're needy, hell on wheels if you're healthy. Subtly, the mother moves again to the center of this auto / biographical text and assumes the position through which Kincaid's serial autobiography renews itself.

Jamaica Kincaid writes in *My Brother* that she, like Lucy, has three brothers. Kincaid is thirteen years older than Devon, her brother who is ill. The three sons her mother had after Kincaid are never really brothers to her: they are always her mother's children and a threat to Kincaid's development. In a parenthetical comment toward the end of the book, Kincaid remarks that her brother Devon's birth impoverished the family: "our family was never the same after his birth" (174). In a move Kincaid considers indefensible, her mother removes her from school so she may care for the other children. Kincaid's abiding sense is that her mother sacrificed her willingly, in this way and others, without concern for her fu-

[16]    Jamaica Kincaid, *My Brother* (New York: Farrar, Straus and Giroux, 1997).

ture. It is an old and deep grievance, but still acute. In Kincaid's writing, it is as if her mother is sacrificing her every day. Kincaid cannot maneuver out of range of this injustice.

When Kincaid relates this story, it comes as she identifies two connections to her brother: one is the ambivalent, at best, influence of their mother's love, the other is their mother's hostility toward memory. When her brother is well enough to leave the hospital, he goes to live with their mother: "and this was wonderful, that he would live with his mother and she would take care of him, but this became another example of the extraordinary ability of her love for her children to turn into a weapon for their destruction" (53). Devon's risk in returning to his mother is quickly joined by an historical grievance of Kincaid's. She inserts her pain as the ready illustration for his danger:

> It has never occurred to her that her way of loving us might not be the best thing for us. . . . Her love for her children when they are children is spectacular, unequaled I am sure in the history of a mother's love. It is when her children are trying to be grown-up people—adults—that her mechanism for loving falls apart; it is when they are living in a cold apartment in New York, hungry and penniless because they have decided to be a writer, writing to her, seeking sympathy, a word of encouragement, love, that her mechanism for loving falls apart. Her reply to one of her children who found herself in such a predicament was "It serves you right, you are always trying to do things you know you can't do." (16–17)

Kincaid's encounters with brother and mother keep throwing her into the past. When she discovers the thread of connection between herself and her brother, she turns to reminiscence. Of an episode in which their mother has succeeded in embarrassing Devon, Kincaid writes: "I wanted to say to him, She doesn't know what she is doing, but I have never been able to say this to myself, I have never been able to forgive her for any of the things she did not know she was doing when she did them to me" (73–74). From there the scene shifts more emphatically to memory and she lays out the narrative of her mother's pulling her out of school: "She does not like memory, I wanted to tell him; you have no memory, I wanted to tell him, she taught you that. Some time before I was sixteen years of age, I might have taken a series of exams that, had I passed them, would have set me on a path that would have led me to be educated at a university, but just before all of that my mother removed me from school" (74). The grievances are pointed: "There was no real reason for me to be removed from school, she just did it, removed me from school." As Kincaid tells it, there may have been some circumstances that would make her mother consider removing her from school, but none justified the action. No real good came of it. The context in which the memory arises bristles with ambiguity: Kincaid's mother is praising her in a backhanded way for helping her brother; yet, Kincaid would not have been able to help her brother at all if she had developed along the path her mother set her on.

While the weight of reminiscence lies heavily on Kincaid, her mother will bear none of the burden of memory (including acknowledging responsibility and making amends). Thus Kincaid is isolated in her memory and pain; she is the only one who keeps account, and it results in her becoming a permanent witness. As is often the case in remembering misery, Kincaid is not set free by her insight. Her memory records her mother's caprice and refusal to examine her decisions and their consequences. As a living monument to this damage, Kincaid remembers alone, which seems to compel her to hold fast to the truth about her mother. It is a complicated legacy, memory, and a view of her mother as profoundly dangerous is something Kincaid has salvaged from the wreckage.

As I have argued, Kincaid's texts end and often begin with death imagery or with the sentiments of memento mori. Death is never far from the scene. In a comment on the composition of *My Brother*, Kincaid explores this proximity: "What I am writing now is not a journal; a journal is a daily account, an immediate account of what occurs during a certain time. For a long time after my brother died I could not write about him. It was really a short time between the time that he became sick and the time he died, but that time became a world" (91–92). Tending to the dying and writing do not occur simultaneously, rather, the attention to death makes the world out of which writing comes. Reflecting in *My Brother* on Devon's imminent death and the possibility that he might be buried near his father, Kincaid insists: "The dead never die, and I now say this—the dead never die—as if it were new, as if no one had never noticed this before" (121). In reference to her hearing of her stepfather's death from her mother, three months after the fact and with an account of the family's poverty, Kincaid comments on the world generated by the liveliest and most life-threatening force, her mother: "In the world I lived in then, my old family was dead to me. I did not speak of them, I spoke of my mother, but only to describe the terrible feelings I had toward her, the terrible feelings she had toward me, in tones of awe, as if they were exciting, all our feelings, as if ours had been a great love affair, something that was partly imaginary, something that was partly a fact; but the parts that were imaginary and the parts that were facts were all true" (118–19).

Devon asks Kincaid, as many of her interviewers have, about the relation between her life and her fiction: Is it autobiographical? His reason for asking is especially pressing as he approaches death under his mother's care and in her house: "He had read in a novel written by me about a mother who had tried and tried and failed and failed to abort the third and last of her male children. And when he was dying he asked me if that mother was his mother and if that child was himself ('Ah me de trow'way pickney'); in reply, I laughed a great big Ha! Ha! and then said no, the book he read is a novel, a novel is a work of fiction; he did not tell me that he did not believe my reply and I did not tell him that he should not believe my reply" (174).

The end of the text makes the move characteristic of Kincaid: she places a body on the threshold of the concluding text, and its discovery is profoundly linked to the possibility of future writing: "When I was young, younger than I am now, I started to write about my own life and I came to see that this act saved my life. When I heard about my brother's illness and his dying, I knew, instinctively, that to understand it, or to make an attempt to understand his dying, and not to die with him, I would write about it" (196). The proximity of her own death (and life) to writing means that a book about her brother's death is never far from a concern that defines her work: how writing can save your life. It also means that in any death scene, her creativity is a living presence: it is catalyzed by the threat of death, indissoluble from it and from mourning. The text concludes by discovering, in the last paragraph, the lost object of this work of mourning and the necessity both to leave the scene and to return to it in future. Yet it is not her brother (who she discovers after his death is probably gay) who provides the final surprise. The work of mourning has turned up an object that connects love, writing, and death: editor, father-in-law, and "perfect reader," William Shawn, the father to supplement the discouraging mother, the principle of family through which to begin her new family, the one to whom she will always write despite his death: "The perfect reader has died, but I cannot see any reason not to write for him anyway, for I can sooner get used to never hearing from him—the perfect reader—than to not being able to write for him at all" (198).

This is an unexpected conclusion. It is as if Kincaid has switched the bodies and replaced the one we expected her to bury and resurrect, her brother's, with another. Yet perhaps it is not surprising that her brother's death proves insufficient; after all, she admits that she does not love him. In her loss of William Shawn, Kincaid discovers a death that makes more of a claim on her, a death capable of replicating the conditions that spur her need to write for her life.

# 5

# Without Names

## An Anatomy of Absence in Jeanette Winterson's *Written on the Body*

*A name makes reading too easy.*
—Michel Foucault, "The Masked Philosopher"

*W*ritten on the Body least resembles autobiography in the context I've developed here. Unlike Allison, Gilmore, and Kincaid, Winterson has neither asserted nor acceded to a primarily autobiographical context for understanding her writing. Following her first autobiographical novel, *Oranges Are Not the Only Fruit*, Winterson wrote the kind of postmodern fiction that does not readily lend itself to autobiographical reading. Why, then, read *Written on the Body* as a limit-case about self-representation? The chapters that precede this one form a context for understanding how Winterson engages autobiography's central issues without reproducing its formal conventions. Indeed, she resists them, not because they are unrelated to her project, but because they are central, and resistance offers a renewable and resilient mode of engagement. Autobiography's attention to names as markers of identity, its tension about the relation between historical verifiability and the limits of memory, its distrust of fantasy, dreams, and the imagination, its multiform history and patchwork present tense all offer Winterson grounds for an experiment in (self-)representation focused on sexuality, love, and loss.

Winterson offers this exchange in *Art and Lies*: "What do Lesbians do in bed? 'Tell them,' said Sophia, the Ninth Muse. Tell them? There's no such thing as autobiography, there's only art and lies."[1] As a response to the injunction to tell what lesbians do in bed, "[t]here's no such thing as autobi-

---

[1]  Jeanette Winterson, *Art and Lies* (Toronto: Knopf Canada, 1994), 141.

ography, there's only art and lies," is a curious reply. Winterson seems to suggest that autobiography lies immediately behind, or within, questions of sexuality and sexual know-how. What lesbians do in bed is a personal question, a subjective question despite its generalizing tone and capital L, an autobiographical question. Yet immediately after coming to the fore, autobiography is made to recede. The circuit from sexuality to autobiography is made with dazzling brevity on the way to "art and lies," and in this moment autobiography is negated and absented in the place perhaps where one is most likely to look for it. Traces of autobiography are significant here. That they keep turning up indicates that autobiography is embedded in both sexuality and artifice and even provides a way to think of how they are related. Indications of autobiography appear in unexpected places or they fail to appear in expected places. "There's no such thing as autobiography" echoes the fervently whispered "there's no such thing as ghosts" as a denial in the presence of uneasy, even downright panicky, belief. There is something discreditable about both autobiography and ghosts—those figures of absence and haunting—and despite the presumed truthfulness of one (autobiography) and unlikeliness of the other (ghosts), one finds recurring assertions that they either do or do not really exist, as if the meaning of that existence were insistently and precisely in question. In facing the meaning of autobiography's existence, Paul de Man in "Autobiography as De-facement" came up with tropes of absence and death. Autobiography, as de Man notes, in its effort to represent life comes inevitably upon its own impossibility. There is a certain gothic quality to his reading that allows for a link to Terry Castle's *Apparitional Lesbian* in which Castle argues that the lesbian is typically represented as a ghostly presence, a specter whose haunting is evidence of both her derealization and persistent presence.[2] In its frequent absenting from the scene of writing and persistent interruptions of it, autobiography, like sexuality, is knowable both in and as absence as well as vivid, self-declaring presence.

I offer this reading of Jeanette Winterson's *Written on the Body* as a limit-case focused on sexed and gendered self-representation. Her book is interesting in this context because it plays with certain expectations about how and whether a lesbian author writes a lesbian text, and what such a

---

[2]   See her Polemical Introduction to *The Apparitional Lesbian* (New York: Columbia University Press, 1993) for a briefing on this thesis. The familiar term "thinly veiled autobiography" further suggests the ghostliness of autobiography. Some readers look for autobiography everywhere, as if it were everywhere, and when they find a certain kind of text they suggest that its art is subordinate ("thinly veiled") to its real existence as autobiography. Writing, in this view, merely drapes the real recalling the metaphors of language as the clothing of thought or existence.

claim might mean. Yet *Written on the Body* is more interested in proliferating questions around that query than in producing answers to it. In so doing, it invokes certain interpretations, expectations, and conventions that attend autobiography even as it reworks those connections for productive kinds of dissonance. It allows the reading effects implied by autobiography to remain lively even as it presses beyond autobiography's formal boundaries. I describe Winterson's text as being in implicit dialogue with autobiography in order to highlight the way certain rhetorical conventions and cultural references or situations catalyze the expectations generated by autobiography, namely, that the writer has a truth to tell and is telling it about the writer's life.

What motivates this contextualization? That Winterson's first book, *Oranges Are Not the Only Fruit*, was widely received as autobiographical has installed the expectation, confirmed by some reviewers and almost all my students, that subsequent texts by Winterson can be read within the context of an autobiographical project, even if Winterson wants to change the rules.[3] Rather than pronounce this interest as false or limited, I want to let it provide a way into the trickier and more expansive discourses of self-representation and the issues raised there through its interrogation of identity as a function of representation, especially in its attention to the materiality of bodies, and the relation of language to the coming-into-being of sexuality and gender.

Let me introduce a comparison to further clarify the context in which I read Winterson's project. As a major influence, Monique Wittig's *Lesbian Body* has been a part of feminist discourse about the body from the beginning of contemporary interest in that topic.[4] *Written on the Body* intersects with a developed stage of this discourse and depends, in my view, on the thinking about the body that precedes it, including Wittig's *Lesbian Body* as its most salient precursor. *Written on the Body* is contemporaneous with a renewed interest in speech-act theory, specifically, the performative as it has been theorized by Judith Butler and others. This interest in the performative links legal studies of injurious speech to the U.S. military's "don't ask, don't tell" policy, and to the contexts in which one must answer the question "who are you?" with a statement that begins "I am."[5] Addi-

---

[3]  Jeanette Winterson, *Oranges Are Not the Only Fruit* (New York: Atlantic Monthly Press, 1987).

[4]  Monique Wittig, *The Lesbian Body*, trans. David Le Vay (Boston: Beacon, 1986; first published in French, Paris: Minuit, 1973).

[5]  See Judith Butler's work on the performative, especially in "Critically Queer," *GLQ* 1 (1993): 17–32. Performatives are those speech acts in which the saying is the doing, as in Searle's example, "I now pronounce you," from the wedding ceremony. A declaration of identity such as "I am a lesbian" is performative of identity in a context in which speech is conduct. This logic underpins the U. S. military's deeply problematic "don't ask, don't tell" policy. I call attention to the performative here to show how Winterson's refusal to make

tionally, both texts explore how and whether texts perform autobiography, how the lesbian author's sexuality motivates the reading of her text as autobiography, and how such impulses might be rethought.

Jeanette Winterson's *Written on the Body* features an ungendered, unnamed narrator who falls in love with a married woman. Monique Wittig's *Lesbian Body* creates a lesbian world in which the lovers explore the possibilities of embodiment. Through an intertextual reading, it is possible to consider what Wittig's strategy of renaming and Winterson's strategy of not-naming reveal about gender, sexuality, and the modes of signifying them, in relation to self-representation. Both Wittig and Winterson deploy one of the most common tropes of autobiography: the intertwined figures of book and body. Wittig writes: "The body of the text subsumes all the words of the female body. . . . To recite one's own body, to recite the body of the other, is to recite the words of which the book is made up" (10). Winterson, too, offers this trope: "I like to keep the body rolled up away from prying eyes. Never unfold too much, tell the whole story. I didn't know that Louise would have reading hands. She has translated me into her own book" (89). Because the bodies in both are anatomized in less than familiar ways, the figure of the book and body suggest texts that one must labor to read well. Wittig names the bodies in question on the title page as "lesbian" and feminine pronouns appear in the text. The body is represented in the mode of becoming lesbian rather than in its possession of any particular parts that make it such. In Winterson, no gender references are permitted about the first-person narrator who nonetheless describes her or his sexual adventures with men and women in some detail. The body in both texts signifies gender and sexuality in shifting allusions to the transparency and opacity of what bodies can tell us about what we "see."

In neither text is the relationship between body and sexual identity primarily referential or mimetic. There is no stable referent, neither anatomical nor metaphorical, that makes the bodies lesbian; no single practice or array of fetishes that proves the body's sexuality as lesbian. Rather, the relationship between identity (what can and cannot be rendered visible when "I am a lesbian" is or is not the primary signifier of sexual identification) and representation (how to tell a story with sexuality at its center without relying upon a familiar way of representing sexuality) becomes the ground for an extended inquiry into the claims to knowledge made by the presence and absence of the names around and through which the body is made to cohere. Evidence of identity, therefore, is located in representational practices of habeas corpus (bringing out the body) that resist

---

such a declaration can be read as resistance in a climate of surveillance and punishment. A performative can be an autobiographical utterance and to decline it is part of Winterson's limit-testing about the representation of sexuality and identity.

a legalistic imperative of proof in favor of signification, that is, of proximate and shifting signifiers that can be read relationally within and among texts. I invoke legal language here to remind us that expectations about whether and how a text is autobiographical are often coded as expectations about whether an author is telling the truth, which is frequently elided with a judgment about how well the author can be said to conform to (or reproduce) hegemonic notions of appropriate identity. This expectation reveals that identity is a function of representation which is thoroughly imbricated in the juridical. Instead of judging whether the body is made intelligible within normative discourses of identity, I want to intervene in those judgments by turning the focus toward how these texts bring out the body. The question, then, is not whether the author is telling the truth, but how the body is used as a truth-text and what truth-claims about identity are made through the body.

Wittig explores ways to signify "lesbian" through what we could call reanatomization, a comprehensive invention and display of and by bodies under the rubric of "the lesbian body." Her refusal of a patriarchal regime of names makes it possible for bodies to dissolve under that system of kinship, which depends upon patrilineage as a system of meaning and value, and to reemerge through a matrix named "lesbian." That the name lesbian titles the project but is not reproduced on every page indicates that the power of this signifier lies in naming the whole text *The Lesbian Body* rather than any single or separable dimension of it. Bodies in this text are always coming apart. They are either described through a cataloguing of parts coming back together, or parts being disjoined limb from limb, and limb from socket. The violence of this disarticulation and rearticulation points up the materiality of language (especially in Wittig's catalogues of body parts), the way language bears upon the body, and makes it knowable (or unknowable). In contrast to Wittig's experiment with the body under the name lesbian, Winterson's ungendered, unnamed narrator declines such an utterance. If Wittig's lesbian body is rendered material by its name, Winterson's textual body coheres around the performative, "I grieve." An intertextual reading of Winterson's and Wittig's representations of bodies makes it clearer how Winterson's signification of desire without sexual identification can be read as a refusal of the patriarchal regime of names and the identities it compels. The body's intelligibility is risked in both; in Wittig by claiming and in Winterson by declining a sexual name. Both, however, work the body for its capacity to figure sexuality in terms that do not reproduce heterosexist claims to knowledge. Wittig's emphasis on naming as the mode through which the lesbian emerges makes it possible to ask of Winterson's choice of not-naming: How, in the context created by reading the texts together, does absence signify?

In order to direct this question toward critical conversations beyond autobiography studies, we need only look to the work being done on the body and the performative, and to some earlier work on the theoretical meanings of presence and absence initiated, from different but not irreconcilable directions, via deconstruction and feminist theory. A fairly diverse group of theorists informs my formulation here of how absence signifies. Feminist critics, for example, have undertaken a critical project of recovering and remembering the erased cultural productions and lives of women. Although some poststructuralist work on absence, notably by Pierre Macherey, Hélène Cixous, and Jacques Derrida, is written at a conceptual distance from the retrieval and archival work of lost, buried, and disappeared writers and subcultures, taken together these projects amount to a massive reconceptualization of evidence. Evidence, following these interventions, may be adduced in and as what is missing, through loss, omission, trauma, or some condensation of these and other phenomena. Interpretive practices have followed these projects and extended them by reading inferentially and circumstantially for remnants, traces, and fetishes of what has to be recognized as a revised real.

In the context I am describing, the revised real emerges through a reconceptualization of evidence. Representations of the real depend upon and are a function of what can be claimed as evidence, in the case of self-representation, of identity, of *who* was *there*, and of how identity can be rendered intelligible. Critical work on bodies is significant here for its claims about how bodies are read as and for evidence of the real. A newly fashioned matrix for reading bodies has merged insights about the body's materiality with claims about how the body performs meaning. Both emphases—upon materiality and performance—underscore that representations of the body are caught up in competing systems of meaning. Although an emphasis on how bodies perform gender, race, and sexuality contends with the insistence that the body possesses these attributes, these positions appear furthest apart in their most abstract formulations. They are surprisingly similar when they situate the body in a realm of material consequences. Whether the body possesses or performs race, gender, and sexuality, the material consequences nonetheless strike with similar intensity. Both *The Lesbian Body* and *Written on the Body* exploit the possibilities of how bodies possess and perform "identity." In both, the ways in which the representation of the body *is* its identity is of central concern.

*Written on the Body* extends the self-representational project Winterson initiated in *Oranges Are Not the Only Fruit*, published in 1985 when she was twenty-six, which won the Whitbread Prize in England for fiction. Yet the stability of "fiction" as a sufficient description of *Oranges* is called into question immediately because the constructed line between first-person fiction and autobiography is barely meaningful as a marker of generic territoriality. In *Oranges*, Winterson trades across this border through her combination of historical events and places (in her and her protagonist's lives) with allegory and fantasy. This intermingling of the imagined and the verifiable articulates a threshold between fiction and autobiography, and an entry point for the text into a category that expands upon the generic limits of both. Protagonist and author are brought up in Lancashire, adopted daughters of an evangelical mother and barely visible father, and both are named Jeanette. In *Oranges*, young Jeanette is recruited into her mother's allegorical pact with the world. Here, she recites her origin story: "I had been brought in to join her in a tag match with the Rest of the World. She had a mysterious attitude towards the begetting of children; it wasn't that she couldn't do it, more that she didn't want to do it. She was very bitter about the Virgin Mary getting there first. So she did the next best thing and arranged for a foundling. That was me" (3). The mother expects the daughter to become an evangelist, and this proceeds more or less according to plan until Jeanette falls in love with Melanie. Once she does so, what she is capable of seeing in herself and the local community of women believers alters. Subsequently, the lesbians in whose midst she has grown up are recognized as such. Jeanette realizes that she shares their sexuality, though what she will make of this at the end of the book is still an open question. She does not reject the carnival-tent atmosphere of evangelism and the otherwordly orientation of her mother, but neither is she accepted by her mother, minister, and church as a lesbian. So in the way of the autobiography, the bildungsroman, the coming-out story, and the heroic quest narrative, she must leave her home to find it. In this case, she heads off to university. The author's notes on the book jacket preview, condense, and displace the same lesbian pilgrim's progress.

Winterson's books and Winterson's body have been conflated by some reviewers and readers in an attempt to gender and name her narrator "lesbian." To do so, readers must detour through the autobiographical, a detour into the intelligible, whereby readers inscribe the identity of the author upon the dissonance in the category of identity in the text. Whereas *Oranges* blends allegory and fantasy as ways to reread the contours within an arguably historical and personal landscape, Winterson's own, intervening works *Sexing the Cherry* and *The Passion* depart from the verifiable details of her life and engage history on a grander scale.[6] In these texts her penchant for allegory is untethered from the Bible and au-

[6] Jeanette Winterson, *The Passion* (New York: Vintage, 1989); *Sexing the Cherry* (New York: Vintage, 1991).

tobiography per se and channeled into meditations upon space, time, and narrative. Her new interests resume and extend what can still be called an autobiographical task in *Written on the Body* insofar as Winterson's first-person narrator returns to some earlier preoccupations with identity and representation first explored via the autobiographical.

Some reviewers have assumed that *Written on the Body* is a sequel to *Oranges*, both of which are claimed as romans à clef. This is less evidence of a critical consensus than a symptom of what kinds of questions get asked when a review is framed through autobiographical assumptions. In the *New York Review of Books*, Winterson's fictionalizing of the self-representational "I" has been reviewed as a literary device.[7] The unnamed and un-gendered narrator is taken as an interesting conceit in a love story focused so centrally upon the body and its materiality. After all, the reasoning goes, it's not like Winterson is really hiding anything with this "I," everyone knows she's a lesbian. While the autobiographicality of *Written on the Body* has not been particularly contested or even really puzzled out in the so-called straight press, some lesbian reviewers have had another point to make. Sarah Schulman, for example, finds the device of the ambiguous narrator an odd and rather unsuccessful refusal by Winterson to take the name of lesbian. For her, *Written on the Body* is like "all fiction based somewhat on real life" and is marred by "lapses of discipline" such as "too many lines of recreated dialogue" which somewhat surprisingly in this review, make the "emotions richer, easier to recognize." Schulman considers the text flawed, if endearing.[8] Schulman solves the ambiguity of the narrator's gender by diagnosing *her* as "a confused, insecure lesbian who can't fully love the woman of her dreams." The problem here is not so much that the narrator isn't identified as a lesbian, but that a lesbian author has an ambiguously gendered narrator. Both reviews concern sexuality, its visibility, and what one makes of it. Yet both breeze past the constitutive and not merely perfunctory impediment Winterson sets in their path. There is a prior question here about autobiography as the generic grid of truth. To claim that the name "lesbian" would solve the questions of name, gender, sexuality, and identity evades the problematic within the representation of identity Winterson engages. In terms of names, *Written on the Body* already claims to be a novel. It is not through the presence of the name "novel" that this text enters into the problematic but through the absence of the name "autobiography" precisely in the places one wishes to find it. Were it present, all competing or disruptive knowledge

7 Gabriele Annan, "Devil in the Flesh," *New York Review of Books*, May 4, 1993, 22–23.
8 Sarah Schulman, "Guilty with Explanation: Jeanette Winterson's Endearing Book of Love," *Lambda Book Review* 3, no. 9 (March–April 1993): 20.

of identity could be compelled to cohere under this name. Identity (the author's, the narrator's, the text's) would become knowable through a grid of intelligibility *already in place*.

I take *Written on the Body* as both a continuation and an expansion of Winterson's interest in self-representation, if in significantly altered terms. The question with which *Written on the Body* begins, "Why is the measure of love loss," expands upon one posed in *Oranges*, which concerns naming: "There are many forms of love and affection, some people can spend their whole lives together without knowing each other's names. Naming is a difficult process; it concerns essences, and it means power." Here, her question was: "But on the wild nights who can call you home? Only the one who knows your name" (170). In *Oranges*, Winterson sought an answer to "who can call you home?" in allegory and fantasy. That narrative moves between the coming-out story and its consequences for Jeanette, and parables in which she chats with advice-giving demons. While her interest in fantasy links *Oranges* to *The Passion*, *Sexing the Cherry*, and *Art and Lies*, a different connection links *Oranges* to *Written on the Body*. In *Written on the Body* the various tensions and problematics are not charted primarily through the alternative plenitude of fantasy, but in the linkage of love and loss. Fantasy's counterpart, anxiety, emerges in the responses induced by an unnamed and ungendered narrator. In *Oranges*, Winterson's questions about power, knowledge, and names; her recurring tropes of home, wild nights, love, and loss; and her exploitation of autobiographical echoes gesture explicitly toward self-representational discourse. In *Written on the Body*, however, she extends the self-representational strategies of *Oranges* into the perverse strategy of not-naming.

The strategy of not-naming raises some related questions about identity and the mechanisms of identification through which identity is ascertained and secured: In what ways does a name indicate presence? Must the absence of a name be linked to loss? Or, to put it more precisely in *Written on the Body*'s terms: When and how can absence be read as something other than loss? When and how does absence signify what one does not possess rather than what one refuses to give? Winterson's text works these questions for a range of possible answers. But there are prior questions here about names and their function within the field of representation. How, within the discourses of self-representation, do names signify identity? What does it mean for a name to identify a subject—to gender it, sex it, make it real? What are the definitional limits of "sex," "gender," and "sexuality" as evidence of the "identity" of an autobiographical subject? Ultimately, these questions can be focused on Winterson's text in a very particular way: they suggest a project interested in the possibilities that attend the representation of identity when names are absent.

*Written on the Body* offers a hard case for testing the meaning of names. Immediately, the lack of disclosure or seeming invisibility of gender foregrounds sexuality as a question. Without the name of gender and the identity it indicates, how are we to know this "I"? When we attempt to infer sexual identity from the narrator's lovers, we are offered bisexuality as a nonidentifying answer to the question of gender: the beloved is a woman and the narrator has had some male and more female lovers. Gender and sexuality do not reduce to each other nor do they confirm *an* identity for the narrator. The refusal to disclose gender and the subsequent interpretation of sexuality as a question moves the reader briskly onto autobiography's familiar ground, where identity is implicated in questions of representation and ontology. What might seem so ontologically *there* as to defy the need of representation becomes, in this text, difficult to name. In this way, Winterson forces the autobiographical to divulge its weirdness and to open onto the wider, and wilder, field of self-representation through the questions above. Through her inquiry into naming, as it instantiates identity as a function of representation, Winterson moves to an unexpected location within self-representation.

The expected claims about names in autobiography emphasize their stabilizing function: a name identifies a person, a family, a history, and focuses attention on the solid corporeality to which it refers. Ultimately the name seems to mark a ground zero of representational veracity: "who *is* the autobiographer?" can be answered by a simple cross-check and verification of the author's name and the protagonist named in the text. If they are identical, you have autobiography. But as Winterson suggests in *Oranges*, the stakes are too high for naming to function as a simple referential anchor that holds the world to the text through the name of the autobiographer: "Naming is a difficult process; it concerns essences, and it means power." Though this may sound like a young lover reaching for "deep meaning," as a comment on naming in autobiography, it is suggestive. In autobiography, the name becomes a symbol of not only the past to which one may lay claim but the past and family that claims you. Such a symbol (and such families) may well be more threatening than comforting. After all, not everyone who writes autobiographically ends up embracing the name as a signifier of familial belonging. Some write in order to destroy the claims upon them made by families, communities, and past experiences. Following in this vein in her feminist intervention in the history of ideas, Denise Riley finds an apt figure in Desdemona whose life depends upon what may be done to her through a name.[9] Desdemona's questioning and querulous signature, "Am I that name?" resonates here as a self-

---

[9]    Denise Riley, *"Am I That Name?"* (Minneapolis: University of Minnesota Press, 1988).

representational signifier that is different from the performative, "I am that name," though comprehensible as part of the same signifying system. "Am I that name?" does not mean the obverse of "I am that name," not, that is, "I am *not* that which men say I am," but "am I?" a question that leads toward an interpretive context in which, presumably, those who know the answer can ensure the consequences that will follow. To find oneself named, pinned in place by that identification, and placed within a community, a family, and a home is precisely what many self-representational writers are trying not simply to represent but to escape. Thus, writers may engage the discourses of self-representation as much to lose a name as to find one. To lose a name is not merely to exchange one set of constraints for a less-familiar one. To remove oneself from a familiar audience and community in an effort to find a more companionable home is not an easy task. Rather, to route self-representation more emphatically and precisely through representation necessarily engages the subject in an altered discursive project, the terms of which are not fully predictable. The writer may well need to reconstruct the very possibilities and grounds for community through this effort.

The terms in which Winterson casts this venture are more concerned with the anxiety provoked by the absence of the name than with sustaining the conceit of an unnamed, ungendered narrator. In other words, if not-naming were merely the coy pose of a clever writer, its ability to generate anxiety might well dissolve within a few chapters. Anxiety remains in lively play, however, because what is missing is the signifying chain of identity that presumably corresponds to a material reality in which identity coheres through the progressive, motivated, and linked signification of sex, gender, and sexuality. Autobiography not only depends upon this signification, it seems to proves its reality. Winterson's strategic omission of the name strikes at the signifying seam between reality and autobiography. Winterson's installation of a speaking subject whose only name is "I" places the reader in a position to question which signifiers cause the subject to unravel and which to cohere, and in what contexts.

Through the absence of names, Winterson raises questions of identity that the presence of names does not really answer. Questions about the ascertainable identities of the narrator, the author, and the text are stabilized by names, but are not identical to them. The questions lie there, redundant, seeking transparency. An answer would throw light, but in doing so would obliterate the opacity through which this narrator emerges. Both the text itself and the topos of gendered and sexual identity here are "written on the body" in such a way that the body cannot simply offer a transparently visible or unambiguously legible proof of "identity," but that does not remove the problem of identification, of establishing how "we" know "one" (a woman, a lesbian, an autobiography) when "we" see "one." The body is usually thought to provide compelling, even irrefutable, proof of sex and gender, and ultimately of unique identity. The body coalesces under the name of sex. The erotic body is mapped through acts, zones, desires, all of which usually cite sex as identification. How then can a book on the body, a love story no less, avoid sexing the subject? While *Oranges* brings out the autobiographical body through naming it as female, as lesbian, as "Jeanette," *Written on the Body* traces a different path through self-representation. Winterson almost seems to be asking how much she can leave out and conserve the autobiographical trace. The experiment here plays at the extreme edge because she chooses to omit both name and sex as she refuses to secure the body's identity beyond that of "lover." It seems improbable to pursue self-representation without names. It not only defies generic conventions and the expectations they install, it risks coherence altogether. But perhaps the limit of coherence at which Winterson plays through figures of the name and the body locates *the* risk worth taking precisely due to the functions both name and body have played in regimes of truth and identity, regimes in which autobiography itself has served.

*Written on the Body* attempts to map the boundary of representation—its limit—in relation to what can and cannot be known and uttered about the lover's body, and between what can be represented through a lover's discourse and what, in the absence of the beloved, is lost and must achieve signification elsewhere. To do so, *Written on the Body* divides into three sections. In the first, the narrator recounts falling in love with Louise, who, when they meet, is married to Elgin, a cancer specialist. The narrator is a hero cast in the Byronic mold; there have been many lovers, mostly women, and many married women. There have also been many heartbreaks. The narrator fears that Louise, too, will become another figure in this romance narrative, but Louise defies expectation and instead of kissing the narrator good-bye, declares that she is leaving Elgin: "My love for you makes my other life a lie." The lovers begin an idyllic stretch that ends abruptly in some awkward and rather implausible blackmail: Louise, it turns out, has leukemia. Elgin tells the narrator that Louise's symptoms have flared, that he and he alone can guarantee her the best medical care, and that his connections offer the best hope for Louise's health. But there is a catch: he will not offer them unless the narrator vanishes. Without consulting Louise, the narrator agrees and the book breaks into its second part, a sustained meditation upon the body. This section consists of four chapters devoted to the body. At their conclusion, the narrative of the first section seems to resume, though the ending invites a revision of this schema.

The excess generated by the absence around naming and gender finds explicit, even hyperbolic, representation in Louise and Elgin, the Married Couple. There is even a detailed account of how Elgin got his name, and he is rendered in stereotypical terms as Jewish. In a similarly schematic way, Louise's gendered representation is a proliferation of formalist attributes, even fetishes, of gender: her red hair, her pale skin, her lovely home, her effects, all amount to a hyperbolic emphasis on her femaleness, on the necessity of saying "she" in reference to Louise. Louise pervades, even invades, the scene as a system of gendered signs. Signifiers of gender proliferate around her; she is an extension of and extends into her home. All this metonymic displacement allows the narrator to find fetishes everywhere: "She dribbled viscous juices down her chin and before I could help her wiped them away. I eyed the napkin; could I steal it? Already my hand was creeping over the tablecloth like something out of Poe" (37). The excessivity of Louise's gendering in the context of the narrator's self-representation casts Louise's "reality" into doubt. She is a gendered object in a hyperreal sense: she is almost a phantasm. Some names attach to her readily, but all depend upon an interpretive context of sexuality that is structured through a significant absence. The problem of knowing Louise's name(s) is consistent with the problem of not knowing the narrator's; both concern the context in which gender and sexuality as evidence of each other is performed. Louise is not presented in a delimited way as a "married woman"; her desire is not thoroughly heterosexualized by this name, and therefore the narrator doesn't pop out from behind namelessness as a fella. Instead, Louise reacts unpredictably in relation to that name, and the reader is offered another possible name for the beloved. She's a real femme, that Louise. With the femme-ing of Louise comes the subtextual encoding of the Casanova-Narrator as a butch lesbian.

Perhaps Terry Castle's reading of the lesbian as apparition permits a two-step reading toward identifying the narrator: if Louise can be read as an apparitional lesbian, then the narrator steps from behind the curtain and reveals herself, too, as such. Louise's extreme womanliness is not precisely what Castle argues for as the lesbian's derealization, but it accomplishes the same spectralization of the character. Obviously, this is an inferential reading, a circumstantial reading, and it is consistent with the opening-up of this reading practice rather than in the narrowing of the evidence into a single proof of the narrator's identity. But such an inference does not, finally, resolve the question. Do lesbians fall in love only with lesbians? Can a reading practice that seeks to open up the categories "married" and "woman" afford to, or be expected to, close down around the category "lesbian"? In other words, things get tricky here precisely because it is the ascription of names to identity, the very code of the juridi-cal, that Winterson is scrambling. Castle's argument works best, I think, for texts other than *Written on the Body*, for in this case it is the unknowa-bility that is interesting. Thus I see less a veiled derealization than a sym-pathetically posed question about realization. While Castle provides an engaging way to identify lesbians in literature, I mean to emphasize here that *Written on the Body*'s signification performs in a different way. The ab-sence of a referential ground zero for the narrator keeps the signification in play, renders interpretation necessary. If the narrator is not readily comprehensible as a "woman," she need not be incomprehensible as a les-bian, and this is the sort of linkage of gender to sexuality as the basis of identification and identity that Winterson wants to keep coming at throughout the text and not, particularly, to resolve. Her questions unfold in this way: Must a reading of sexuality be routed through a gender proof? How great is the distance (interpretive, representational, self-rep-resentational) between the names woman and lesbian? Both questions concern the interpretive space opened up between sexuality and gender, between identity and names. It is a space Winterson will not suture.

Since Winterson will not suture this space, what meanings are gener-ated and circulate here? The space ambivalently evokes both loss and omission; namelessness may seem like the space that marks where a name was lost as much as the space of its refusal or obliteration. Such ambiva-lence between loss and refusal leads in two directions. In one direction, if one believes that a name has been lost, then its former presence registers as that which one formerly possessed or knew. The "lost" name becomes a pretext for nostalgia, which gestures toward a narrative with an origin (toward myth) and installs the repetition of loss as a central motif, whether this is figured as the "return" of or to what was lost, or the repe-tition of its loss. In a different direction, namelessness memorializes an-other struggle. Here the absence of a name does not signify loss, but a suc-cessful evasion of the fixity implicit in naming, and a redirection of the representation of identity. Nostalgia and this provisional freedom from fixity are welded together in *Written on the Body*, and both circulate through the representation of gender and sexuality.

In this context Winterson's narrator raises the question of narcissism by turning from the other or others to the self, toward the narrator's own pain rather than toward an external love object. The narrator's own body is now the only place where Louise's body can be known and, function-ally, is. In this extreme incorporation that apprehends another as the self and that merges self and other to the point of absorption, Winterson seems to be flirting with something rather more controversial than char-acter development. By coding the narrator as narcissistic, she gestures toward the discourses of sexology and their inscription of homosexuality as pathology, most notably, as narcissism. However, I find no simple identification grid here: if narcissism, then lesbianism. The connection is implicit in the discourses of sexuality, and interpretive practices of reading for the possibility of lesbian representation make much of inference. Even as the specter of narcissism is raised in this text, however, Winterson eludes the trap that Freud set because the subject to whom narcissism would attach engages self-representation differently. This isn't, then, simply a story of "women who love too much" or "lesbian without very good boundaries." The text frustrates those conclusions, even as it suggests them, as Winterson constructs a discussion of the beloved's body by a lover without the name to which narcissism might attach.

Following the first section of *Written on the Body*, the narrator's body is removed from one narrative, a straightforward tale of complicated love, and another self-representational discourse in which to measure love and loss is called for. Winterson does all that can be done with the questions that I have suggested animate the first section of the book, and then raises the representational stakes. The narrative breaks when Louise becomes ill and the narrator presumes to choose Louise's future for her. At this point, Louise's body is on the verge of becoming the body in pain, and, as a body saturated in a materiality with consequences, a body that demands another discourse for representation. Winterson removes Louise in order to focus primarily on how the narrator experiences the pain of loss. The narrator has lost a body that in this text is primary. While it is not originary per se as either a maternal or infantile body, it is a primary love object nonetheless, and, insofar as it is absent, mourned, and central, is a fetish for the body logic that is generated by the context of a central loss.[10]

The text moves to an engagement with representing the self in relation to representing trauma. The pain of lost love—amplified by the narrator's decision to heed Elgin's blackmail without consulting Louise, the narrator's disappearance, and then Louise's—combines with the way the narrator can imagine Louise's illness. Lost love and leukemia become analogues with different textual references. Bereft of Louise's body, which the narrator imagines changing in relation to disease, the narrator enters a textual universe where all constructions of the body are simulacral. The narrator reads books on grief and mourning that advise sleeping with a pillow to blunt the pain of the beloved's absence. In addition, the narrator pores over medical literature about bodies and illness. In contrast to the self-help books' emphasis on the beloved's absent body, the medical texts

---

[10]    In this context, see Teresa de Lauretis's *Practice of Love* (Bloomington: Indiana University Press, 1994) for a discussion of loss and fantasy in lesbian representation and reading.

construct a present, if simulacral, body through a rhetoric of parts and their functions.

Following the opening, unnamed narrative section, there are four lessons in the anatomy of absence entitled "The Cells, Tissues, Systems and Cavities of the Body," "The Skin," "The Skeleton," and "The Special Senses." Each section begins with a *Gray's Anatomy*-like description: "The CLAVICLE OR COLLAR BONE: THE CLAVICLE IS A LONG BONE WHICH HAS A DOUBLE CURVE. THE SHAFT OF THE BONE IS ROUGHENED FOR THE ATTACHMENT OF THE MUSCLES. THE CLAVICLE PROVIDES THE ONLY BONY LINK BETWEEN THE UPPER EXTREMITY AND THE AXIAL SKELETON" (129). What follows are reminiscences in the presumed present tense of narration from which the narrator has recounted the story. Memory combines with grief to produce a discourse in which the partial presences conjured by memory combine within the sliding invention of imagination. Memory goes beyond reporting and becomes self-invention. The turn toward the other via memory is a turn toward the self as the producer of counterimages and also as the locus of grief. The absence of the beloved within this present tense is now embraced and becomes the occasion for both memory and self-representation: "It was a game, fitting bone on bone. . . . Bone of my bone. Flesh of my flesh. To remember you it's my own body I touch. Thus she was, here and here" (129–30).

Even with this renewed emphasis upon the materiality of the body, upon the names by which the body can be described beneath the surface, sex is still not announced. *Written on the Body* refuses to hint at sexual identification through sexual difference. Here is the narrator on the presumptive appeal of sexual difference: "I thought difference was rated to be the largest part of sexual attraction but there are so many things about us that are the same" (129). The invocation of sexual difference suggests the old chestnut that "opposites attract," which is shorthand for the logic of heterosexism in which sexual difference is the fetish that, ironically and illogically, grounds heterosexuality. In the narrator's embrace of sameness, an unmarked body offers no "clues" to gender and sexuality. Although this is the sentence I have heard quoted as "proof" that the narrator is a lesbian, consider how it continues to deflect that gaze and to pursue a different discourse of sexuality than one that assigns names to sexual identities. No erotogenics follows from conventionally sex-marked sites, body parts, zones—no penis, labia, clitoris, breasts, but also no anus, no nipples. No "source" sites or parts from which substitutes are drawn— the site of pleasure and pain is, more comprehensively, the body. If there is a fetish, and why wouldn't there be, it would be the body as the displaced locus of embodied knowledge, the material with which eros develops, the real that aches. If I say, as Winterson's narrator might, "I ache for you," do you want to know, precisely, what part hurts? Winterson's language helps to locate a different source of desire—the "I" rather than the specified, named person, who in desire has desire. It is not "Jeanette" or the genitals ("jeanette-als"?) so much as the self-representational "I," the capacity for saying "I," that constructs pleasure and pain.

Through its emphasis upon the "I," the anatomy lessons continue to explore autobiography, if in different terms from the first section in which absences in the narrative could be filled, as some reviews of the text suggest, with information from Winterson's life. The lessons anatomize absence and indicate, however, that this is a self-representational project that capitalizes on the shared "I" of autobiography and first-person fiction in which the "I" forms an opening, an orifice through which the self-representational pours. It is impossible to say, though, which is hole (the self-representational? narrative?) and which is rim in this reading because the "I" of the narrator generates meaning in both locations.[11] Perhaps most pertinent to *Written on the Body* is the way in which this "I" functions as a body part in a way that is consistent with the text's erotogenics and is no more or less a mark of the real than the other body parts represented here. It is not that Winterson claims there is no materiality to bodies and sex, the representations of other characters besides the narrator suggest as much. Rather, the text makes it possible to consider the materiality of language through the representation of the narrator. The materiality of names does not totalize the materiality of bodies and sex, and the materiality of bodies and sex is not totalizable under names.

In this context, we can ask if Winterson succeeds in taking up the project that Judith Butler adumbrates in the conclusion to her essay, "The Lesbian Phallus": "For what is needed is not a new body part, as it were, but a displacement of the hegemonic symbolic of (heterosexist) sexual difference and the critical release of alternative imaginary schemas for constituting sites of erotogenic pleasure."[12] Butler rereads narcissism and the phallus to uncover two meanings: (1) that Freud links pain to love when he detours through hypochondria in his discussion of narcissism, and (2) that Freud's and Lacan's use of the phallus depends not upon the equivalence or nonequivalence of phallus to penis, but upon the logic of expropriability and substitution. That is, the phallus is not the signifier of the signified worth having, but the signifier of investiture. As such, according to Butler, other phalluses or other assignations of the phallus are certainly

---

[11]    See Lacan's "The Subversion of the Subject," in *Écrits: A Selection*, trans. Alan Sheridan (New York: Norton, 1977), for a fuller discussion of this dynamic, especially 299, 304, 315–16.

[12]    See her discussion in "The Lesbian Phallus and the Morphological Imaginary," in *Bodies That Matter* (New York: Routledge, 1993), 91.

possible and would become productive of other imaginary morphologies. Through this reading, Butler makes clear that the lesbian phallus is not a new body part, but a signifier of alternative morphologies, of imaginary bodies with pleasures that are not predicated on their reproduction of what she calls the "hegemonic symbolic of (heterosexist) sexual difference." To enlist Butler in reading the body logic I am describing in *Written on the Body*, the "I" does not underwrite the coherence of the body any more than any body part does, though taken together, all gesture toward a materiality that motivates signification. They do not so much refer to a total object of which they are all parts so much as the function that produces them, here, a representation of the body, and a materiality of sex rendered without the names of sexual difference-as-identity.

At this critical intersection, Wittig's work offers a significant counterpoint to Winterson's. Compare the interpenetrative possibilities in the named lesbian body in Wittig to the unnamed in Winterson. A representative moment in Wittig: "The women lead m/e to your scattered fragments, there is an arm, there is a foot, the neck and head are together, your eyelids are closed, your detached ears are somewhere, your eyeballs have rolled in the mud, I see them side by side, your fingers have been cut off and thrown to one side, I perceive your pelvis, your bust is elsewhere, several fragments of forearms the thighs and tibiae are missing. . . . I announce that you are here alive though cut to pieces, I search hastily for your fragments in the mud, m/y nails scrabble at the small stones and pebbles, I find your nose a part of your vulva your labia your clitoris, I find your ears one tibia then the other, I assemble you part by part, I reconstruct you . . ." (79–80).[13] The beloved's violent bodily dispersal and her recuperation are repeated throughout the book. The lesbian body is capable of infinite disarticulation and reassembly under the name of lesbian. Wittig's pleasure in cataloguing the lesbian body, its organs, functions, and intimate anatomy, form the rhetoric of a series of prose poems or block-style fragments. Without the name of lesbian, this body does not cohere. It would merely be destroyed, its resurrection outside the logic of identity explored in this text. However, the grieving lover may always collect the beloved and restore her to health within the embrace of the lesbian body as a system of representation.

In this sense Butler's reading of Lacan can illuminate what Winterson and Wittig are doing with names. As Butler points out: "For Lacan, names, which emblematize and institute this paternal law, *sustain* the integrity of the body. What constitutes the integral body is not a natural

---

[13] *The Lesbian Body* was translated by David Le Vay who is described in the foreword as an anatomist and surgeon.

boundary or organic telos, but the law of kinship that works through the name. In this sense, the paternal law produces versions of bodily integrity; the name, which installs gender and kinship, works as a politically invested and investing performative. To be named is thus to be inculcated into that law and to be formed, bodily, in accordance with that law."[14] This presumption of bodily coherence through sex and the name are refused and reworked by Wittig's, and Winterson's (if in a very different way) inscription of the lesbian body. Without the phallus, without genitals, or hierarchized erogenous zones, Wittig gives us a body ripped and ripping open that nonetheless persists under the name of "lesbian." A name is generated here that is also part of the pieces from which all of the lesbian body may be reworked. Its pleasures are in its continuity. Winterson's narrator declines the performative because the narrator's identity cannot logically be identified by that utterance. To declare a name and a gender would give the narrator the status of all narrated objects, including Louise, and the project would implode. Winterson gives us bodies in pain: the text of Louise's leukemic body is set beside the narrator's grieving figure.

It is important to raise again, and in altered terms, why the refusal of names, especially in a climate of detection, is significant. When we remember how emphatically the name goes to kinship, and how the enforced linking of names to kinship structures makes legally binding familial ties out of arrangements such as marriage, and through this construction legalizes acts that would be crimes were they committed against nonkin, we might well conclude that the call for names is less about establishing referentiality than the kinship structures and juridical discourses that follow from them. Names for identity and body parts belong to an order of signification that is a social order. To resist these specific names, at the very least, is to resist that social ordering. In *The Lesbian Body* the resistance to the social ordering that includes patriarchal kinship focuses on linking changed names to a changed body, and, implicitly, to changes in the social body. The patrilineal names are refused along with the regimes of the body they impose. Wittig breaks down the body and catalogues it, reanatomizes it as lesbian, and undertakes an epic and violent reworking of the acts of love, their embodied knowledge, and their complex pleasures. In the absence of patronymic traditions, the body breaks down. In fact, bodily integrity itself is risked. This makes possible the emergence of an altogether different bodily coherence, one not organized around the phallus as the symbolic signifier of value.

I should clarify here that my interest in Lacanian psychoanalysis is sub-

---

[14]    Butler, *Bodies That Matter*, 72.

ordinate to my interest in Butler's reading of it. I intend her reading to operate as a pivot, a way to turn from psychoanalysis, while acknowledging its relevance, toward an alternative reading. A Lacanian morphology misses the pressure points of Wittig's experiment, for although it could be suggested that Wittig seems to start and stay within the logic of a return to the mirror stage by representing a body in pieces, it seems more plausible that the lesbian body as *le corps morcelé* is on the verge of cohering differently. Through this representational location and tactic, Wittig undertakes a sustained project in signification. Her emphasis does not fall simply upon putting the body together differently; that is, she is not trying to come through the mirror stage *to* and *as* something / someone / someplace different. Rather, the project is sited there and stays there, inhabiting its function and techniques and working the contours of signification for the persistence and appearance of the disallowed—the lesbian body, a body the subject is prohibited from forming. The repetition is key here. Wittig can disassemble and reassemble the lesbian body from any part. Thus a psychoanalytic reading reaches a particular limit when confronted with *The Lesbian Body*. As an alternative to a Lacanian reading and as a supplement to Butler, I would suggest that the logic through which Wittig's lesbian body coheres is fractal.

Fractal geometry offers a way to describe irregular shapes (sometimes called "pathological" in Euclidean geometry) that are self-similar, that is, shaped identically at their micro and macro levels. Fractal geometry has been used, for example, to demonstrate that the shape of the English coastline at one-hundred-mile segments or at one-mile or one-foot segments is identical to its overall shape. The point in my reading of *The Lesbian Body* as a shape that is comprehensible through fractal geometry is to claim that no fetishized part of the body stands in for or represents the whole (as through synecdoche); rather, as I read Wittig, the lesbian body at every order is identical in morphology to every other order of magnitude. Each part is identical to any other part in shape and therefore the body can be recognized as lesbian from *any* fragment and can also regenerate the largest organization of the body from any fragment. From any body part, including the "I," the whole project of writing autobiography without names could be generated.

In *Written on the Body*, the grieving lover has left the wounded beloved and cannot recollect her. Parts and functions of the body become occasions for meditations upon loss without the prospect of reconstruction. Whereas Wittig has refused patrilineal names and instituted a discourse of the endlessly explorable lesbian body, Winterson seems to go under its interdict and lose a name. Winterson's narrator cannot reach the beloved, but can only move further away, study books on grieving, and wait. The narrator is returned to one body: the narrator's own. This *I*'s discourse on the body does not bridge the violence of separation, but leaves the *I* on one side of the abyss with only the body s / he can touch as evidence of the other's presence . . . and absence. There are similar tropes in both texts, but one difference remains the place of the name and the morphological equivalence between identity and name that both will claim. For Wittig, "lesbian" is the signifier of bodily coherence that incorporates violent dismemberment but permits the pleasure of putting the body back together. Without the signifier of lesbian in *Written on the Body*, the lover's identity persists through and as the absence of Louise, a monument to breaking up: "I am alone on a rock hewn out of my own body" (9).

Following the four lessons on the anatomy of absence, *Written on the Body* returns to the story. It is March and Elgin has promised to call with news about Louise's condition. But something has shifted, and it is not just what was left of the plot. Interruptions in the style of the lessons recur in the narrative as it drives toward an ending that is distinct from the storytelling style of the first section and informed by the self-reflexivity of the second section's excursion into the body. The ending reflects on the process of writing (perhaps the most narcissistic gesture of all because it entails the representation of the self to the self and an engagement with the gap that structures representation), and the identity that emerges from this shift in the third section is the author-identity which, Foucault argues, is always disappearing: the identity signified by the autobiographical performative "I am writing."[15]

The third section breaks from the confines of storytelling to become more self-reflexive, almost an allegory of storytelling, and finds Winterson resuming her interest in fantasy. The differing form of each section offers differing strategies for writing on the body and as such form an experiment in alternative morphologies (of the lover's body, of the body of the writing, of sexuality). Whereas the first section is more conventional in narrative terms and the second section meditates upon anatomy and absence, the third section is disorienting in terms of time, and in its willingness to turn phantasmatic Louise loose as the uncanny. When the narrator finally decides to find Louise and set it all right, attempts to track her down turn up only traces and dead ends. The places where the narrator might find Louise are now, more than ever, the narrator's own body. Yet Louise, phantasmatic in the first section, and spectral in the second, is now, curiously enough, "back."

[15]   Foucault, "What Is an Author?"

Louise returns in the penultimate paragraph, paler and thinner, but alive. But the shimmering real into which Louise enters is loaded with signifiers of writing and textuality. Winterson concludes:

> This is where the story starts, in this threadbare room. The walls are exploding. . . . I stretch out my hand and reach the corners of the world. . . . Beyond the door, where the river is, where the roads are, we shall be. We can take the world with us when we go and sling the sun under your arm. Hurry now, it's getting late. I don't know if this is a happy ending but here we are let loose in open fields. (190)

In its conclusion, *Written on the Body* appears to be more prequel than sequel to *The Lesbian Body*. The lovers have reunited and their bodies grow to incorporate the world that can now contain them both. Here, to be "let loose in open fields" may signify the same expansive and fictive desire for limitlessness that namelessness has signified throughout the text. Winterson's refusal to anchor the narrator through the name "lesbian," or her textual practice through the name "autobiography," has allowed for a particular inquiry into the limits of intelligibility within the representation of identity. Nonetheless, the ending turns back upon the project itself as the narrator wonders: "I don't know if this is a happy ending."

This hesitant moment may well suggest the next best question to pose within the terms of what I have been describing as Winterson's project. We should allow this moment its charm: Could a narrator who asks "why is the measure of love loss?" resist asking whether the story has a happy ending? Still, and with no damage to pleasures besides charm, I am concluding that *Written on the Body* allows for an exploration of figures of facticity. Winterson has assembled a code for reading around the nexus of identity. She plays with the semiotics of naming as an i.d. code, and investigates the slippage between names and things in a way that reworks the meanings among sex, gender, sexuality, and autobiography as problematical, uncertain, even enigmatic. To emphasize the connection to Wittig, we should remember that Wittig has argued that women are made knowable through the category of "sex" as a forcible interpretive act and that "sex" is a category she considers thoroughly political, without ontology, and constituted through a violent assault on the grounds of ontology.[16] For her "[t]he category of sex does not exist a priori, before all society. And as a category of dominance it cannot be a product of natural

---

[16] Monique Wittig, "The Category of Sex," in *The Straight Mind and Other Essays* (Boston: Beacon, 1992), 1–8.

dominance but of the social dominance of women by men, for there is but social dominance" (5). "Sex" as it prefigures "gender" and the autobiographical body for women is not primarily, then, a lived construction so much as a nonlived obstruction.[17]

Thus, to "be" a woman already indicates a kind of material violence. Winterson and Wittig reject autobiography as the narrative account of a woman's subjection. That Winterson chooses to tell a love story focused upon the intensity of embodied longing without a gender marker may mean less that the narrator doesn't feel like a lesbian than that she doesn't feel like a woman in precisely the way that Wittig does not, and, therefore, refuses that identification. For Wittig, the name "lesbian" trumps patriarchal kinship, makes it impossible for it to tell its story. Writing twenty years later, Winterson is more skeptical about whether a different name (and the substitute order it proclaims) escapes the juridical. In this she plays poststructuralist to Wittig's structuralist. For Winterson, a name is still a name and while namelessness may not smash the juridical, it sure throws a wrench in the works. Taken intertextually, Winterson's and Wittig's work frames a question for self-representation and lesbian representation: if the continued possibility of self-representation is currently being renegotiated through autobiography without names, is this a happy ending? "I don't know," as a self-reflexive signature of dubious tone, indicates the need to read absences and the resistance to conventions of autobiographical, gendered, and sexual representation as revisions of the real.

17   See my *Autobiographics* for an elaboration of this point.

# CONCLUSION

# The Knowing Subject and an Alternative Jurisprudence of Trauma

I have elucidated some of the historical and theoretical contexts for understanding how autobiographical limit-cases develop their meanings, clarified some of the issues that arise when self-representation and the representation of trauma coincide, identified texts that suggest an engagement with autobiography's central concerns and a refusal of autobiography's form and the judgments it imports. And, over the course of the study, I have offered a method for discerning self-representation in texts that do not engage the issues of truth, identity, ethics, and knowledge through conventional autobiography. By positing that the demands that trauma and the self make upon each other might require alternative forms through which to represent both, I hope to have contributed an argument for the significance of limit-cases to the studies of trauma and autobiography. By intensifying, multiplying, and maximizing the paradoxes within such notions as representativity, limit-cases yield new forms of knowledge about several critical issues that impinge on self-representation and trauma: truth, subjectivity, kinship, violence, law, and love. Ultimately, limit-cases constitute an alternative jurisdiction for self-representation in which writers relocate the grounds of judgment, install there a knowing subject rather than a sovereign or representative self, and produce an alternative jurisprudence about trauma, identity, and the forms both may take.

In 1980 Michel Foucault agreed to an interview with *Le Monde* in its series on leading European intellectuals, with one condition: he would remain

143

anonymous. For the purposes of identification in the interview, Foucault was "the masked philosopher."[1] Considering that an intellectual's prominence was a criterion for being selected as an interviewee, Foucault's choice of anonymity was an especially acute mechanism for examining how names think for us. As he explained, "A name makes reading too easy." While Foucault admitted to "nostalgia for a time when, being quite unknown, what I said had some chance of being heard" (321), his refusal of a name would go nostalgia one better. It would re-create reading as a highly charged anonymous encounter in which reader and writer would be compelled to discover their relation to each other in the present tense. *You* don't know *me*, anonymity insists: now what? The encounter, as Foucault imagined it, would not be one-sided; both reader and writer would risk transformation: "The effects of the book might land in unexpected places and form shapes that I had never thought of" (321). Foucault's experiment in opening up a space of possibility by refusing to name himself recalls Winterson's effort to see what could be discovered about identity in the absence of names.[2] Like Winterson, Foucault links our habit of letting names think for us to the same settled habits of thought that produce truth as a received doctrine. For Foucault, philosophy is the activity that makes it possible to rethink our relations to truth: "What is philosophy if not a way of reflecting, not so much on what is true and what is false, as on our relations to truth?" (327). For Winterson and the authors I have discussed, limit-cases offer the same opportunity to reflect on how knowledge about truth is produced, by whom, and in what forms. They do so in part by refusing the name "autobiography" and the intelligibility it would impose.

The truthfulness of knowledge about the self and trauma as it arises in relation to self-representation immediately confronts the issue of judgment. The association of autobiography with representativeness, confession, and testimony suggests some of why this should be so. So does the history of identifying memory as a central and vulnerable location of identity, and trauma as a threat to the self due to how it injures memory. The prevalence of judgment is threaded through the recurring emphases in my study's limit-cases—kinship, law, violence, identity, and love—and

---

[1]    Michel Foucault, "The Masked Philosopher," published in French in *Entretiens avec Le Monde*, 1984; I am quoting from Michel Foucault, *Ethics*, vol. 1, ed. Paul Rabinow (New York: New Press, 1997), 321–28.

[2]    In the interview, Foucault also proposes "a game: that of the 'year without a name.' For a year, books would be published without their authors' names. The critics would have to cope with a mass of entirely anonymous books" (321). It is interesting to imagine what would happen to a "memoir boom" in such a year, and, specifically, the fate of the books I describe as limit-cases.

offers a way to connect them to each other as well as to the prohibitions on speech that structure trauma. In requiring testimony to take certain forms, judgment defines what cannot be said as much as what can, and, in establishing these forms as truthful, produces form as the grounds for experimentation.

Criticism takes the form of judgment as it meets self-representational records and seeks to name them, attempts to answer whether they are telling the truth rather than how, and deems certain ventures out-of-bounds. I would not argue that critical judgments are exclusively or necessarily negative. Rather, the discourses in which judgment arises, including literary and cultural criticism, participate in establishing the forms of knowledge and truth telling from which some who seek to represent trauma and the self swerve in the very effort to tell a truth. When judgment constrains self-representation, disallows or stigmatizes the inventiveness necessary to live to tell the story, or simply views the autobiographer as raw material for a verdict, then writers do well to structure the grounds for an alternative hearing. Swerving from these constraints makes other engagements possible, as Foucault no doubt discovered when he spoke as the masked philosopher. Upon his unmasking, how many were surprised to discover this as his dream for criticism? "I can't help but dream about a kind of criticism that would not try to judge but to bring an oeuvre, a book, a sentence, an idea to life; it would light fires, watch the grass grow, listen to the wind, and catch the sea foam in the breeze and scatter it. It would multiply not judgments but signs of existence; it would summon them, drag them from their sleep. . . . It would bear the lightning of possible storms" (323). Such a criticism would be especially attentive to those books in which the writer undertook the ethical project Foucault adumbrated as the "care of the self," which he linked with the techniques and practices (or "technologies") that make it possible for one to become other than what one is ("On écrit pour être autre que ce qu'on est").

The ethics of self-representational projects are perhaps most familiar in the kinds of cases I have not discussed: those in which a falsehood is presented in the guise of truth. In these projects, a fraud is perpetrated in the name of autobiography. I want to emphasize how different these cases are from the limit-cases I describe. The same dynamics of judgment extend to these projects and, indeed, suggest why someone would choose autobiography as a form in which to make a truth-claim. However, attempting to confer the status of truth on an invented narrative and to assert an autobiographical identity is precisely what Allison, Gilmore, Kincaid, and Winterson do not do. I am sensitive to the dangers of claiming as fact works about trauma that are fictionalized. Let me repeat, then, that even if I might discuss those works within the same dynamics I have been describing about truth telling, the limit-cases I study here do the opposite of what those would-be autobiographers do: they choose not to stand as the representative or sovereign self of autobiography. Theirs is a critique of that position and the truth and knowledge produced through it.

In Foucault's terms, ethics could entail self-transformation: "I would like it to be an elaboration of the self by the self, a studious transformation, a slow and arduous transformation through a constant care for the truth."[3] Limit-cases are almost always about this transformational activity. They expose the insufficiency of viewing ethics and law primarily as a code of conduct. They examine the relations among people that exist in the presence of trauma and attempt to historicize the relations from which trauma has emerged in order to conceive of a self who can differ from the identity trauma imposes. Limit-cases pose the questions "how have I lived? how will I live?" in relation to the social and psychic forms within which trauma has been present. They offer histories of harm and the individual that differ from legal ones and which are, strictly speaking, inadmissible as testimony. In their swerving from an overtly testimonial form to an alternative one that draws on both legal and literary knowledge, and in their siting of this new form in an alternative jurisdiction to the contemporary memoirs of trauma or contemporary legal cases about abuse within families, limit-cases produce an alternative jurisprudence to understand kinship, violence, and self-representation. It is, in that context, extratestimonial. Narrow legal remedies are not sought, nor are they desired. What, after all, would Jamaica Kincaid's Annie John and Lucy want to do to their mother other than survive her? What does Mikal Gilmore want from the state that executed his brother other than that his family not be understood exclusively in the catastrophe of that execution? What does Dorothy Allison want from her stepfather other than the justice that comes from telling her story? Limit-cases are testimonial projects, but they do not bring forward cases within the protocols of legal testimony. They offer an alternative; they cannot do otherwise.

Without recourse to locations outside the law, these stories could not be told. When writers establish an alternative jurisdiction for narratives in which self-representation and the representation of trauma coincide, they produce what we can think of as an alternative jurisprudence by a knowing subject. I use "knowing" to suggest a process, even an ethic, that is not directed toward a judgment in which the subject is "known," but through which it models an engagement with what is difficult, compelling, in-

---

[3]  Foucault, "The Concern for Truth," in *Foucault Live* (New York: Semiotext(e), 1969), 461; quoted in Foucault, *Ethics*, 1: xxxix.

tractable, and surprising. The knowing subject works with dissonant materials, fragmented by trauma, and organizes them into a form of knowledge. I would call this an alternative jurisprudence to the knowledge of trauma and the self that is produced in legal contexts because it contributes a critical knowledge of the law and speaks to the relations that underpin how we live. This linkage, if not necessarily the critique of it, derives in the legal tradition from Blackstone's reading of Aristotle, for whom "jurisprudence, or the knowledge of those laws, is the principal, and most perfect branch of ethics."[4]

In a similar vein, Peter Goodrich defines "minor jurisprudences" as forms of legal knowledge that coexist alongside law but which lack law's dominant authority in the present.[5] Some of these jurisprudences arose within jurisdictions (places, forms, or courts) whose existence has been lost or destroyed. Goodrich's example of the courts of love in medieval France is instructive: although a literature of these courts and their conduct survives, their historical existence is dubious in part because nothing like them exists now. When a jurisdiction is lost, and the forms within which its jurisprudence is produced are disestablished, then the status of that knowledge becomes illegitimate, its very existence rendered dubious, its historicity recast as fiction. Limit-cases carve out a jurisdiction in which illegitimate subjects tell stories in forms marked by elements of fiction. In their exposure of the link between illegitimacy and fiction in self-representational projects, limit-cases expose the conditions in which alternative forms of knowledge about justice are compelled to appear, and how subjects who produce this knowledge are marked.

I call attention to limit-cases in this way because they offer an alternative form of jurisprudence about trauma and the self that is in the process of being forgotten even as it emerges. I memorialize it here against the competing histories of the present moment that may well erase its difference from the contemporary production of memoir or the study of trauma, and to notice both the work it does and the potential it has to reorganize what justice and knowledge look like in the context of trauma. Reading back from the vantage point of *Written on the Body*, we can see how limit-cases call attention to colonial powers and the force of social and psychic individuation, family relations and their entanglements with cultural and historical forms of violence, petty legalism and the terrors law can impose. Our relation to these makes us what we are and our ability to absorb them and tell our stories in ways that make these forms make

---

[4]  William Blackstone, *Commentaries on the Laws of England* (Boston: T. B. Waits and Sons, Printers, 1818), 27.
[5]  Peter Goodrich, *Law in the Courts of Love* (London: Routledge, 1996).

sense describes the method for becoming a sovereign self, the representative man of autobiography, the one who can say "this is who I am and how I came to be this way." Instead of asking how one becomes the sovereign self, a juridical notion that makes law into the fundamental basis of identity, limit-cases reveal the judgment sovereignty harbors and the way sovereignty is out of bounds for a self who emerges through a critique of law. Power is brought to bear through the sovereign self, the one who can impose the very conditions of living on an other, whose knowing prohibits other forms of knowing and acting. Instead of an assertion of identity as that which makes sense within structures and relations marked by violence, limit-cases present identity as it develops against the grain of the sovereign self, the principles of law that underlie it, and the trauma they inflict and permit. The knowing self in contrast to the sovereign or representative self does not ask who am I, but how can the relations in which I live, dream, and act be reinvented through me?

# Bibliography

Adams, Henry. *The Education of Henry Adams: An Autobiography*. Boston: Houghton Mifflin, 1918.

Allison, Dorothy. *Bastard Out of Carolina*. 1992. New York: Plume, 1993.

———. *Skin: Talking about Sex, Class, and Literature*. Ithaca: Firebrand Books, 1994.

———. *Trash*. Ithaca, New York: Firebrand Books, 1988.

———. *Two or Three Things I Know for Sure*. New York: Dutton, 1995.

Alpert, Judith L., ed. *Sexual Abuse Recalled: Treating Trauma in the Era of the Recovered Memory Debate*. Northvale, N.J.: Jason Aronson, 1995.

Althusser, Louis. *The Future Lasts Forever*. Paris: Stock/IMEC, 1992.

———. "Ideology and Ideological State Apparatuses." Translated by Ben Brewster. In *Critical Theory since 1965*, edited by Hazard Adams and Leroy Searle, 239–50. Tallahassee: University Press of Florida, 1986.

Anderson, Benedict. *Imagined Communities: Reflections on the Origin and Spread of Nationalism*. London: Verso 1983, 1991.

Angelou, Maya. *All God's Children Need Traveling Shoes*. New York: Random House, 1986.

———. *Gather Together in My Name*. New York: Random House, 1974.

———. *I Know Why the Caged Bird Sings*. New York: Random House, 1969.

Annan, Gabriele. "Devil in the Flesh." *New York Review of Books*, May 4, 1993, 22–23.

Anzaldúa, Gloria. *Borderlands / La Frontera: The New Mestiza*. San Francisco: Spinsters/Aunt Lute, 1987.

Arens, W. *The Original Sin: Incest and Its Meaning*. New York: Oxford University Press, 1986.

Armstrong, Louise. *Kiss Daddy Goodnight: A Speak-out on Incest*. New York: Hawthorn Books, 1978.

———. *Rocking the Cradle of Sexual Politics: What Happened When Women Said Incest*. Reading, Mass.: Addison-Wesley, 1994.

Ashley, Sandi. *The Missing Voice: Writings by Mothers of Incest Victims*. Dubuque, Iowa: Kendall/Hunt, 1992.

Barnett, Pamela E. "Figurations of Rape and the Supernatural in *Beloved*." *PMLA* 112.3 (spring 1997): 418–27.

Barrios de Chungara, Domitila. *Let Me Speak! Testimony of Domitila, a Woman of the Bolivian Mines*. New York: Monthly Review Press, 1978.

Barthes, Roland. *A Lover's Discourse: Fragments*. Translated by Richard Howard. New York: Hill and Wang, 1985.

Bass, Ellen, and Laura Davis. *The Courage to Heal: A Guide for Women Survivors of Child Sexual Abuse*. New York: Harper & Row, 1988.

Bauby, Jean-Dominique. *The Diving Bell and the Butterfly: A Memoir of Life in Death*. 1997. New York: Vintage Books, 1998.

Bell, Vikki. *Interrogating Incest: Feminism, Foucault, and the Law*. New York: Routledge, 1993.

Berlant, Lauren. *The Anatomy of National Fantasy: Hawthorne, Utopia, and Everyday Life*. Chicago: University of Chicago Press, 1991.

Bernheimer, Charles, and Claire Kahane, eds. *In Dora's Case: Freud—Hysteria—Feminism*. 1985. 2d. ed. New York: Columbia University Press, 1990.

Blackstone, William. *Commentaries on the Laws of England*. Boston: T. B. Waits and Sons, Printers, 1818.

Blume, E. Sue. *Secret Survivors: Uncovering Incest and Its Aftereffects in Women*. New York: Wiley, 1990.

Briere, John. *Child Abuse Trauma: Theory and Treatment of the Lasting Effects*. Newbury Park, Calif.: Sage Publications, 1992.

Brown, Laura. "Not Outside the Range: One Feminist Perspective on Psychic Trauma." In *Trauma: Explorations in Memory*, edited by Cathy Caruth, 100–112. Baltimore: Johns Hopkins University Press, 1995.

Bryant, Marcella. *Ancient Child: Poetry about Incest*. Austin, Tex.: Plain View Press, 1989.

Buell, Lawrence. "Autobiography in the American Renaissance." In *American Autobiography: Retrospect and Prospect*, edited by Paul John Eakin, 47–69, Madison, Wisconsin: University of Wisconsin Press, 1991.

Butler, Judith. *Bodies That Matter*. New York: Routledge, 1993.

———. "Critically Queer." *GLQ* 1 (1993): 17–32.

———. *The Psychic Life of Power: Theories in Subjection*. Stanford: Stanford University Press, 1997.

Butler, Sandra. *Conspiracy of Silence: The Trauma of Incest*. San Francisco: New Glide Publications, 1978.

Caruth, Cathy, ed. *Trauma: Explorations in Memory*. Baltimore: Johns Hopkins University Press, 1995.

———. *Unclaimed Experience: Trauma, Narrative, and History*. Baltimore: Johns Hopkins University Press, 1996.

Casey, Edward S. *Remembering: A Phenomenological Study*. Bloomington: Indiana University Press, 1987.

Castle, Terry. *The Apparitional Lesbian*. New York: Columbia University Press, 1993.

Chernin, Kim. *In My Father's Garden: A Daughter's Search for a Spiritual Life*. Chapel Hill: Algonquin Books, 1996.

———. *In My Mother's House*. New Haven: Ticknor & Fields, 1983.

———. *My Life As a Boy*. Chapel Hill: Algonquin Books, 1997.

Cliff, Michelle. *Abeng*. New York: Penguin Books, 1991.

———. *No Telephone to Heaven*. New York: Vintage Books, 1989.

Conroy, Frank. *Stop-Time*. New York: Viking Press, 1967.

Cornell, Drucilla. *The Imaginary Domain: Abortion, Pornography, and Sexual Harassment*. New York: Routledge, 1995.

Cover, Robert. "Violence and the Word." *Yale Law Journal* 95.8 (July 1986): 1601–29.

Culbertson, Roberta. "Embodied Memory, Transcendence, and Telling: Recounting Trauma, Re-establishing the Self." *New Literary History* 26 (1995): 169–95.

Cutting, Linda Katherine. *Memory Slips: A Memoir of Music and Healing*. New York: Harper Perennial, 1998.

Daniels, April, and Carol Scott. *Paperdolls: Healing from Sexual Abuse in Mormon Neighborhoods*. Salt Lake City: Palingenesia Press, 1992.

De Lauretis, Teresa. *Practice of Love*. Bloomington: Indiana University Press, 1994.

De Man, Paul. "Autobiography as De-facement." *Modern Language Notes* 94, no. 5 (1979): 919–30.

Dimock, Wai-chee. *Residues of Justice*. Berkeley: University of California Press, 1996.

Dinsmore, Christine. *From Surviving to Thriving: Incest, Feminism, and Recovery*. Albany: State University of New York Press, 1991.

Djebar, Assia. *Women of Algiers in Their Apartment*. 1980. Translated by Marjolijn de Jager. Charlottesville: University Press of Virginia, 1992.

Doyle, Laura. *Bordering on the Body: The Racial Matrix of Modern Fiction and Culture*. New York: Oxford University Press, 1994.

Duggan, Lisa, and Nan Hunter. *Sex Wars: Sexual Dissent and Political Culture*. New York: Routledge, 1995.

Eakin, Paul John, ed. *American Autobiography*. Madison: University of Wisconsin Press, 1991.

Eribon, Didier. *Michel Foucault*. Translated by Betsy Wing. Cambridge, Mass.: Harvard University Press, 1991.

Eskridge, William N., and Nan D. Hunter. *Sexuality, Gender, and the Law*. New York: Foundation Press, 1997.

Felman, Shoshana, and Dori Laub. *Testimony: Crises of Witnessing*. New York: Routledge, 1992.

Ferguson, Moira. *Colonialism and Gender from Mary Wollstonecraft to Jamaica Kincaid*. New York: Columbia University Press, 1993.

Fineman, Martha. *The Neutered Mother, the Sexual Family, and Other Twentieth-Century Tragedies*. New York: Routledge, 1995.

Foucault, Michel. *Birth of the Clinic: An Archaeology of Medical Perception*. Translated by A. M. Sheridan. New York: Pantheon, 1973.

——. *Discipline and Punish: The Birth of the Prison*. Translated by Alan Sheridan. New York: Random House, 1977.

——. *Ethics: Subjectivity and Truth*, Volume 1. Edited by Paul Rabinow. Translated by Robert Hurley et al. New York: New Press, 1997.

——. *Herculine Barbin*. Paris: Gallimard, 1978.

——. *The History of Sexuality. Vol. 1, An Introduction*. Translated by Robert Hurley. New York: Random House, 1978.

——. *Madness and Civilization: A History of Insanity in the Age of Reason*. Translated by Richard Howard. New York: Vintage 1988.

——. "What Is an Author?" Translated by Josué Harari. In *The Foucault Reader*, edited by Paul Rabinow, 101–20. New York: Pantheon, 1984.

——, ed. *I, Pierre Rivière, having slaughtered my mother, my sister, and my brother*. Translated by Frank Jellinek. New York: Random House, 1975.

Fraser, Sylvia. *My Father's House: A Memoir of Incest and Healing*. 1987. New York: Ticknor & Fields, 1988.

Freedy, John R., and Stevan E. Hobfoll, eds. *Traumatic Stress: From Theory to Practice*. New York: Plenum Press, 1995.

Freud, Sigmund. *Dora: An Analysis of a Case of Hysteria*. New York: Collier Books, 1963.

——. "Mourning and Melancholia" (1917). In *General Psychological Theory*, 164–79. New York: Collier Books, 1963.

——. *Therapy and Technique*. New York: Collier Books, 1963.

Freyd, Jennifer J., *Betrayal Trauma: The Logic of Forgetting Childhood Abuse*. Cambridge, Mass.: Harvard University Press, 1996.

Fuller, Patsy. "The Social Construction of Rape in Appeal Court Cases." *Feminism and Psychology* 5.2 (1995): 154–61.

Ganzarain, Ramon C., and Bonnie J. Buchele. *Fugitives of Incest: A Perspective from Psychoanalysis and Groups*. Madison, Conn.: International Universities Press, 1988.

Gates, Henry Louis, Jr., ed. *Reading Black, Reading Feminist*. New York: Penguin, 1990.

Gilbert, Sandra M. *Wrongful Death: A Memoir*. New York: Norton, 1997.

Gilmore, Leigh. *Autobiographics: A Feminist Theory of Women's Self-Representation*. Ithaca: Cornell University Press, 1994.

Gilmore, Mikal. *Shot in the Heart*. New York: Doubleday, 1994.

Glass, James M. *Shattered Selves: Multiple Personality in a Postmodern World*. Ithaca: Cornell University Press, 1993.

Goldstein, Eleanor C., and Kevin Farmer. *True Stories of False Memories*. Boca Raton: SIRS, 1993.

Goodrich, Peter. *Law in the Courts of Love: Literature and Other Minor Jurisprudences*. London: Routledge, 1996.

———. *Oedipus Lex: Psychoanalysis, History, Law*. Berkeley: University of California Press, 1995.

Gordon, Linda. *Heroes of Their Own Lives: The Politics and History of Family Violence, Boston, 1880–1960*. New York: Viking, 1988.

Grealy, Lucy. *Autobiography of a Face*. Boston: Houghton Mifflin, 1994.

Haaken, Janice. *Pillar of Salt: Gender, Memory, and the Perils of Looking Back*. New Brunswick: Rutgers University Press, 1998.

———. "The Recovery of Memory, Fantasy, and Desire: Feminist Approaches to Sexual Abuse and Psychic Trauma." *Signs* 21.4 (summer 1996): 1069–94.

Hacking, Ian. "The Making and Molding of Child Abuse." *Critical Inquiry* 17 (winter 1991): 253–88.

———. *Rewriting the Soul: Multiple Personality and the Sciences of Memory*. Princeton: Princeton University Press, 1995.

Halperin, David. *Saint Foucault: Toward a Gay Hagiography*. New York: Oxford University Press, 1995.

Hartman, Saidiya. *Scenes of Subjection*. New York: Oxford University Press, 1997.

Harrison, Kathryn. *The Kiss*. New York: Avon Trade Books, 1998.

Hedges, Lawrence E. *Remembering, Repeating, and Working through Childhood Trauma: The Psychodynamics of Recovered Memories, Multiple Personality, Ritual Abuse, Incest, Molestation, and Abduction*. Northvale, N.J.: Jason Aronson, 1994.

Hellman, Lillian. *Pentimento*. Boston: Little, Brown, 1973.

———. *An Unfinished Woman: A Memoir*. Boston: Little, Brown, 1969.

Herman, Judith. *Trauma and Recovery*. New York: Basic Books, 1992.

Hirsch, Marianne. *Family Frames: Photography, Narrative, and Postmemory*. Cambridge, Mass.: Harvard University Press, 1997.

Holloway, Karla F. C. "The Body Politic." In *Subjects and Citizens*, edited by Michael Moon and Cathy Davidson, 481–95. Durham: Duke University Press, 1995.

Jamison, Kay Redfield. *An Unquiet Mind*. New York: Knopf, 1995.

Johnson, Barbara. "My Monster, My Self." In *A World of Difference*, 144–54. Baltimore: Johns Hopkins University Press, 1987.

Johnson, Janis Tyler. *Mothers of Incest Survivors: Another Side of the Story*. Bloomington: Indiana University Press, 1992.

Kaplan, Alice. *French Lessons*. Chicago: University of Chicago Press, 1993.

Kaplan, Caren. "Resisting Autobiography: Out-Law Genres in Transnational Feminist Studies." In *De / Colonizing the Subject: The Politics of Gender in Women's Autobiography*, edited by Sidonie Smith and Julia Watson, 115–38. Minneapolis: University of Minnesota Press.

Karr, Mary. *The Liar's Club: A Memoir*. New York: Viking, 1995.

Kaysen, Susanna. *Girl, Interrupted*. New York: Turtle Bay Books, 1993.

Kincaid, Jamaica. *Annie John*. New York: Farrar, Straus and Giroux. First Plume Printing, 1986. First published in slightly different form in the *New Yorker*, 1983.

———. *At the Bottom of the River*. New York: Farrar, Straus and Giroux, 1983.

———. *The Autobiography of My Mother*. New York: Farrar, Straus and Giroux, 1996.

———. *Lucy*. New York: Farrar, Straus and Giroux, 1990. First Plume printing, 1991.

———. *My Brother*. Farrar, Straus and Giroux, 1997.

———. *A Small Place*. New York: Farrar, Straus and Giroux, 1988.

Kingston, Maxine Hong. *The Woman Warrior: Memoirs of a Girlhood among Ghosts*. New York: Knopf, 1976.

Knapp, Caroline. *Drinking: A Love Story*. New York: Dial Press, 1996.

Kristeva, Julia. *Powers of Horror: An Essay in Abjection*. New York: Columbia University Press, 1982.

———. *Revolution in Poetic Language*. 1974. Translated by Margaret Waller. New York: Columbia University Press, 1984.

Lacan, Jacques. *Écrits: A Selection*. Translated by Alan Sheridan. New York: Norton, 1977.

———. *The Four Fundamental Concepts of Psycho-Analysis*. Edited by J.-A. Miller. Translated by Alan Sheridan. New York: Norton, 1978.

Langer, Lawrence. *Admitting the Holocaust*. New York: Oxford University Press, 1994.

Layton, Lynne. "Trauma, Gender Identity and Sexuality: Discourses of Fragmentation." *American Imago* 52.1 (1995):107–25.

Lejeune, Philippe. *Le pacte autobiographique*. Paris: Seuil, 1975.

Lentricchia, Frank, *The Edge of Night*. New York: Random House, 1994.

Lévi-Strauss, Claude. *The Elementary Structures of Kinship*. Boston: Beacon Press, 1969.

Lionnet, Françoise. *Autobiographical Voices: Race, Gender, Portraiture*. Ithaca: Cornell University Press, 1989.

———. "Of Mangoes and Maroons: Language, History, and the Multicultural Subject in Michelle Cliff's *Abeng*." In *De / Colonizing the Subject: The Politics of Gender in Women's Autobiography*, edited by Sidonie Smith and Julia Watson, 321–45. Minneapolis: University of Minnesota Press, 1992.

———. *Postcolonial Representations: Women, Literature, Identity*. Ithaca: Cornell University Press, 1995.

Lispector, Clarice. *An Apprenticeship, or The Book of Delights*. Austin: University of Texas Press, 1986.

Loftus, Elizabeth F., and Katherine Ketcham. *The Myth of Repressed Memory: False Memories and Allegations of Sexual Abuse*. New York: St. Martin's Press, 1994.

———. *Witness for the Defense: The Accused, the Eyewitness, and the Expert Who Puts Memory on Trial*. New York: St. Martin's Press, 1994.

Lorde, Audre. *Zami: A New Spelling of My Name*. Trumansburg, N. Y.: Crossing Press, 1983.

Macey, David. *The Lives of Michel Foucault: A Biography*. New York: Pantheon Books, 1993.

Mailer, Norman. *The Executioner's Song*. Boston: Little, Brown, 1979.

Martens, Tony. *Characteristics and Dynamics of Incest and Child Sexual Abuse; with a Native Perspective by Brenda Daily and Maggie Hodgson*. Edmonton, Alberta: Nechi Institute, 1988.

McCarthy, Mary. *Memories of a Catholic Girlhood*. New York: Harcourt Brace, 1957.

McCourt, Frank. *Angela's Ashes: A Memoir*. New York: Scribner's, 1996.

Mason, Mary. "The Other Voice." In *Autobiography: Essays Theoretical and Critical*, edited by James Olney, 207–35. Princeton: Princeton University Press, 1980.

Menchú, Rigoberta. *I, Rigoberta Menchú: An Indian Woman in Guatemala*. Edited by Elisabeth Burgos-Debray. Translated by Ann Wright. London: Verso, 1984.

Miller, Jacques-Alain. "The Analytic Experience: Means, End, and Results." In *Lacan and the Subject of Language*, edited by Ellie Ragland-Sullivan and Mark Brache. New York: Routledge, 1991.

Miller, Nancy K. *Bequest and Betrayal*. New York: Oxford University Press, 1996.

———. "Mothers, Daughters, and Autobiography: Maternal Legacies and Cultural Criticism." *Mothers in Law: Feminist Theory and the Legal Regulation of Motherhood*, edited by Martha Fineman and Isabel Karpin, 3–26. New York: Columbia University Press, 1995.

Moraga, Cherríe. *Loving in the War Years*. Boston: South End Press, 1983.

Morrison, Toni. *Beloved*. New York: Plume, 1988.

Mulvey, Laura. "Visual Pleasure and Narrative Cinema." In *Visual and Other Pleasures*, 14–26. Bloomington: Indiana University Press, 1989.

Nabokov, Vladimir. *Speak, Memory: A Memoir*. New York: Grosset & Dunlap, 1951.

Nathan, Debbie, and Michael Snedeker. *Satan's Silence: Ritual Abuse and the Making of a Modern American Witch Hunt*. New York: Basic Books, 1995.

Norris, Christopher. *What's Wrong with Postmodernism*. Baltimore: Johns Hopkins University Press, 1990.

Ovaris, Wendy. *After the Nightmare*. Holmes Beach, Fla.: Learning Publications, 1991.

Paton, Douglas, and John M. Violanti. *Traumatic Stress in Critical Occupations: Recognition, Consequences, and Treatment*. Springfield, Ill.: Charles C. Thomas, 1996.

Price, Michelle. "The Psychoanalysis of an Adult Survivor of Incest." *American Journal of Psychiatry* 52.2 (June 1, 1992): 119–36.

Quinby, Lee. "The Subject of Memoirs." In *De / colonizing the Subject*, edited by Sidonie Smith and Julia Watson, 297–320. Minneapolis: University of Minnesota Press.

Raine, Nancy Venable. *After Silence: Rape and My Journey Back*. New York: Crown, 1998.

Randall, Margaret. *This Is about Incest*. Ithaca: Firebrand Books, 1987.

Renvoize, Jean. *Incest: A Family Pattern*. London: Routledge & Kegan Paul, 1982.

Riley, Denise. *"Am I That Name?" Feminism and the Category of "Women" in History*. Minneapolis: University of Minnesota Press, 1988.

Rodriguez, Richard. *Days of Obligation: An Argument with My Mexican Father*. New York: Viking, 1992.

———. *Hunger of Memory*. Boston: D. R. Godine, 1982.

Rose, Jacqueline. "Dora: Fragment of an Analysis." *In Dora's Case: Freud—Hysteria—Feminism* 1985. 2d ed. Edited by Charles Bernheimer and Claire Kahane, 128–48. New York: Columbia University Press, 1990.

Rosenthal, Bernard. *Salem Story: Reading the Witch Trials of 1692*. New York: Cambridge University Press, 1993.

Rousseau, Jean-Jacques, *Confessions*. Translated by J. M. Cohen. New York: Penguin, 1953.

Rubin, Gayle. "The Traffic in Women: Notes on the 'Political Economy' of Sex." In *Toward an Anthropology of Women*, edited by Rayna R. Reiter, 157–210. New York: Monthly Review Press, 1975.

Schulman, Sarah. "Guilty with Explanation: Jeanette Winterson's Endearing Book of Love." *Lambda Book Review* 3.9 (Mar.–Apr. 1993): 20.

Schwartz, Nina. *Dead Fathers: The Logic of Transference in Modern Narrative*. Ann Arbor: University of Michigan Press, 1994.

Shell, Marc. *The End of Kinship: "Measure for Measure", Incest, and the Idea of Universal Siblinghood*. Stanford: Stanford University Press, 1988.

Simmons, Diane. *Jamaica Kincaid*. New York: Twayne, 1994.

Skorczewski, Dawn. "What Prison Is This? Literary Critics Cover Incest in Anne Sexton's "Briar Rose." *Signs*, winter 1996, 309–42.

Slater, Lauren. *Prozac Diary*. New York: Random House, 1998.

Smith, Sidonie. "Identity's Body." In *Autobiography and Postmodernism*, edited by Kathleen Ashley, Leigh Gilmore, and Gerald Peters, 266–92. Amherst: University of Massachusetts Press, 1994.

———. "Memory, Narrative, and the Discourses of Identity in *Abeng* and *No Telephone to Heaven*." In *Postcolonialism and Autobiography*, edited by Alfred Hornung and Ernstpeter Ruhe, 37–59. Amsterdam: Editions Rodopi, 1998.

Smith, Sidonie, and Julia Watson, eds. *De/Colonizing the Subject: The Politics of Gender in Women's Autobiography*. Minneapolis: University of Minnesota Press, 1992.

———. *Getting a Life*. Minneapolis: University Minnesota Press, 1996.

———. *Women, Autobiography, Theory: A Reader*. Madison: University of Wisconsin Press, 1998.

Sommer, Doris. "Sacred Secrets: A Strategy for Survival." In *Women, Autobiography, Theory: A Reader*, edited by Sidonie Smith and Julia Watson, 197–207. Madison: University of Wisconsin Press, 1998.

Spence, Donald P. *Narrative Truth and Historical Truth: Meaning and Interpretation in Psychoanalysis*. New York: Norton, 1982.

———. *The Rhetorical Voice of Psychoanalysis: Displacement of Evidence by Theory*. Cambridge, Mass.: Harvard University Press, 1994.

Spivak, Gayatri. "Three Women's Texts and Circumfession." In *Postcolonialism and Autobiography*, edited by Alfred Hornung and Ernstpeter Ruhe, 7–22. Amsterdam: Editions Rodopi, 1998.

Spring, Jacqueline. *Cry Hard and Swim: The Story of an Incest Survivor*. London: Virago, 1987.

Stein, Gertrude. *The Autobiography of Alice B. Toklas*. New York: Harcourt Brace, 1933.

———. *Everybody's Autobiography*. New York: Random House, 1937.

Stevens, Lynne. "Bringing Order to Chaos: A Framework for Understanding and Treating Female Sexual Abuse Survivors." *Violence against Women* 3.1 (Feb. 1997): 27–45.

Stoll, David. *Rigoberta Menchú and the Story of All Poor Guatemalans*. Boulder, Colo.: Westview Press, 1998.

Styron, William. *Darkness Visible: A Memoir of Madness*. New York: Random House, 1990.

Suleiman, Susan Rubin. *Budapest Diary: In Search of the Motherbook*. Lincoln: University of Nebraska Press, 1997.

Sullivan, Mercer L. "Biography of Heinous Criminals: Culture, Family, Violence, and Prisonization." *Journal of Research in Crime and Delinquency* 33.3 (Aug. 1996): 354–77.

Terr, Lenore. *Too Scared to Cry*. New York: Harper & Row, 1990.

———. *Unchained Memories: True Stories of Traumatic Memories, Lost and Found*. New York: Basic Books, 1994.

———. "What Happens to the Memories of Early Trauma? A Study of Twenty Children under Age Five at the Time of Documented Traumatic Events." *Journal of the American Academy of Child and Adolescent Psychiatry* 27 (1988): 96–104.

Torgovnick, Marianna. *Crossing Ocean Parkway: Readings by an Italian American Daughter*. Chicago: University of Chicago Press, 1994.

Tompkins, Jane. *A Life in School: What the Teacher Learned*. Reading, Mass.: Addison-Wesley, 1996.

Twitchell, James B. *Forbidden Partners: The Incest Taboo in Modern Culture*. New York: Columbia University Press, 1987.

Van der Kolk, Bessel, Alexander C. McFarlane, and Lars Weisaeth, eds. *Traumatic Stress: The Effects of Overwhelming Experience on Mind, Body, and Society*. New York: Guilford Press, 1996.

Veeser, H. Aram, ed. *Confessions of the Critics*. New York: Routledge, 1996.

Weintraub, Karl. *The Value of the Individual*. Chicago: University of Chicago Press, 1978.

Wilson, Elizabeth. "Not in This House: Incest, Denial, and Doubt in the White Middle-Class Family." *Yale Journal of Criticism* 8 (1995): 35–58.

Wilson, Melba. *Crossing the Boundary: Black Women Survive Incest*. Seattle: Seal Press, 1994.

Winterson, Jeanette. *Art and Lies*. Toronto: Alfred A. Knopf Canada, 1994.

———. *Oranges Are Not the Only Fruit*. New York: Atlantic Monthly Press, 1987. First published by Pandora, London, 1985.

———. *The Passion*. New York: Vintage, 1989. First published by Bloomsbury Press, London, 1987.

———. *Sexing the Cherry*. New York: Vintage, 1991. First published by Bloomsbury, London, 1989. First published in the United States by the Atlantic Monthly Press, New York, 1990.

————. *Written on the Body*. New York: Knopf, 1993. First published by Jonathan Cape, London, 1992.

Wittig, Monique. "The Category of Sex." In *The Straight Mind and Other Essays*. Boston: Beacon, 1992: 1–8.

————. *The Lesbian Body*. Translated by David Le Vay. Paris: Minuit, 1973. Boston: Beacon, 1986.

Wolff, Tobias. *In Pharaoh's Army: Memories of the Lost War*. New York: Knopf, 1994.

Woolf, Virginia. *A Room of One's Own*. New York: Harcourt, Brace, 1929.

Young, Iris Marion. *Justice and the Politics of Difference*. Princeton: Princeton University Press, 1990.

Žižek, Slavoj. *Looking Awry: An Introduction to Jacques Lacan through Popular Culture*. Cambridge, Mass.: MIT Press, 1991.

# Index

Freud, Sigmund (*continued*)
  on melancholia, 67–68
  on memory, 28
  on transference, 89, 89n–90n
Freyd, Jennifer, 27–28, 30
*Future Lasts Forever, The* (Althusser), 38–42

Gender. *See also* Sex; Sexual identity;
    Sexuality
  body as proof of, 131
  definitional limits of, 128
  language and, 122
  politics of, and study of shell
    shock/hysteria, 33
  trauma studies and, 26
  Winterson on, 13
Gender politics
  and study of hysteria, 26
  truth telling and, 21
Gilmore, Gary, 5, 13, 71, 74–95, 97
Gilmore, Mikal, 5, 8, 9, 23, 71–95, 114, 145,
    146. *See also Shot in the Heart*
*Girl, Interrupted* (Kaysen), 18
Goodrich, Peter, 50–51, 53, 147

Haaken, Janice, 25–26
Hacking, Ian, 25
Haraway, Donna, 98n
Harrison, Kathryn, 23–24
Haunting
  as disordering of time, 82
  family, 72–73
  by family culture, 92
  lesbian in, 121
Hawthorne, Nathaniel, 10
Hellman, Lillian, 11, 18, 96
*Herculine Barbine* (intro. Foucault), 37
Hirsch, Marianne, 93n
History, boundary with memoir, 36
*History of Sexuality, The* (Foucault), 34, 37
Holocaust
  generational component of, 93
  memory of, 47
Hong Kingston, Maxine, 10, 18
Howard, Jacob, 21
Hysteria
  Freud's work on, 25n
  and shell shock, 25–26, 33

"I." *See also* Self; Subject
  disturbances of, 36
  as focus of memoir, 2
  in hybrid texts, 17
  in Kincaid's work, 103
  as masculine construct, 72
  national, 18

and politics of memory/autobiography,
    24
  ruptured boundaries of, 71–72
  in various genres, 11
  Winterson's fictionalizing of, 127
  in *Written on the Body,* 136
*I, Pierre Rivière* (ed. Foucault), 35–38
*I, Rigoberta Menchú,* 4. *See also* Menchú,
    Rigoberta
Identity
  family and, 114
  memory and, 32–33, 144
  and namelessness, 144
  naming and, 113, 120, 128, 140
  not-naming and, 128
  role of chance in, 91
  sex/gender and, 123–24
  sexual, 123–24, 130–31
  splitting of, 103
  in Winterson's work, 123–24, 130–34
Identity politics, trauma narratives and, 48
Illegitimacy
  Allison's hermeneutics of, 69–70
  class and, 61
  of law, 52
  law's investment in, 50
  legal violence and, 60
  shame and, 61, 69
  in South Carolina's legal code, 54
Incest, 5. *See also* Child abuse; Sexual
    abuse
  child's reporting of, 58
  class and, 57, 57n, 61
  clinical/social implications of, 26
  consent/agency and, 58–59, 58n
  cultural meanings of, 56
  in law, 69
  law's investment in, 50
  legal violence and, 60
  legal visibility of, 52, 57
  personal/legal ramifications of, 13
  psychoanalysis's use of, 69
  self-representational accounts of, 53
  shame and, 61, 69
Individualism, American, 19
Individuation, in Kincaid's work, 106–7
Institutions, unconscious of, 51
Interrogator, role in testimony, 4–5

*Jane Eyre* (Brontë), 11
Judgment, and constraint of self-represen-
    tation, 145
Judicature, autobiography as, 43
Juridical
  Foucault's notion of, 48
  in Winterson's work, 142

Trauma (*continued*)
  formulations of, 7
  Freudian meanings of, 27
  generational component of, 93
  collective experience of, 30
  healing and, 15
  historical, 27
  jurisprudence of, alternative to, 143–48
  language of, 93
  limit-cases in study of, 143
  memory and, 8–9, 24–33
  passive voice and, 67
  of powerlessness, 50
  real versus imagined in, 46
  reconception of, 49
  redefinition of, 25
  representativeness and, 19–24
  and ruptured boundaries, 71–72
  self-representation and, 9, 48–49
  threat to self, 144
  unspeakability of, 46
  upsurge in publications about, 16
  in women's everyday lives, 26–27
  writing about, 15
Truth
  knowledge about, 144–45
  law and, 51
Truth telling
  in autobiography, 38–39, 47
  autobiography's relation to, 101
  cultural power of, 3n
  expectations about, 124
  in Kincaid's work, 101, 102
  and law, 102
  legalistic definition of, 3
  memory as, 39–40
  reliance on, 42
  in trauma studies, 47
*Two or Three Things I Know for Sure* (Allison), 45, 62

*Unchained Memories* (Terr), 30
Unconscious
  of institutions, 51
  of law, 51, 68
  relation to dead, 72–73
*Unfinished Woman, An* (Hellman), 11

Valéry, Paul, 11–12
van der Kolk, Bessell, 29
Veracity. *See also* Truth; Truth telling
  judgments about, 48
Victimization, grammar of, 67
Violence
  erotics of, 59–60
  of illegitimacy, 55
  of law, 52
  sex and, 59–60
  and shattering of time, 93
  subculture and, 56–57
  voyeurism and, 75n
Voyeurism, 71
  and texts on violence, 75n

*Walden* (Thoreau), 10
Whitman, Walt, 10, 18
Wilson, Elizabeth, 57n
Winterson, Jeanette, 5, 9, 120–42, 145. *See also Written on the Body*
  and absence of names, 144 (*see also* Naming, refusal of)
  and fictional "I," 127
  identity in, 123–24, 130–34
  loss in, 134
  metonymy in, 132
  naming and gender and, 13
  self-representation and, 128, 131
Wittig, Monique, 123–24, 137–38, 141
*Woman Warrior* (Kingston), 18
Women
  autobiographical challenges to, 21
  everyday trauma of, 26–27
  law's violence toward, 52
  as legal subjects, 68
  trauma accounts of, 23–24
Wordsworth, William, 89
Writing
  invisibility in autobiography, 36
  as life saving, 119
*Written on the Body* (Winterson), 9, 120–42, 147

*Zami: A New Spelling of My Name* (Lord), 16

The author gratefully acknowledges permission to use the following material:

Excerpts from *Bastard Out of Carolina* by Dorothy Allison. Copyright © 1992 by Dorothy Allison. Reprinted by permission of Dutton, a division of Penguin Putnam Inc.

Excerpts from *Lucy* by Jamaica Kincaid. Copyright © 1990 by Jamaica Kincaid. Reprinted by permission of Farrar, Straus and Giroux, LLC and The Wylie Agency, Inc.

Excerpts from *My Brother* by Jamaica Kincaid. Copyright © 1997 by Jamaica Kincaid. Reprinted by permission of Farrar, Straus and Giroux, LLC and The Wylie Agency, Inc.

Excerpts from *Annie John* by Jamaica Kincaid. Copyright © 1985 by Jamaica Kincaid. Reprinted by permission of Farrar, Straus and Giroux, LLC and Vintage/Random House UK.

Excerpts from *Shot in the Heart* by Mikal Gilmore. Copyright © 1994 by Mikal Gilmore. Reprinted by permission of the author and Doubleday, a division of Random House, Inc.

Excerpts from *Written on the Body* by Jeanette Winterson. Copyright © 1994 by Vintage Books. Reprinted by permission of the author and International Creative Management, Inc.

An earlier version of chapter 3 appeared as "Last Words: Transference and the Auto/biographical Demand in Mikal Gilmore's *Shot in the Heart*" in *American Imago* 55, no. 2 (1998): 227–298. © 1998. Reprinted by permission of The Johns Hopkins University Press.

An earlier version of chapter 4 appeared in *Postcolonialism and Autobiography*, ed. Alfred Hornung and Ernstpeter Ruhe (Amsterdam: Rodopi, 1998): 211–231. Reprinted by permission.

An earlier version of chapter 5 appeared as "An Anatomy of Absence" in *Genders* 26 (1997): 224–251. Reprinted by permission of New York University Press.